Three-Dimensional Needlepoint

Three-Dimensional Needlepoint

Gale Litvak

Designed and illustrated by
Lynn Yost
Photography by David Arky

G. P. Putnam's Sons/New York

For my parents, with love and appreciation

Library of Congress Cataloging in Publication Data

Litvak, Gale.
    Three-dimensional needlepoint.

    1. Canvas embroidery. I. Title.
TT778.C3L58   1984   746.44'2   83–22958
ISBN 0–399–12926–X

Printed in the United States of America

Contents

Introduction

Plastic canvas for needlepoint is a recent innovation. Unlike traditional woven needlepoint canvas, which frays, plastic canvas can be cut into self-contained shapes. These shapes can be assembled to create wonderful three-dimensional objects. Stitching is quick because the canvas mesh is large, and, since the plastic cannot become distorted, neither blocking nor mounting is required. In addition to its other virtues, when plastic canvas needlepoint is stitched with most yarns, it is washable and hard wearing.

This book is a comprehensive introduction to the realm of three-dimensional needlepoint. The first section explains how to get started and tells you everything you will need to know about working with plastic canvas. Step-by-step instructions follow for twenty-two distinctive projects, each exemplifying a unique facet of plastic canvas needlepoint.

The exciting items you will learn to make include unusual picture frames; charming candlesticks; an elegant scallop shell box stitched with luxurious ribbon yarn; beautiful butterfly place mats, coasters, and napkin rings; a trio of toy dinosaurs; and a unique three-story dollhouse that could become a family heirloom. There are projects for the experienced needlepointer as well as for the novice. Each project is graded. Beginner projects require easy stitches, and the canvas constructions are simple. Intermediate projects have one area of complexity—either the stitching or the construction. Advanced projects are complex in stitching as well as in construction.

Getting Started

Materials and Equipment

Plastic Canvas

Plastic canvas is a rigid yet flexible molded clear or opaque material. The widely spaced horizontal and vertical plastic threads intersect at right angles, forming a grid. Each two adjacent intersecting horizontal and vertical threads of the grid outline a square-shape hole. The point at which one horizontal thread intersects one vertical thread is called a mesh.

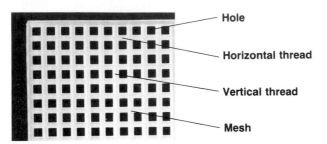

Plastic canvas comes in two gauges—7 mesh and 10 mesh. The gauge is determined by the number of meshes horizontally in one inch of canvas. The gauge can also be determined by counting the number of holes in a one-inch horizontal or vertical row on the canvas. The size of the horizontal and vertical plastic threads and the holes between the threads are larger on 7-mesh canvas than on 10-mesh canvas. Each mesh size of plastic canvas is available in sheets of varying linear dimensions and hole counts.

Plastic canvas is made by several manufacturers, and the sheet dimensions and gauges may vary slightly from one to another. It is therefore important to use only one brand of canvas when working a project.

Each project in this book specifies canvas from a particular manufacturer. If you must substitute, be careful to select canvas with the same mesh and hole count as the canvas that is recommended.

Mesh size	Canvas sheet size	Hole count
10 Mesh (10 holes/in.)	8″ × 10″	80 × 100
	10½″ × 13½″	116 × 136
	11″ × 14″	110 × 140

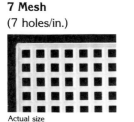

Actual size

Mesh size	Canvas sheet size	Hole count
7 Mesh (7 holes/in.)	10½″ × 13½″	70 × 90
	12″ × 18″	80 × 120
	13½″ × 21½″	90 × 145

Actual size

Marking Pens

Shapes are cut out of plastic canvas sheets prior to stitching. For cutting ease and accuracy, the edges of the shapes should be outlined on the canvas prior to cutting.

The potential care of the needlepoint object must be considered when you are choosing a canvas marker. To prevent bleeding during washing, outlines must either be removed before stitching or be permanent enough to be washed with detergent.

Most types of markers are not suitable for use on plastic canvas because they will not adhere to the nonporous surface. There are, however, two kinds of markers that work best. The first type, china or glass markers, adhere to plastic canvas but are not permanent. Errors can easily be corrected while you are outlining, and after cutting, the outlines can be removed with a soft cloth and warm water. The second type, opaque paint markers, adhere to plastic canvas and are impervious to water and detergent. Turpentine can be used to correct errors in outlining. Marvy Deco Color Opaque Paint Markers are the markers I have found best for consistent opaque color. Those with narrow points work effectively on both 7-mesh and 10-mesh canvas. Choose a marker color similar to the yarn color you will use to overcast and assemble the edges of a project, in case the canvas peeks through. If many yarn colors are used for overcasting and assembly, match the marker color to the palest yarn color or use a white, light gray, or silver marker.

Beware of the many brands of magic markers called permanent. Most of these markers are impervious only to water, not to phosphate or detergent. These markers may be used if you intend to remove the outlines from the canvas prior to stitching. Erase the lines with turpentine. If you do not erase the lines before stitching, such a marker may be used safely only on a project that will not be washed with soap or detergent.

Cutting Tools

Due to the thickness and rigidity of plastic canvas, medium-weight dressmaker's shears are best for cutting around the outside edges of the canvas shapes. Sometimes a project will require an interior cutout and it will be difficult to use scissors. In such cases, use a mat or craft knife to cut the outline edges. Use small embroidery scissors for cutting yarn. For removing stitching mistakes, use the point of an embroidery scissors or a seam ripper.

Needles

Tapestry needles are best for the stitching and assembly of plastic canvas. These needles have blunt points and large eyes for easy threading. They come in graduated sizes; the larger the needle, the lower the number. A no. 16 needle is best for both stitching and assembly on 7-mesh canvas. A no. 18 needle is best for stitching on 10-mesh canvas, and a no. 20 needle is recommended for assembly.

A weaving needle, which is a large version of the tapestry needle, is recommended for assembling long, narrow tubes on some 7-mesh canvas projects. The five-inch-long shaft of the needle can enter and maneuver in a narrow cylinder that is too small to accommodate a hand.

Yarns

In general, the yarns that are suitable for traditional needlepoint can be used for needlepoint on plastic canvas. The large mesh sizes and rigidity of plastic canvas, however, make it possible to use many nontraditional yarns as well.

Yarns are described by many characteristics. One is fiber content—the material used to create the yarn, such as wool, cotton, rayon, acrylic, Dacron, acetate, or polyester. The fiber affects the luster of the yarn, its durability, and its washability. Diameter, or weight, is another characteristic. Yarns range from narrow to thick and are described as fine, medium, or heavy weight. Several strands of a fine yarn may be worked together, creating a heavier yarn.

A third characteristic is ply. Individual pieces of yarn are called strands. One strand of yarn may be composed of several yarn elements that are twisted together, or plied. The individual elements of a plied yarn are called plies. Plied yarns are better for needlepoint than unplied yarns because they resist breaking during stitching and provide durable wear.

A fourth characteristic is elasticity—the ability the yarn has to stretch and relax. Yarns that have great elasticity, although they are not used for traditional needlepoint, may be used on plastic canvas because of its rigidity. The yarn can be stretched while stitching without distorting the canvas.

Most of the projects in this book are of a utilitarian nature, and therefore the yarns suggested were selected on the basis of their washability. They fall into six general categories: Persian yarn, knitting worsted, craft yarn, pearl cotton, ribbon, and metallic yarn.

Persian yarn or Persian-type yarn is a fine-weight yarn composed of three 2-ply strands. The strands may be separated and used individually, or several strands may be used together, creating a heavier weight yarn. Persian yarn or Persian-type yarn is best suited for stitching on 10-mesh canvas.

Knitting worsted, medium weight and 4-ply, can be an acrylic or a wool yarn. It is soft and elastic and may be used on both 7-mesh and 10-mesh canvas. Depending on the stitch being worked and the canvas mesh, one or two strands are used.

Craft yarns are heavyweight and usually lustrous. One strand is used for all stitches. Since craft yarns are thick, they are suitable only for 7-mesh canvas.

Size 3 pearl cotton is a lustrous, fine-weight, 2-ply yarn, equal in thickness to two strands of Persian yarn. Individual or multiple strands may be used for stitching on both 7-mesh and 10-mesh canvas.

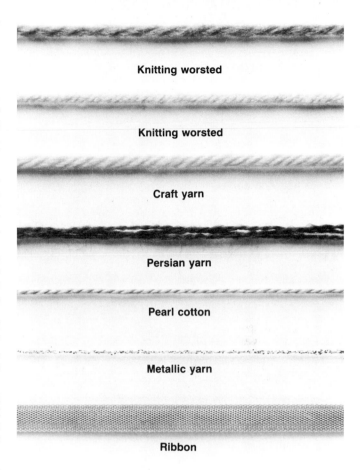

Knitting worsted

Knitting worsted

Craft yarn

Persian yarn

Pearl cotton

Metallic yarn

Ribbon

Ribbon can be used as yarn on plastic canvas. When it is stitched, lustrous, quarter-inch rayon ribbon creates a crinkled, uneven surface. A single strand of ribbon works well for stitching on 10-mesh canvas. Two strands are needed for 7-mesh canvas.

Metallic yarn, which is fine weight and synthetic, is best suited for 10-mesh canvas. Stitches may be worked using single or multiple strands.

Project Materials

Listed at the beginning of the instructions for each project are the specific basic materials required. General supplies that are needed for all projects, such as cutting tools and canvas markers, are not listed. The plastic canvas required is listed by the manufacturer, brand name, color, canvas mesh and hole count, sheet size, and quantity. Yarns are listed by the manufacturer, brand name, color number and name, and required yardage.

Every individual stitches differently—some tighter, others looser. The yardages given are therefore approximately 10 percent greater than the amount of yarn that was used to create the model. Suggested needles for stitching each project are listed, too.

In addition to these basic supplies, many projects require materials for assembly and finishing. These, too, are listed at the beginning of each project.

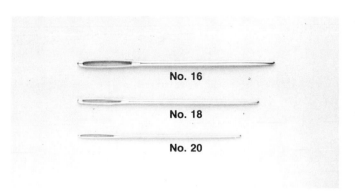

No. 16

No. 18

No. 20

Working with Canvas

The Cutout Diagrams

Each project has several pieces that must be cut from sheets of plastic canvas prior to stitching. Instructions for how these pieces are to be cut from the canvas are given at the beginning of each project on one or more cutout diagrams. These diagrams are graphic representations of sheets of plastic canvas. The horizontal and vertical lines on the cutout-diagram grids represent the plastic threads of the canvas.

Under the heading Materials at the beginning of the instructions for each project, the number of plastic canvas sheets required is specified as well as the canvas mesh, its linear dimensions, and the hole count of each sheet. The cutout diagrams for the project duplicate these specifications, matching the mesh, linear dimensions, and hole count of each piece of canvas. In general, one diagram represents one sheet of canvas. Sometimes, however, one diagram represents more than one sheet of canvas. The number of sheets of canvas to be cut following a cutout diagram is listed below it.

The cutout diagram illustrates the best way to cut each piece of canvas with a minimum of canvas waste. Each piece to be cut is outlined on the diagram. The name of each piece is in its center. At least two canvas holes horizontally and/or vertically separate each piece on the diagram. In many cases, an edge of a piece is also the edge of the canvas. Some pieces have outline edges in the center, within which large Xs are enclosed. These areas represent canvas that is to be cut from the centers of these pieces.

Sometimes cutout diagrams represent sheets of canvas that are not full size. Trim the canvas, matching the hole count of the cutout diagram, prior to marking the pattern pieces on the canvas. These pieces of excess canvas may be used for other projects or as sample canvas to test a project's stitches.

Marking the Canvas

Transfer each cutout diagram to its corresponding sheet of canvas, working one diagram at a time. Place the sheet of canvas on top of a dark sheet of paper on a flat surface. Make sure that the length and width hole count of the canvas matches the length and width hole count of the diagram. Using a china marker or an opaque paint marker, mark the outline edges of the pieces on the canvas, working one piece at a time and matching the outlines of the edges on the diagram. Find the correct placement of the piece outlines on the canvas by counting the squares on the cutout-diagram grid and matching this count to the corresponding holes on the canvas.

Cutting the Pieces

Using dressmaker's shears and working one piece at a time, cut out each piece along the outside edges of the marked plastic threads that form the edge. Cut close to the threads so the edges are smooth. Cut corners and stepped edges carefully, turning the canvas as necessary. After each piece is cut, trim any thread nubs that extend beyond the edges of the piece.

Place any piece that has a center to be cut out on top of a heavy piece of cardboard. Using a mat or craft knife, cut out this center piece along the outside edges of the marked plastic threads that form the edge. Cut carefully, turning the canvas as necessary.

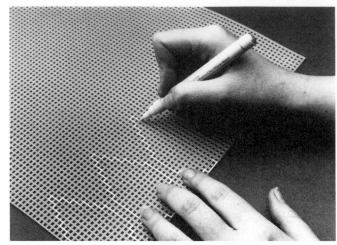
Marking the canvas.

Cutting the canvas.

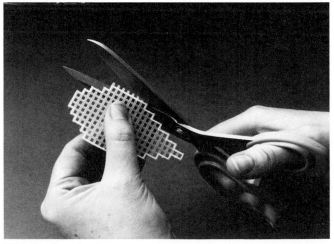
Trimming thread nubs.

Stitching

After cutting, each piece is worked with a broad range of needle-point stitches. The stitches are created by yarn crossing the meshes and threads of the canvas vertically, horizontally, and diagonally. Each stitch creates a different surface design.

Creating a needlepoint stitch in plastic canvas is a two-step process. First, the needle holding the yarn is inserted in a hole in the canvas from the wrong side of the canvas, and the yarn and needle are pulled through the hole from the right side. To complete the stitch, the needle is inserted in a different hole on the right side of the canvas, and the needle and the yarn are then pulled through this hole from the wrong side. The yarn that remains on the right side of the canvas forms the stitch.

So that the stitches cover the canvas and appear uniform, the yarn has to be worked at an even tension. If the yarn is too loose, stitches will bulge on the surface and potentially snag. If the yarn is too tight, it will not cover the canvas adequately and the canvas may curve or buckle.

Different stitches require different weights of yarn to cover the canvas. In general, stitches that are worked horizontally or vertically require a heavier yarn than a stitch that is worked diagonally. A fine- or medium-weight yarn can be used as a heavyweight yarn by working two or more strands together.

For stitching ease, the yarn should be worked in short lengths. Use 18-inch yarn lengths to work stitches that cover one canvas mesh or thread. Up to 36-inch lengths of yarn may be used to work stitches that cover several canvas meshes or threads.

Thread the yarn through the needle by folding a short length back on itself at one end to form a loop. Push this loop through one side of the needle eye. Pull it through the eye from the other side, leaving a yarn tail extended from either side.

When you are using one strand of yarn or an odd-numbered group of strands, align these tails so one is short and one is long. The long tail is secured to the back of the canvas prior to stitching. When a stitch requires two strands of yarn, cut one strand twice as long. After threading the needle, pull the strands so the tails are even. Stitch, working the two strands as one. This allows the needle to pass smoothly through the canvas holes.

For stitches that require more than two strands of yarn, cut half the number of strands, twice as long. Thread the needle and work as recommended with two strands of yarn.

To secure yarn tails prior to stitching, leave a 2-inch tail of yarn when entering the yarn from the wrong side of the canvas. Lay this tail against the back of the canvas parallel to the canvas threads that will be covered by the stitching. To secure the tail, cover it with the first few stitches worked.

To end a length of yarn, pull the needle and the yarn through the canvas to the wrong side. Slide the needle under several stitches, pulling the yarn tight to secure it. Remove the needle and clip the remaining yarn close to the stitched surface.

While you are working the stitches, the length of yarn in the needle may twist, resulting in kinks or knots. This twisting also tightens the yarn, making the stitches appear thin. To relax the yarn, let the yarn and the needle dangle. While they are dangling, the yarn will spin and untwist itself.

The Stitches

Needlepoint stitches are created by inserting the needle through the holes of the canvas and laying the yarn over the canvas threads or meshes vertically, horizontally, or diagonally. A stitch is one line of yarn covering one or more canvas threads or meshes, or sets of several lines of yarn, each a stitch in itself, grouped together to form distinct patterns. Collectively, the needlepoint stitches cover the surface of the canvas. To do so, adjacent stitches in group patterns and adjacent rows of stitches share common holes.

As a means of presentation, stitches are categorized by how the yarn individually or in groups crosses the threads of the canvas. *Diagonal stitches* cross the canvas diagonally. *Straight stitches* cross the canvas vertically or horizontally. *Crossing stitches,* composed of at least two stitches, cross the canvas and each other vertically, horizontally, or diagonally. *Composite stitches* are stitches that combine both diagonal and straight stitches. *Surface stitches* are stitches that are worked on top of a previously stitched ground of another stitch. *Edge overcasting stitches* are stitches specific to needlepoint on plastic canvas that are used to cover the outline edge threads of the canvas pieces.

The stitches presented within each category are the stitches used to work the projects in this book, not a comprehensive listing of needlepoint stitches. The stitch descriptions are limited to the way the stitches are used in the projects.

The grid diagrams accompanying the stitch descriptions are graphic representations of pieces of plastic canvas. The horizontal and vertical lines on the diagram grids represent the horizontal and vertical threads of the canvas. The lines over the grids represent stitches. Insert the needle and the yarn from the wrong side of the canvas to the right side at each number 1 and all the odd numbers. Insert the needle and the yarn from the right side of the canvas to the wrong side at each number 2 and all the even numbers. The numbers describing the sequence of stitch formation are listed by rows. The stitching sequence for each row begins with the number 1.

It is important when stitching a piece to note the top/bottom orientation of the canvas. Most stitches are worked with the top of the piece at the top of the canvas. Some stitches are worked in alternating rows and the canvas is turned upside down. When this occurs, the word *Top* appears upside down on the diagram.

The sequence on each of the stitch diagrams is written for right-handed people. Left-handers can use the diagrams by turning them upside down. Follow the numerical sequences as they are written and the row directions as they are shown, after reversing them.

Before beginning a project, it is best to try each stitch on a piece of extra canvas of the same gauge, using the recommended yarn. If the stitches do not cover the canvas adequately, loosen the tension of your stitches or add additional strands of yarn.

Starting a piece of yarn.

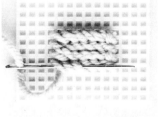

Ending a piece of yarn.

Diagonal Stitches

The yarn in diagonal stitches slants diagonally across one or several canvas meshes or threads. The stitches that slant across one canvas mesh are flat and regular. The stitches that cross two or more canvas meshes and threads are raised and have a padded appearance. Diagonal stitches are used as outline, background, and decorative stitches.

Tent Stitch

The tent stitch is the most common of all the needlepoint stitches. It is used as both an outline stitch and a background stitch. The stitch is formed by slanting the yarn diagonally over one canvas mesh. The traditional direction of the angle is from lower left to upper right. There are three methods of working the tent stitch—half-cross stitch, continental stitch, and basketweave stitch. Each may be used to work an area of any length and width. All three methods achieve the same effect on the right side of the canvas. The variation occurs on the wrong side of the canvas, where each method has a different appearance and a different degree of yarn coverage.

The diagonal of the tent stitch can be worked in a second direction, lower right to upper left. When this direction occurs on the stitch diagrams for a project, twist the diagram a quarter turn, so the diagonal of the tent stitch appears in the traditional lower left to upper right slant. Turn the pattern piece to match the placement of the stitch diagram.

Half-cross stitch may be worked in horizontal or vertical rows. When working horizontally, work odd rows with the canvas in its normal top/bottom position. Work even rows with the canvas turned. To work half-cross stitch vertically, twist the diagram a quarter turn and follow the stitching sequence. Rows of half-cross stitch may be any length.

The stitches on the wrong side of the half-cross stitch are straight stitches over one canvas thread. This method of working the tent stitch uses the least yarn.

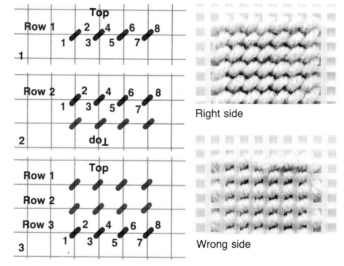

Right side

Wrong side

Continental stitch may be worked in either horizontal or vertical rows. For horizontal rows, the odd rows are worked with the canvas in its normal top/bottom position. Work the even rows with the canvas turned. To work continental stitch vertically, twist the diagram a quarter turn and follow the stitching sequence. Rows of continental stitch may be any length.

The stitches on the wrong side of the continental stitch are diagonal stitches over two canvas meshes and one canvas thread, creating a heavy padding. This method uses more yarn than half-cross stitch.

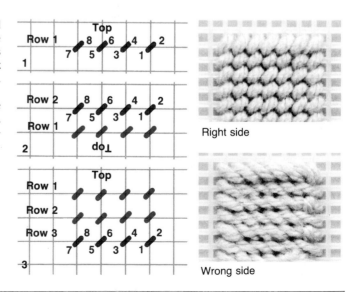

Right side

Wrong side

Basketweave stitch is worked across diagonal rows of canvas meshes. The first row is a single stitch. Each succeeding row is one stitch longer than the previous row. The second row and all the even rows are worked down. The third row and all the succeeding odd rows are worked up. The first stitch of each odd row is worked across the canvas mesh directly below the mesh covered by the last stitch of the previous down row. The first stitch of each even row is worked across the canvas mesh directly left of the mesh covered by the last stitch of the previous up row.

The stitches on the wrong side of the basketweave stitch are alternating horizontal and vertical straight stitches covering two canvas threads. The stitch pattern resembles woven fabric. This method uses the most yarn.

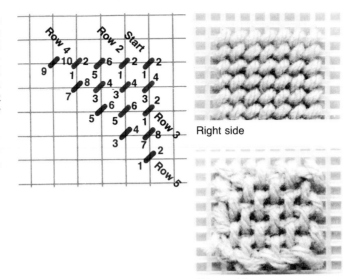

Right side

Wrong side

Slanted Gobelin Stitch

Slanted gobelin stitch is a diagonal stitch worked over a minimum of two canvas meshes and two canvas threads. The traditional slant of the diagonal is from lower left to upper right. This is a versatile stitch that may be worked horizontally or vertically. The stitch may be used to form short or elongated rectangular bands or squares. The first and last stitches of any slanted gobelin stitch unit are always tent stitches. The outline edges of any slanted gobelin stitch unit are always straight. The diagonal of the slanted gobelin stitch may be worked in a second direction, lower right to upper left. The method of working the stitches in this second direction is diagramed as reversed slanted gobelin stitch. The horizontal and vertical rows for both slanted gobelin stitch and reversed slanted gobelin stitch may be lengthened or shortened by adding or subtracting the longer diagonal stitches.

Horizontal rows of slanted gobelin stitches are diagramed worked left to right. They may be worked right to left by treating the last stitch as the first, making the last step the first step of the sequence. Horizontal rows of reversed slanted gobelin stitches may be worked in the opposite direction by similarly reversing the stitching sequence.

Vertical rows of slanted gobelin stitches are diagramed worked top to bottom. They may be worked bottom to top by treating the last stitch as the first, making the last step of the sequence the first. Vertical rows of reversed slanted gobelin stitches may be worked in the opposite direction by similarly reversing the stitching sequence.

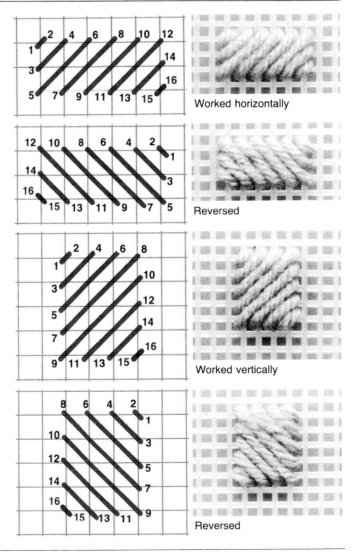

Worked horizontally

Reversed

Worked vertically

Reversed

Mosaic Stitch

The mosaic stitch is composed of three diagonal stitches, two short and one long, that produce a neat textured square. The first and last stitches of each three-stitch block are tent stitches. The center stitch is a diagonal stitch that slants across two canvas meshes and two canvas threads. The slant of the diagonal for each of the three stitches is from lower left to upper right. The mosaic stitch is worked horizontally in rows of any length and is usually used as a background stitch. Follow the stitching sequence diagramed for each row, turning the canvas upside down to work the even-numbered rows.

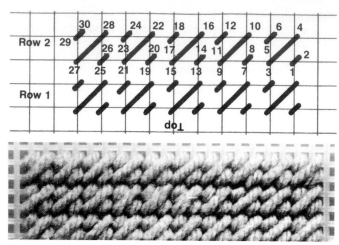

Mosaic Stitch

Cashmere Stitch

The cashmere stitch is composed of four diagonal stitches that repeat in rows to produce a rectangular block pattern. The first and last stitches of each four-stitch block are tent stitches. The center two stitches are diagonal stitches that slant across two canvas meshes and two canvas threads. The slant of the diagonal for each of the four stitches is from lower left to upper right. The cashmere stitch is worked horizontally in rows of any length and is used as a textured background stitch. Follow the stitching sequence diagramed for each row, turning the canvas upside down to work the even-numbered rows.

Cashmere Stitch

Diagonal Satin Stitch

Diagonal satin stitch is a slanted stitch worked over a minimum of two canvas meshes and two canvas threads. The traditional slant of the diagonal is from lower left to upper right. This decorative stitch may be worked horizontally or vertically. The diagram shows it worked horizontally. The first and last stitches of any diagonal satin stitch unit are always tent stitches. A diagonal satin stitch pattern always has one straight edge and one stepped edge.

The diagonal of the diagonal satin stitch may be worked in a second direction, lower right to upper left. The method of working this stitch in this second direction is diagramed as reversed diagonal satin stitch. The horizontal and vertical rows of stitches for both the diagonal satin stitch and the reversed diagonal satin stitch may be lengthened or shortened by adding or subtracting the longer diagonal stitches.

Horizontal rows of diagonal satin stitches are diagramed worked left to right. They may be worked right to left by treating the last stitch as the first, making the last step the first step of the sequence. Horizontal rows of reversed diagonal satin stitch may be worked in the opposite direction by reversing the sequence.

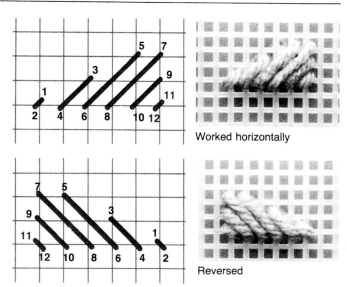

Worked horizontally

Reversed

Diagonal Satin Variation

Diagonal satin variation is a more secure method of working the diagonal satin stitch when the individual slanting yarn lines of the stitch span extended lengths of canvas. The stitch is worked in two steps. The first step is worked with long and short diagonal stitches, slanting in one direction, that alternate in a zigzag pattern. In the second step, short stitches are worked next to the short stitches of the first step, completing the diagonal line.

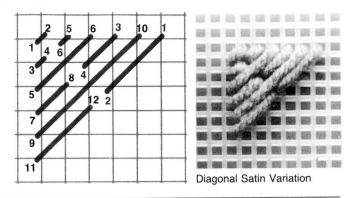

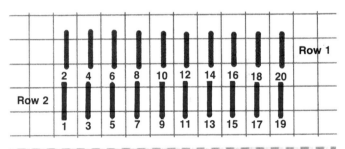

Diagonal Satin Variation

Straight Stitches

Straight stitches are worked either horizontally or vertically over one or more canvas threads. Straight stitches are used to outline, as background, and as decorative stitches.

Gobelin Stitch

Gobelin stitch is worked either horizontally or vertically over one or more canvas threads. The stitches are created in rows that form short or elongated rectangular bands or squares. Worked over several canvas threads, gobelin stitches cover the canvas quickly and have a heavy padded appearance. The outline edges of any gobelin stitch unit are always straight.

The diagram shows the gobelin stitch worked vertically over two canvas threads, creating horizontal rows. Following the same method, the stitches may be worked over fewer or more canvas threads, thus reducing or enlarging the height of the row.

The first row and all the odd-numbered rows are worked from right to left. The second row and all the even-numbered rows are worked from left to right. Each of these rows may be worked starting at the opposite end by treating the last stitch of the row as the first, making the last step of the sequence the first.

To work the gobelin stitch horizontally, creating vertical rows, twist the diagram a quarter turn and follow the stitching sequence.

Gobelin Stitch

Mitered Gobelin

Connected rows of gobelin stitches worked horizontally and vertically are used to outline areas. The rows intersect at the corners, forming a mitered edge. A single slanted gobelin stitch is added to cover the angle of this edge. To form the mitered corners of two intersecting gobelin stitch rows, work the angled edge of the bottom row first, with vertical stitches. Then work the angled edge of the side row with horizontal stitches, adding one horizontal stitch on the top. Work the slanted gobelin stitch to cover the mitered edge. Now continue working the horizontal gobelin stitches upward, completing the vertical row. Work the other mitered corners in the same way as you come to them.

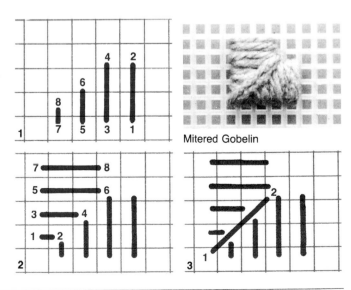

Mitered Gobelin

Satin Stitch

The satin stitch is formed by groups of stitches, worked either horizontally or vertically, over at least one, but usually several, canvas threads. A group of these stitches is worked diagonally, with individual stitches covering different numbers of canvas threads, thus creating a stepped edge. A group of satin stitches may be worked with one straight edge and one stepped edge, or with two stepped edges. Satin stitches may be worked in unconnected or connected rows. The range of stitch patterns in satin stitch is extensive. Individual patterns create distinct decorative textures.

The examples of satin stitches worked vertically are developed in rows that go right to left or left to right. Each of these rows may be worked starting at the opposite end by treating the last stitch of the row as the first, making the last step of the sequence the first. To work satin stitch horizontally, twist the diagrams a quarter turn and follow the stitching sequence. Satin stitches worked horizontally are developed in rows that work up or down. Each of these rows may be worked starting at the opposite end by treating the last stitch of the row as the first, making the last stitch of the sequence the first.

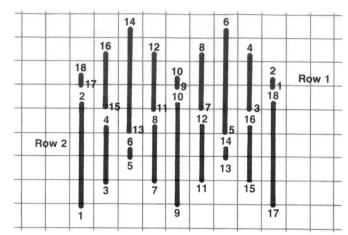

Connected rows

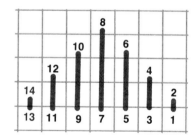

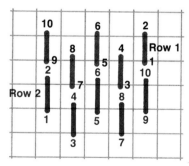

Unconnected row

Brick Stitch

The brick stitch is composed of two offset vertical straight stitches of the same length. Each of the stitches crosses the same number of canvas threads. This stitch has an even, regular appearance and is quick to work.

When working brick stitch two sets of offset stitches are worked zigzag in one row. Rows of brick stitch may be any length, and the pattern may be used to fill large areas by repeating the two rows diagramed. The first row and every odd row are worked from right to left and the second row and every even row are worked from left to right. Each of these rows may be worked starting at the opposite end by treating the last stitch of the row as the first, making the last step of the sequence the first. The example shows the offset vertical straight stitches of the brick stitch worked over two canvas threads. The stitches may be worked over four canvas threads as well.

Brick Stitch

Parisian Stitch

The Parisian stitch is composed of two alternating long and short straight stitches worked in two zigzag rows. The long and short stitches are placed in opposite positions in each of the rows. The Parisian stitch has an irregular overall texture and may be worked vertically or horizontally. The diagram shows Parisian stitch worked vertically in horizontal rows. Rows of Parisian stitch may be any length. The pattern may be used to fill large areas by repeating the alternating rows.

The diagram shows the first row and every odd row worked from right to left and the second row and every even row worked from left to right. Each of these rows may be worked starting at the opposite end by treating the last stitch of the row as the first, making the last step of the sequence the first.

To work the Parisian stitch horizontally in vertical rows, twist the diagram a quarter turn and follow the stitching sequence as diagramed.

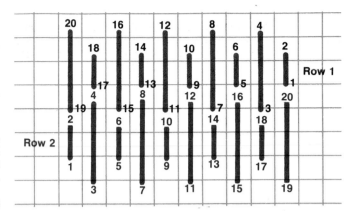

Parisian Stitch

Hungarian Diamond Stitch

The Hungarian diamond stitch is composed of long and short vertical straight stitches that repeat in two offset rows to produce an overall diamond pattern. Individual diamonds are created in units of odd-numbered stitches. The diamond-shape units in each row are separated by one canvas hole.

Rows of Hungarian diamond stitch may be any length. The pattern may be used to fill large areas by repeating the two offset rows.

The diagram shows the first row and every odd row worked from right to left and the second row and every even row worked from left to right. Each of these rows may be worked starting at the opposite end by treating the last stitch of the row as the first, making the last step of the sequence the first.

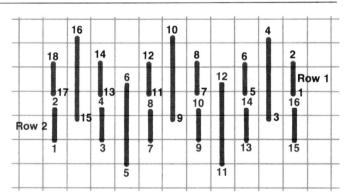

Hungarian Diamond Stitch

Crossing Stitches

Crossing stitches are composed of at least two stitches that cross a canvas thread or mesh and another stitch horizontally, vertically, or diagonally. As a result of this layering of stitches, crossing stitches have a raised surface and are very durable. They are slow to work, however. Crossing stitches are used as outline stitches, background stitches, and decorative stitches.

Cross Stitch

The cross stitch is the simplest of the crossing stitches. It is composed of two stitches that cross diagonally over the same canvas mesh and each other. The upper stitch of the cross stitch slants, like tent stitch, from lower left to upper right. Cross stitches are used as outline, background, and decorative stitches.

Cross stitch may be worked in either horizontal or vertical rows. Each row is worked in two directions. The bottom diagonal stitches in the row are all worked first. These stitches are then crossed by the top diagonal stitches. Rows of cross stitch may be any length. The stitch may be used to fill large areas by repeating the row of cross stitches.

The diagram shows cross stitch worked horizontally. To work cross stitch vertically, twist the diagram a quarter turn and work step 2 of each row sequence first, followed by step 1.

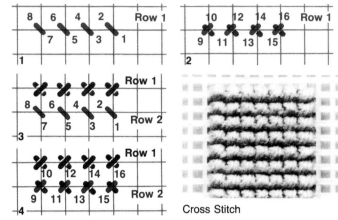

Cross Stitch

Double Cross Stitch

The double cross stitch is composed of two separate cross stitches, one worked diagonally and the other worked horizontally and vertically. The two stitches of the diagonal stitch cross two canvas meshes and threads and are worked first. Then the two straight stitches are worked to cross two canvas threads. The horizontal straight stitch is the last stitch worked. Single double cross stitches are used as decorative stitches.

Double Cross Stitch

Rhodes Stitch

This is a raised stitch composed of six diagonal stitches that each cross two canvas meshes and three canvas threads. The stitches are worked in a counterclockwise order along the outlines of a square. Each stitch, after the first, crosses over all the previous stitches, forming an uneven accumulation of layers. Single Rhodes stitches are used as decorative stitches. The appearance of the Rhodes stitch is dependent on the way the individual stitches are worked. Follow the stitching sequence carefully.

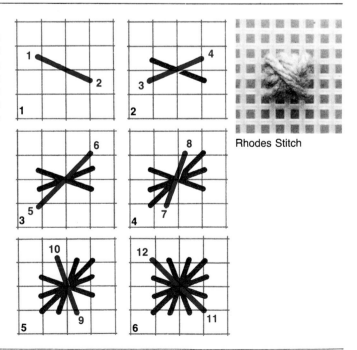

Rhodes Stitch

Double Leviathan Stitch

The double leviathan stitch is composed of several diagonal stitches and straight stitches that cross each other, forming large raised squares. The stitch is worked in small and large versions. The small version is worked in eight stitches. The large version is worked in twelve stitches. The appearance of the double leviathan stitch is dependent on how the individual stitches are worked. Follow the stitching sequences carefully.

The small double leviathan stitch is worked over four canvas threads horizontally and vertically. It is composed of six diagonal stitches and two straight stitches. The diagonal stitches are worked first. The horizontal and vertical straight stitches cross over all the diagonal stitches. The horizontal straight stitch is worked last.

Single small double leviathan stitches are used as decorative stitches. The stitch may be worked in rows, too, creating a highly textured block design.

The large double leviathan stitch is worked over six canvas threads horizontally and vertically. It is composed of ten diagonal stitches and two straight stitches. The diagonal stitches are worked first. The horizontal and vertical straight stitches cross over all the diagonal stitches. The horizontal straight stitch is worked last. This stitch is used singly as a decorative stitch.

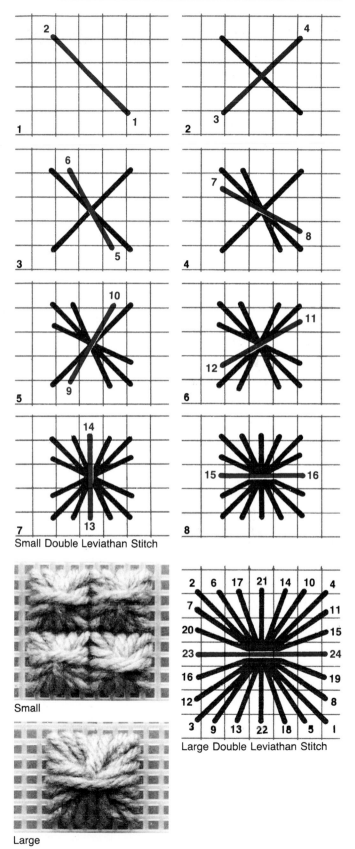

Small Double Leviathan Stitch

Small

Large

Large Double Leviathan Stitch

Composite Stitches

Composite stitches are stitches formed by combining one or more diagonal and straight stitches. The pattern of each stitch is created by the varying combinations of stitches. Each stitch has its own character and decorative use.

Algerian Eye Stitch

The Algerian eye stitch has four diagonal stitches that cross one canvas mesh and four straight stitches that cross one canvas thread. The stitches are worked in clockwise order around a common hole. To work the stitch sequence, bring the needle and the yarn up through the numbered holes from the wrong side of the canvas. Bring the needle and the yarn down through the common hole, or center, marked with the letter C, from the right side of the canvas. Individual Algerian eye stitches are used as decorative stitches.

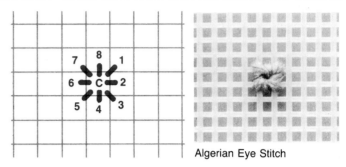

Algerian Eye Stitch

Backstitch

The backstitch is an outline stitch worked in single rows of straight and diagonal stitches. Rows may be worked straight or combined, horizontally, vertically, or diagonally. Straight stitches may cross one or several canvas threads. Diagonal stitches may cross one canvas mesh or several canvas meshes or threads. Rows of backstitch may be any length.

The examples show a row of diagonal backstitch starting at the top of the row and working down. The row of horizontal backstitch is worked from right to left. Each of these rows may be worked starting at the opposite end by treating the last stitch of the row as the first, making the last step of the sequence the first. To work backstitch vertically, twist the horizontal backstitch diagram a quarter turn and follow the stitching sequence.

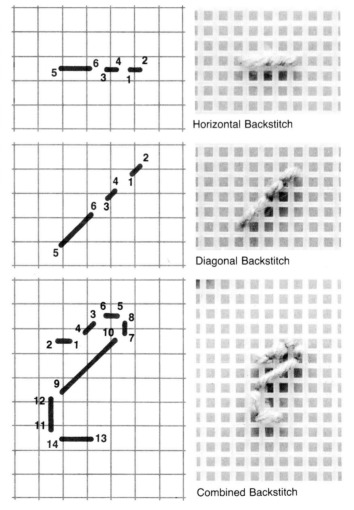

Horizontal Backstitch

Diagonal Backstitch

Combined Backstitch

Surface Stitches

Surface stitches are raised stitches worked on top of a tent-stitch ground. These highly textured stitches are used to add decorative details.

French Knot

The French knot is a rounded, raised stitch that is created by wrapping the yarn around the needle and pulling the needle through. To work a French knot, bring the needle and the yarn through a hole from the wrong side of the canvas. With the needle in your right hand, hold the yarn taut with your left. Twist the yarn around the needle twice. Pull the yarn gently to tighten the twists. Slide the twists down to the point of the needle and insert the needle through the hole in the canvas from which it emerged. Still holding the yarn taut, pull the yarn and the needle through to the back of the canvas. The size of a French knot depends on the number of yarn twists around the needle. To make a larger knot, increase the number of twists.

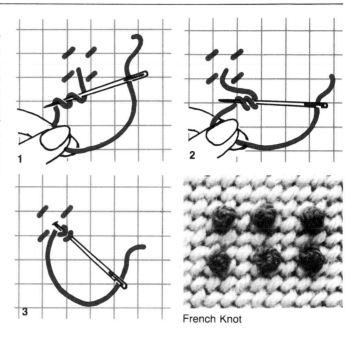

French Knot

Edge Overcasting Stitches

After a piece of plastic canvas has been stitched, an outline of horizontal and vertical plastic threads is visible along the edges. To finish the piece, these outlining threads are overcast with yarn. On flat projects, the edge threads are overcast after stitching. On dimensional projects, the edge threads on each of the pieces may be overcast prior to assembly, during assembly, or after assembly. The stitches described in this section are used to overcast the edge plastic threads on the canvas pieces following stitching and either prior to assembly or after assembly. When working these edging stitches, secure the starting and ending tail of yarn by sliding the needle under the stitches on the wrong side of the canvas.

Whip Stitch

The whip stitch is the stitch most commonly used to overcast the horizontal and vertical threads that outline the edges of the plastic canvas pieces. It is a wrapping stitch, worked through the holes along the edges of the canvas, that covers the outlining plastic threads. The number of stitches worked through each hole depends on the shape of the threads being covered.

The edge of a plastic canvas piece is a linear grid composed of intersecting horizontal and vertical threads. When one horizontal thread intersects with one vertical thread, a corner is formed. When one horizontal thread intersects with two vertical threads or one vertical thread intersects with two horizontal threads, a point is formed.

The outline edges of a piece may be straight or stepped. Two types of corners occur on a piece with stepped edges. Inside corners occur at the bottom of steps. Outside corners occur at the top of steps. On straight-edge pieces, the corners are all outside corners.

To work the whip stitch along a straight edge, attach the yarn

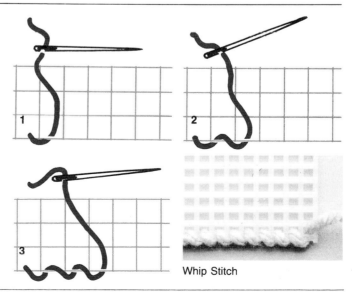

Whip Stitch

to the wrong side of the canvas and bring the needle and the yarn through the first hole on the edge, from the wrong side of the canvas. To work the first stitch, bring the needle through the second hole on the edge from the wrong side of the canvas to the right side of the canvas. To work the second stitch, bring the needle through the third hole on the edge, from the wrong side of the canvas. Each whip stitch is worked the same way as these two stitches. Work one stitch in each hole along straight edges and the holes adjacent to inside corners. Work three whip stitches in the holes at the outside corners. Work five whip stitches in the holes at points. Always work as many stitches as necessary to cover the canvas.

Always work the whip stitch carefully so the outlining plastic threads along the edges of the canvas pieces do not split. As you work each stitch, pull the yarn and the needle gently through each hole. If the plastic thread adjacent to a hole does split, skip that hole and work a stitch in the next hole of the sequence. Then go back and work a stitch in the skipped hole, holding the split plastic thread in place. If the thread moves and the stitch does not cover it, remove this stitch and the stitch worked in the succeeding hole. Now work a stitch over the interior plastic thread parallel to the split thread, one hole in from the edge hole with the split thread. Then continue working whip stitch as before, in the holes along the plastic edges.

The edges of the pieces are often overcast in more than one color yarn. The color of the whip stitch to be worked in each hole is shown on the stitch diagrams by the line of color on the edge outline adjacent to each hole. Work the yarn colors as they appear, in consecutive sequence.

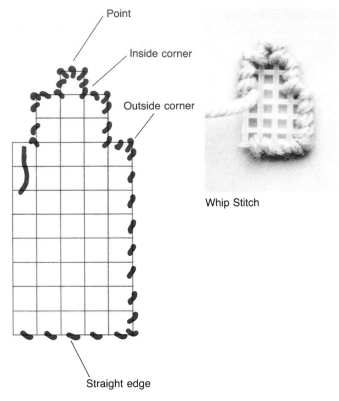

Point

Inside corner

Outside corner

Straight edge

Whip Stitch

Edging Stitch

The edging stitch is a crossing stitch used to overcast the plastic thread on a straight canvas edge. Individual stitches interlace with each other as they are worked, creating a raised edge.

The stitch is worked in two forward/backward steps, through alternating canvas holes. Insert the needle and the yarn from the wrong side of the canvas to the right side at hole 1 and pull the needle through. Move forward two holes and insert the needle from the wrong side of the canvas to the right side at hole 3 and pull the needle through to the right side. Now move back one hole and insert the needle from the wrong side of the canvas to the right side at hole 2 and pull it through to the right side. Move forward again two holes and insert the needle from the wrong side of the canvas to the right side at hole 4 and pull it through to the right side. Move back again one hole and insert the needle at hole 3. Continue working in this two-holes-forward, one-hole-back zigzag sequence (5, 4, 6, 5, 7, 6, 8, etc.) until the edge is complete, always inserting the needle from the wrong side of the canvas to the right side.

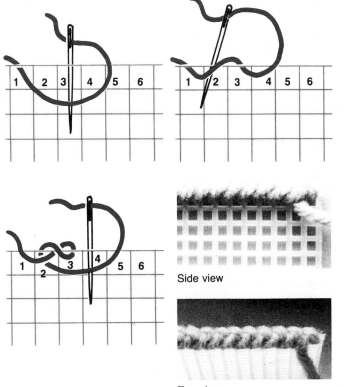

Side view

Top view

Project Stitching Instructions

Each project has a series of stitch diagram charts showing the stitches and yarn colors that should be used to work each plastic canvas piece. The charts are graphic representations of the plastic canvas pieces. The horizontal and vertical lines of the grids represent the plastic threads of the canvas. When a chart is larger than one page, the shape is split and the common center thread is represented by a dotted line.

Overlaid on these grids are horizontal, vertical, and diagonal lines in varying shades, which represent the individual stitches to be worked. The color of each of these overlaid lines indicates the yarn color in which the stitch is to be worked. A color code matching the yarn color names to the linear color of the represented stitches is next to the diagram grids.

Overlaid color lines on the outline edges of the grids indicate edges of the piece that are to be overcast before assembly. Small dots in the centers of squares represent French knots.

In addition to the charts, each project has specific written instructions for stitching each piece of plastic canvas. A recommended sequence for working each piece, including the stitches used and the yarn color and weight in which each stitch is worked, is listed next to each piece.

Do not be concerned if you make an error when you are stitching. If you catch the error while working a stitch, remove the yarn from the needle and pull out the incorrect stitches. Then rework the stitches using the same yarn. If you find a mistake after a piece is completed, the incorrect stitches must be cut out and reworked with new yarn. To cut the stitches, use a seam ripper or the point of the embroidery scissors. On the right side of the piece, slide the cutting tool carefully under the stitches, between the canvas threads and the yarn. Cut through the stitches carefully, working a few stitches at a time. Remove the cut stitches from the wrong side of the canvas, securing the yarn tails for the stitches that remain. Now work the correct stitches.

Usually the sequence in which the stitches are worked on pieces with many stitches or colors begins with the outlining details and ends with adding the background stitches. Using an opaque paint marker in the color of the stitches to be worked, you can mark the placement of the detail stitches on the canvas before stitching. Place small dots in the center of the canvas meshes to be covered by tent stitches or cross stitches. Place dots in the centers of the sets of outside threads to be covered by each of the satin stitches. Place lines across the outside threads that will be covered by rows of gobelin or diagonal gobelin stitches. When marking the stitches on the canvas, be sure to count the holes and threads carefully, matching the markings to the stitch placement on the stitch diagram charts.

Stitches are usually not worked across the threads that are adjacent to the single holes at the points of the plastic canvas pieces. These threads will be covered when the edges of the pieces are overcast or assembled.

Assembling the Pieces

All the projects in this book must be assembled after the canvas pieces have been stitched. In some cases, the plastic edges of two pieces are joined. In others, the plastic edge of one piece is joined to an interior plastic thread on another piece. Sometimes the plastic edges to be assembled are overcast; often they are not. The interior plastic threads may be stitched or unstitched.

The methods for assembling plastic canvas projects are divided into two categories—joining and tacking. Joining methods are used when the outline plastic edges to be assembled are not overcast and the interior plastic threads are unstitched. Tacking methods are used when the plastic edges are overcast and the interior plastic threads are stitched.

The joining category is subdivided into two additional categories—flush joins and overlap joins—based on how the joins are formed. Flush joins occur when the outline edges and the interior threads of the pieces to be joined are adjacent to one another. Overlap joins occur when the edges and threads to be joined overlap each other.

When you are working any joining method, start and end yarn tails by securing the yarn under several stitches on the wrong side of the canvas. Sometimes by the end of the assembly process a piece is completely closed and the yarn cannot be ended on the wrong side. To end this last piece of yarn, insert the needle from the right side of the project into the last hole to be joined through the interior of the piece and out a hole on the right side

nearby. Pull the needle and the yarn out of this hole and clip the yarn close to the stitching.

Joins are usually worked in the color yarn that was used for the pattern stitching adjacent to the edges being joined. When more than one yarn color is used, end the yarn for one color and start the next color as directed.

Work carefully when joining so as not to split the outline plastic threads at the edges of the canvas pieces. To prevent splitting on 10-mesh canvas, work the joins using a tapestry needle one size smaller than you used for stitching.

Corners occur when the adjacent edges of three canvas pieces are joined. Rows of joining stitches on each two adjacent edges start and end in the holes at corners. To prevent the plastic edge threads from splitting at corners, work the stitches in each hole slowly, pulling the needle through gently.

If the thread along the edge of one hole to be joined splits, work the joining stitch over the interior plastic thread parallel to the split thread one hole in from the edge hole. Work the following stitches through the holes along the outline plastic edges of the pieces, as before.

Sometimes the straight edges of three canvas pieces or the straight edges of two canvas pieces and one straight interior thread are joined at once. When this occurs, work the joins in the flush-joining methods for two straight edges or one straight edge and one straight interior thread.

Flush Joins

The edges on plastic canvas pieces are either straight or stepped. Flush joins are made on various combinations of edges: two straight edges, two stepped edges, and a straight and a stepped edge. The stitching methods to create the joins on each of these combinations are related yet different.

Joining two straight edges. Flush joins between pieces with two straight edges can be created by using tent stitch, gobelin stitch, or cross stitch.

The tent-stitch method is worked like a row of half-cross stitch. Lay the edges of the two pieces to be joined side by side. Secure the yarn to the wrong side of the piece on the left and bring the needle through the bottom hole on the edge, to the right side of the piece. Insert the needle on the right side in the first hole on the bottom of the right piece, making one straight stitch. Pull the needle through to the wrong side of the piece. Insert it again, from the wrong side, in the first hole on the bottom of the left piece. Make the first diagonal stitch by inserting the needle from the right side in the second hole on the right piece. Pull it through to the wrong side. Make the second stitch by inserting the needle through the second hole on the left piece, from the wrong side, and the third hole on the right piece, on the right side. Continue making stitches in this way until you reach the ends of the pieces. Add an additional straight stitch, joining the two top holes, as

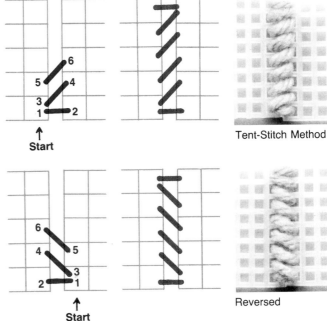

Tent-Stitch Method

Reversed

the first two holes were joined. This sequence of working creates a tent stitch that slants from lower left to upper right.

To create a tent stitch with the opposite slant, follow the same stitching sequence, starting with the first hole on the bottom of the right canvas piece. The tent-stitch method can be worked quickly, because by holding the two pieces to be joined at an angle, the needle can exit from one hole and enter another in one hand motion.

Working the needle for the tent-stitch method.

The cross-stitch method of joining is worked like the cross-stitch pattern stitch. Instead of working all the bottom diagonal stitches first and then crossing them with the top diagonal stitches, in this method of joining, the two stitches that make each cross are completed before the next cross is worked.

Insert the needle through a hole on the wrong side of the canvas pieces at 1 and all the odd numbers. Insert the needle in a hole on the right side of the canvas pieces at 2 and all the even numbers. This joining method is very slow because of the double number of stitches to be made.

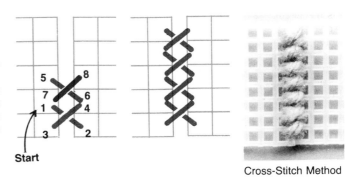

Cross-Stitch Method

The gobelin-stitch method is worked like the gobelin stitch, over one canvas thread. Lay the edges of the two pieces to be joined side by side. Secure the yarn to the wrong side of the piece on the left and bring the needle up through the bottom hole, to the right side of the piece. Insert the needle on the right side in the first hole on the bottom of the right piece. Pull the needle through to the wrong side of the piece. To make the second stitch, insert the needle from the wrong side into the second hole on the left piece. Pull the needle through and insert it from the right side into the second hole on the right piece. Pull the needle through to the wrong side. Continue in this way until you reach the ends of the pieces. This method is slower to work than the tent-stitch method because the needle must go up through one hole and down through another in two hand motions.

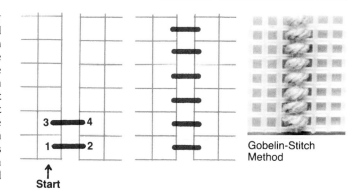

Gobelin-Stitch Method

The tent-stitch and gobelin-stitch methods are related. On the wrong side, the tent-stitch method forms a gobelin stitch. On the wrong side, the gobelin-stitch method forms a tent stitch. The diagonal stitches in both methods affect the alignment of the canvas pieces. The pieces will never be level; one piece will always be slightly higher than the other.

Joining two stepped edges. Flush joins between two canvas pieces with stepped edges are worked in horizontal straight stitches, like the straight-edge gobelin-stitch method. There is one variation: The inside corners on the steps, as well as the straight edges, are joined. A straight stitch is worked across the edges in the holes adjacent to two matched inside corners.

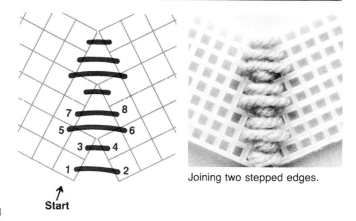

Joining two stepped edges.

To join two stepped-edge pieces, lay the pieces side by side, placing the outside corners of the steps on each piece together. Work straight stitches through the matched edge holes of the pieces, across the angled spaces between the matched corners. The straight stitches will be longer at the bases of the angle and narrower at the points. As you move from one step to the next, work one straight stitch joining the holes adjacent to the inside corners of that step.

Pieces with stepped edges will be angular when joined, curving inward or outward. As with straight-edge pieces joined by the gobelin-stitch method, the top and bottom edges of the two joined stepped-edge pieces will not be level. The edge of one piece will always be slightly higher than the edge of the other.

Joining a straight edge and a stepped edge. Flush joins between a canvas piece with a straight edge and a canvas piece with a stepped edge are worked in a combination of straight stitches and diagonal stitches. This occurs because the hole count on the edges is not equal. There is no precise working method for this flush join. Work the join predominantly in straight stitches, and work diagonal stitches as necessary to cover the edge threads of the stepped piece. Always work a stitch in the hole against the inside corner of a step. As necessary, work more than one stitch in the holes of the straight-edge piece so that the edges of the stepped-edge piece are completely covered. Work the straight stitches over one canvas thread. Work the diagonal stitches over one canvas mesh.

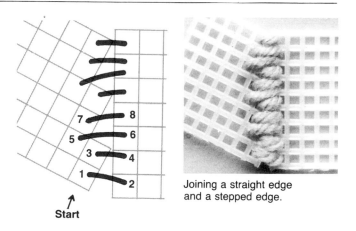

Joining a straight edge and a stepped edge.

The piece of canvas with the straight edge used in these joins may be flat or a cylinder. If the piece is flat, its edge when joined to the stepped edge of the second canvas piece will curve to conform to the angular or curving shape of the stepped-edge piece. When the straight-edge piece is a cylinder, the stepped-edge piece is attached to the top of the cylinder as a cap.

Joining a straight edge to an interior thread. Flush joins also occur when the straight edge of one pattern piece is joined to the interior thread of another pattern piece. The interior thread may be one horizontal or vertical thread on the canvas or a combination of horizontal and vertical threads forming a stepped outline.

To work a join along a straight interior thread, place the straight edge of the canvas piece perpendicular to the interior canvas thread, matching the lengths of the two threads. Join them by working in tent stitch or gobelin stitch over both threads, treating them as one. As with straight-edge joins, tent stitch worked on the right side of the piece with the interior thread creates gobelin stitches on the wrong side. Gobelin stitch worked on the right side of the edge with the interior thread creates tent stitch on the wrong side. In either stitch, these joins are slow to work, since the needle must enter and exit from each hole in each piece with one hand motion.

In the assembly instructions, where the join is visible and contributes to the design of the object, a particular joining stitch is recommended. When no stitch is recommended, work the stitch you prefer.

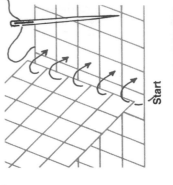

Tent-Stitch Method

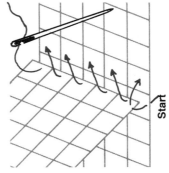

Gobelin-Stitch Method

Joining a straight edge to a stepped interior edge. Flush joins between a straight edge and a stepped outline of interior threads must be worked in a combination of straight and diagonal stitches, like the flush join of a straight-edge piece and a stepped-edge piece. Work this join predominantly in straight stitches. Work diagonal stitches as necessary to cover the stepped outline of the interior threads, and always work a stitch in the hole adjacent to the inside corner of a step. As necessary, work more than one stitch in the holes of the straight-edge piece so the stepped outline of the interior threads is covered. Work the straight stitches over one canvas thread. Work the diagonal stitches over one canvas mesh.

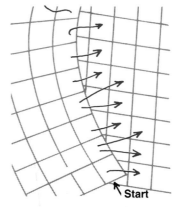

Joining a straight edge
to a stepped interior edge.

Overlap Joins

The second joining category, overlap joins, is created when two plastic canvas pieces are laid on top of each other, matching at least one column of holes and two threads in each layer. To join these pieces, the threads of each layer are treated as one and stitched together. Two flat pieces may be joined by overlapping, or the edges of one piece may be overlap joined, thereby forming a cone or a cylinder. In overlap joins, the edge threads of each layer of canvas are joined to an interior thread on the second layer of canvas.

Overlap joins are usually visible joins worked in the yarn that was used to stitch the canvas. The joining stitches are predominantly tent stitch and gobelin stitch. Sometimes cross stitch and backstitch are used. In the assembly instructions, when the method of stitching contributes to the design of the project, the stitch to work an overlap join is recommended. When no stitch is recommended, work the stitch you prefer.

One-hole overlap join

Two-hole overlap join

Blind backstitch method. When overlap joins are hidden, they are worked in a particular stitching method called blind backstitch, using a fine yarn. This method, which is a combination of vertical backstitches and horizontal gobelin stitches over one canvas thread, joins the two layers of canvas tightly. After the join is complete, it is stitched over with pattern stitches and so becomes invisible.

To work the blind backstitch method of overlap joining, work backstitch vertically over the threads in the column of overlapped holes on the two canvas pieces. Then work two rows of horizontal gobelin stitch, joining the two matched threads of each layer. Joined in each row of horizontal gobelin stitches are an edge thread and an interior thread of each layer.

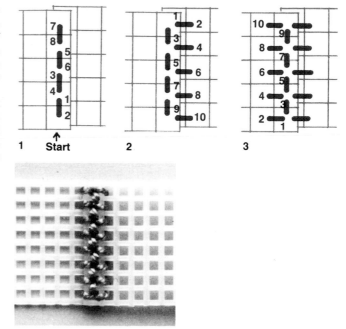

Blind Backstitch Method

Tacking

Tacking, the second method for assembling plastic canvas pieces, is primarily an overstitching method. Piece edges are joined to piece edges or interior threads in much the same way as with flush joining. The major difference between flush joining and tacking is that in tacking, the edges and threads to be joined have been overcast or stitched prior to assembly. Tacking is used to assemble pieces when it would be difficult to use joining methods.

Tacking is predominantly used to join the straight or stepped edge of a piece to the straight or stepped interior thread of a second piece. The stitches are worked in a fine yarn matching the yarn color of the stitches on the edges and threads to be joined. Tacking stitches are gobelin stitch and tent stitch worked in the same manner as these stitches are worked in flush joining when joining piece edges to piece interior threads. Tacking stitches worked in either method appear to be invisible. When the stitches might be visible, a method is recommended in the assembly instructions. When no method is recommended, choose the one you prefer. When the word *blind* is used before a recommended tacking stitch, it indicates that the stitch is worked under pattern stitches on the right side of the canvas. The tacking stitches will be hidden by the pattern stitches.

When two overlapped pieces are assembled by tacking, backstitch is used. As with assembling by joining methods, start and end yarn tails in tacking by securing the yarn under several stitches on the wrong side of the canvas.

The figure-eight stitch. When the edges of two pieces are to be joined—two straight edges or a straight edge and a stepped edge—a stitch specific to tacking is used. The figure-eight stitch is a wrapping stitch in which the needle and yarn are always inserted through the holes on the wrong side of the pieces to be joined. Its zigzag appearance is less visible on these edges than tent stitch or gobelin stitch.

To work the stitch, place the edge of the two pieces to be joined side by side. Insert the needle, from the wrong side, in the first hole on the bottom of the left piece. Pull the needle through to the right side. Now insert the needle, from the wrong side, into the first hole on the bottom of the piece on the right. Pull the needle through. Now insert the needle, from the wrong side, into the second hole on the left piece. Pull the needle through. Insert the needle, from the wrong side, into the second hole on the right piece. Pull the needle through. Continue inserting the needle in opposite holes in this zigzag fashion until stitches are worked in all the holes.

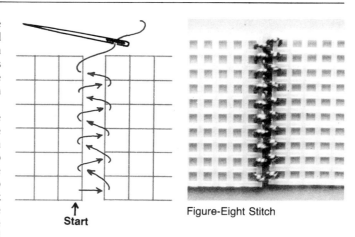

Figure-Eight Stitch

Project Assembly Instructions

Step-by-step assembly instructions are included with each project. The order in which the canvas pieces are to be joined is specified. The assembly methods for each join are listed along with the recommended yarn color and weight to be used.

When you are assembling projects, be aware of the orientation of each canvas piece; each has a right side and a wrong side. The right side is the surface with the pattern stitches. On the assembly illustrations, the right side of a piece is white, the wrong side is gray. The top in the illustrations is the same as the top edge indicated by the arrow next to the stitch diagram chart of each piece.

Interior threads of the canvas pieces that are to be used for assembly don't have overlaid stitch lines on the stitch diagrams.

In the assembly instructions, when two straight edges are to be joined, a method is recommended when the stitch is integral to the design of the piece. Generally the method is not indicated. You may choose the stitch that you prefer.

Most straight-edge flush joins are visible joins worked in the yarn that was used for pattern stitching. Sometimes a join is worked in a finer yarn and is intended to be invisible. When this occurs, the word *blind* is added to the name of the stitching method. In most cases, these blind joins are overstitched in a second joining method, using a heavier yarn. An overstitched blind join is worked when the join requires extra strength.

Care and Cleaning

The stitched areas of all the projects in this book may be hand washed using cold or warm water and a mild detergent. Prior to washing, remove any detachable nonstitched accessories. Soak the object in soapy water and rinse it thoroughly. To remove the excess water, gently pat with a towel. To dry, place the object on a drying rack or on a towel on a flat surface. Do not wash or dry any plastic canvas needlepoint in a washing machine or dryer; the temperature and tumbling will cause distortion. Never have plastic canvas needlepoint professionally dry-cleaned. The cleaning fluids may dissolve the canvas.

Despite the inherent rigidity of plastic canvas, dimensional objects may distort if crushed. When packing or storing an item made of plastic canvas needlepoint, stuff the interior with wads of unprinted paper to maintain its shape. Center it in a packing carton or box and pad it firmly on all sides with additional paper to prevent any movement.

Design Flexibility

Projects in this book can be personalized by changing the colors of the recommended yarns to reflect your own taste. You can also use yarns other than the ones recommended. If you substitute yarns, keep in mind the gauge of the canvas and the stitches to be used. In general, fine- and medium-weight yarns may be used on 10-mesh canvas, and fine-, medium-, and heavyweight yarns may be used on 7-mesh canvas.

On 10-mesh canvas, use one or two strands of a fine-weight yarn such as Persian yarn, metallic yarn, or pearl cotton to work diagonal, crossing, and composite stitches. Use two or three strands to work straight, edge overcasting, assembly, and surface stitches. For medium-weight yarns such as knitting worsted and $1/4$-inch ribbon, use one strand of yarn to work all the stitches.

On 7-mesh canvas, several strands of fine-weight yarns are required to work each stitch. Use two to four strands to work diagonal, crossing, and composite stitches. Use three to six strands for straight, edge overcasting, assembly, and surface stitches. For medium-weight yarns, use one strand for diagonal, crossing, composite, and surface stitches. Use two strands for straight, edge overcasting, and joining stitches. With a heavy craft yarn on 7-mesh canvas, use one strand of yarn for all stitches.

When you substitute yarns, be sure to test each stitch to be worked on a sample of the canvas to be used prior to stitching the project. Each stitch should cover the meshes and the threads of the canvas well. Adjust the working tension and the weight of the yarn for each stitch, adding or subtracting strands as necessary, until the stitches look right.

When you substitute yarns, you may have to adjust the yardage quantities that have been recommended. The yardage remains the same for each color only if the substituted yarn is the same weight as the recommended yarn and the yarn is used for the same stitches. When the stitches remain the same, more yarn will be required if you use a finer yarn. If you use a heavier yarn, less yarn will be required.

Projects may be altered, too, by changing the canvas mesh. A project worked on 7-mesh canvas may be miniaturized by using 10-mesh canvas instead. A project worked on 10-mesh canvas may be enlarged by working it on 7-mesh canvas. A project that is enlarged will increase approximately a third in each dimension. A project that is reduced will decrease approximately a third in each dimension. The scale cannot be changed effectively for all the projects. The ones to try are the dinosaurs, the strawberry baskets, the shell box, the grand piano container, and the pencil case. You may have to substitute yarn weights and quantities when changing the project size. When you increase the size of a project you will need more yarn in a heavier weight. When you reduce the size, you may need less yarn in a finer weight.

Similarly, the cutout diagrams as maps for cutting sheets of canvas will no longer be applicable. Use them only for determining the shapes of the pieces to be cut. When you increase the size of a project, you will need more than the recommended number of sheets of canvas. Be sure to buy canvas in sheets large enough to accommodate the hole count of the largest pattern piece to be cut. When you reduce a project, the canvas quantity required may be the same or less than the amount recommended.

The Projects

This unusual pencil case, which is simple to make, can hold pencils and other school supplies, crayons, or even the pieces of a jigsaw puzzle.

Decorative and practical, these three strawberry baskets are surprisingly easy to stitch and to construct.

Here's a butterfly table setting—place
mats, trivet, napkin rings, coasters and
carrier—that will make any meal an occasion.

Zinnia candlesticks, both small and large, are pretty, easy to stitch and to construct, and can be made in any colors that suit your decor or your fancy.

This charming gingerbread house holds
recipe cards and is sure to add a cheerful
note to your kitchen.

Here's a wise owl that will always tell you what time it is.

Mother Goose's Old Woman's Shoe makes a whimsical wall hanging that will display six of your favorite photographs.

This elegant lace-look picture frame is
stitched with ribbon and gold yarn and
holds two photographs.

The Victorian lamppost, right top, displays four photographs. The Victorian house, right, is an unusual cover for your photograph album.

A most unusual container, this miniature grand piano can hold a note pad, paper clips, or hairpins, or serve as a candy dish.

This scallop shell box, which is stitched with silky ribbon, is a lovely object in which to keep your trinkets or treasures.

This trio of dinosaurs—Tyrannosaurus, Stegosaurus, and Dimetrodon—make sturdy pets that are sure to delight any child.

This magnificent three-story dollhouse, its design based on a Georgian town house, will surely become a prized family heirloom.

The roof of the house has an unusual feature—a charming skylight, which is repeated on the ceiling of the bedroom.

The walls of the bedroom are covered with a pretty needlepointed ''wallpaper,'' which coordinates with the needlepointed ''rug.''

In the living room there are two windows,
subtly patterned walls, and "carpeting."
The ceiling is needlepointed in white.

Shuttered windows add dimension to the
kitchen, which has patterned walls and
a matching "tile" floor.

Strawberry Baskets
Beginner

These bright berries, in three graduated sizes, are perfect for storing oddments or precious collectibles. You can make one or all three for a whimsical touch of summer all year round. These strawberries are easy to stitch—only four basic stitches are used—and the construction is surprisingly simple.

Materials/Large Strawberry Basket

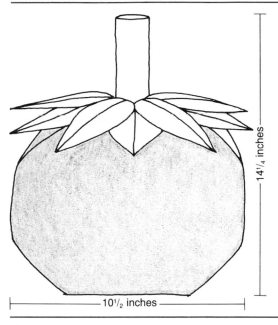

- Columbia-Minerva FashionEase clear 7-mesh plastic canvas: six sheets 10½" × 13½" (70 holes × 90 holes)
- Columbia-Minerva FashionEase Yarn for Needlepoint:

#0014 Red	246 yards
#0007 Yellow	52 yards
#0015 Lime	77 yards
#0016 Leaf Green	33 yards

- Bernat 1–2–3 Ply Persian Type Yarn:

#N27–835 Lime	1 yard (or any Persian yarn that matches #0015 Lime)
#N21–896 Leaf Green	24 inches (or any Persian yarn that matches #0016 Leaf Green)

- no. 16 tapestry needle

- weaving needle

Cutout Diagrams/Large Strawberry Basket

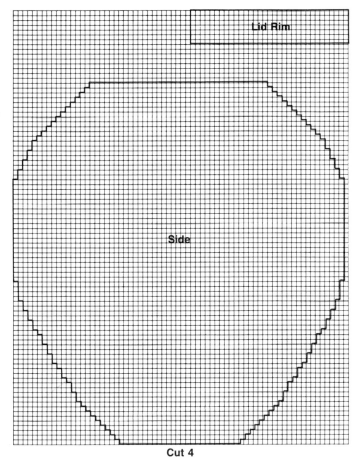

Lid Rim

Side

Cut 4

Pattern Pieces

Follow the cutting diagrams carefully, making sure to count the holes accurately and to cut the right number of pieces.

1. Base. Cut one piece 25 holes wide × 25 holes high.
2. Sides. Cut four pieces 69 holes wide × 75 holes high.
3. Lid. Cut one piece 41 holes wide × 41 holes high.
4. Lid Rims. Cut four pieces 33 holes wide × 7 holes high.
5. Stem. Cut one piece 31 holes wide × 36 holes high.
6. Stem Cap. Cut one piece 10 holes wide × 10 holes high.
7. Leaves. Cut ten pieces 19 holes wide × 40 holes high.

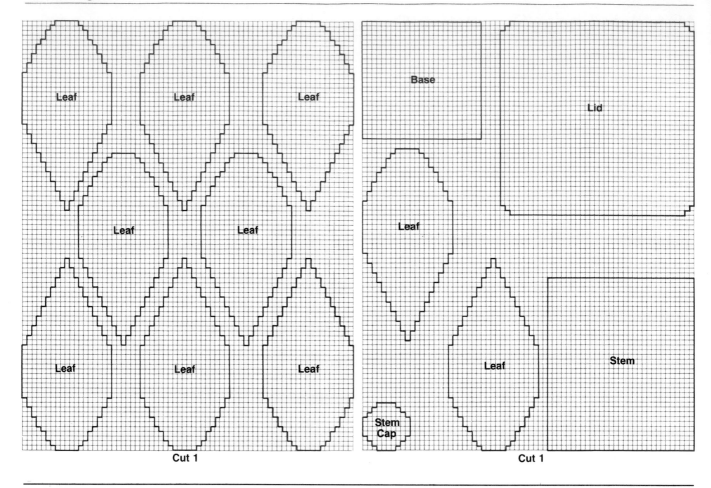

Cut 1   Cut 1

Stitching Diagrams/Large Strawberry Basket

Stitches Used

Tent stitch (see page 12)
Diagonal satin stitch (see page 14)
Brick stitch (see page 16)
Backstitch (see page 20)
Whip stitch (see page 21)

The Stitching

Work with one strand of FashionEase yarn and stitch the pieces as
diagramed in the following order:

1. Work the base of the strawberry in tent stitch, using Red yarn.

2. Work the stem cap piece in tent stitch, using Leaf Green yarn.

3. Work the four sides of the strawberry in brick stitch. Following
   the diagram carefully, put in the markings first with Yellow yarn,
   then do the background with Red yarn. Overcast the edge of
   each piece with Red yarn as diagramed.

4. Work the four pieces of the lid rim in tent stitch, using Red yarn;
   then overcast the bottom edge of each piece as diagramed.

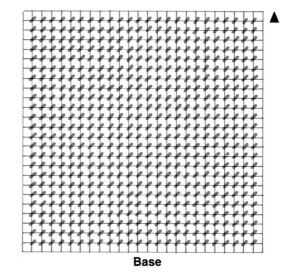

Base

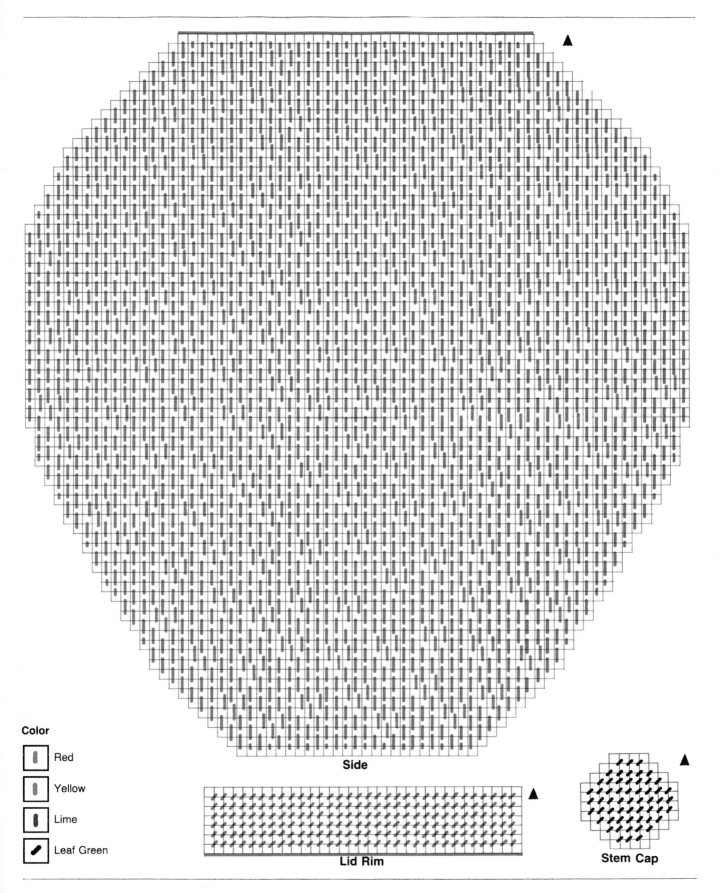

Side

Lid Rim

Stem Cap

Color

Red
Yellow
Lime
Leaf Green

5. Work the piece for the stem in tent stitch, using Leaf Green yarn. (The unstitched plastic thread will be used in the assembly.)

6. Work the piece for the lid in tent stitch. Stitch the center first, using Leaf Green yarn. Work the rest in Red yarn. Overcast the edges, using Red yarn. (The unstitched plastic threads will be used in the assembly.)

7. Work the leaves in diagonal satin stitch, using Lime yarn. Overcast the edges of the leaves, using Lime yarn. Backstitch the centers of the leaves as diagramed, using Leaf Green yarn.

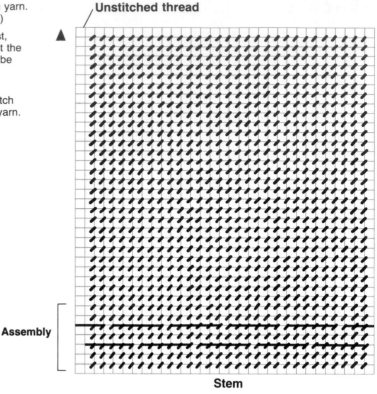

Unstitched thread

Assembly

Stem

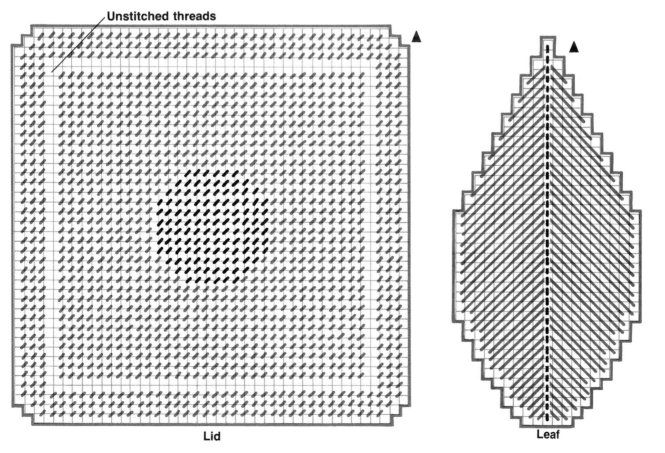

Unstitched threads

Lid

Leaf

Materials/Medium Strawberry Basket

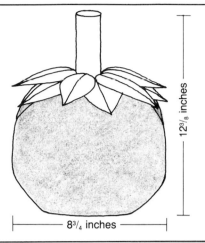

- Columbia-Minerva FashionEase clear 7-mesh plastic canvas:
  four sheets 10½" × 13½" (70 holes × 90 holes)
  one sheet 10½" × 13½" cut to 5" × 10½" (35 holes × 70 holes)

- Columbia-Minerva FashionEase Yarn for Needlepoint:

#0014 Red	160 yards
#0007 Yellow	34 yards
#0015 Lime	48 yards
#0016 Leaf Green	28 yards

- Bernat 1–2–3 Ply Persian Type Yarn:

#N27–835 Lime	1 yard (or any Persian yarn that matches #0015 Lime)
#N21–896 Leaf Green	24 inches (or any Persian yarn that matches #0016 Leaf Green)

- no. 16 tapestry needle

- weaving needle

Cutout Diagrams/Medium Strawberry Basket

Pattern Pieces

Follow the cutting diagrams carefully, making sure to count the holes accurately and to cut the right number of pieces.

1. Base. Cut one piece 19 holes wide × 19 holes high.
2. Sides. Cut four pieces 57 holes wide × 63 holes high.
3. Lid. Cut one piece 35 holes wide × 35 holes high.
4. Lid Rims. Cut four pieces 27 holes wide × 6 holes high.
5. Stem. Cut one piece 31 holes wide × 31 holes high.
6. Stem Cap. Cut one piece 10 holes wide × 10 holes high.
7. Leaves. Cut ten pieces 15 holes wide × 29 holes high.

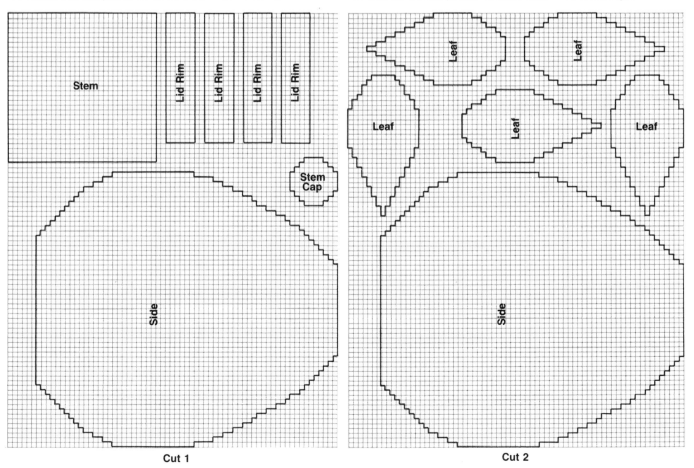

Cut 1   Cut 2

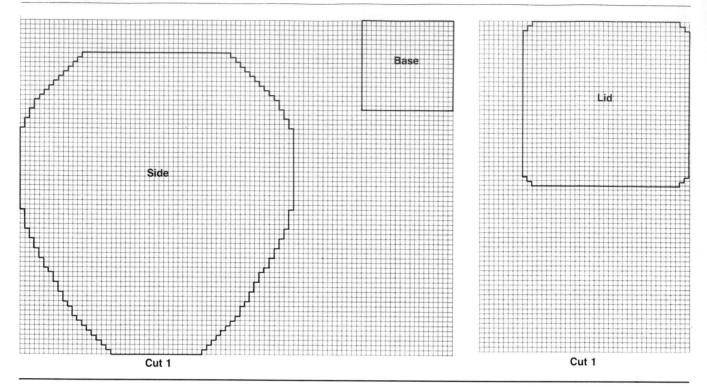

Base

Lid

Side

Cut 1

Cut 1

Stitching Diagrams/Medium Strawberry Basket

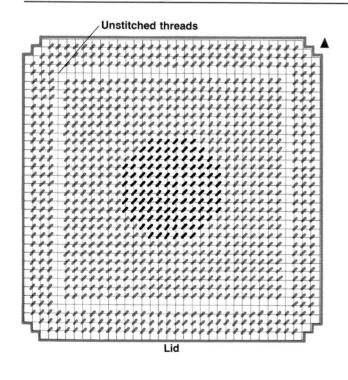

Unstitched threads

Lid

Stitches Used

Tent stitch (see page 12)
Diagonal satin stitch (see page 14)
Brick stitch (see page 16)
Backstitch (see page 20)
Whip stitch (see page 21)

The Stitching

Work with one strand of FashionEase yarn and stitch the pieces as diagramed in the following order:

1. Work the base of the strawberry in tent stitch, using Red yarn.

2. Work the stem cap piece in tent stitch, using Leaf Green yarn.

3. Work the four sides of the strawberry in brick stitch. Following the diagram carefully, put in the markings first with Yellow yarn, then do the background with Red yarn. Overcast the edge of each piece with Red yarn as diagramed.

4. Work the four pieces of the lid rim in tent stitch, using Red yarn; then overcast the bottom edge of each piece as diagramed.

5. Work the piece for the lid in tent stitch. Stitch the center first, using Leaf Green yarn. Work the rest in Red yarn. Overcast the edges, using Red yarn. (The unstitched plastic threads will be used in the assembly.)

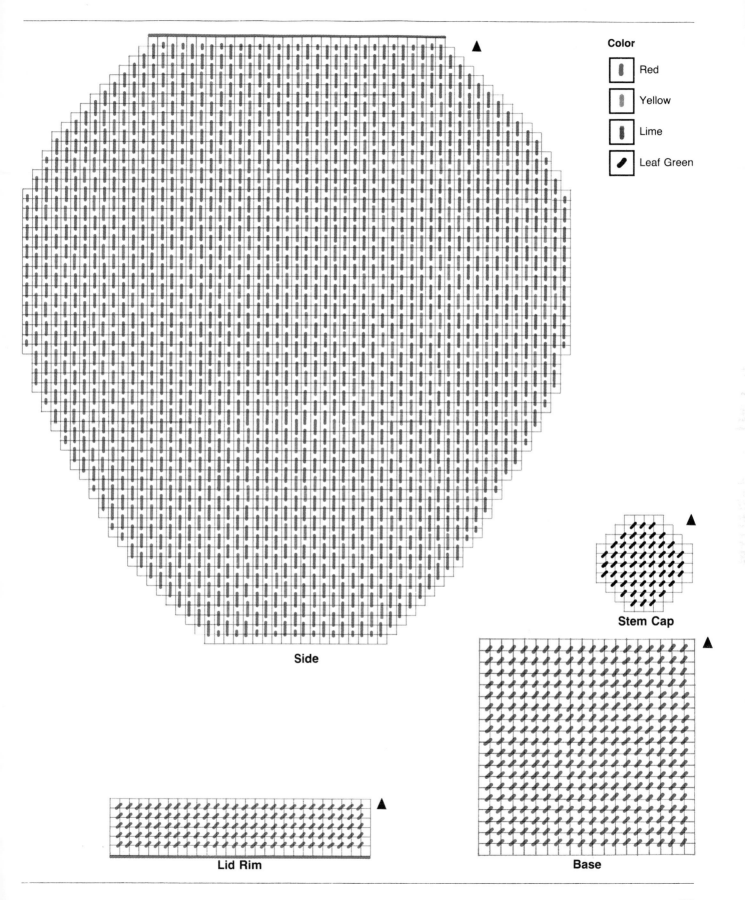

Color

Red

Yellow

Lime

Leaf Green

Side

Stem Cap

Lid Rim

Base

6. Work the piece for the stem in tent stitch, using Leaf Green yarn. (The unstitched plastic thread will be used in the assembly.)

7. Work the leaves in diagonal satin stitch, using Lime yarn. Overcast the edges of the leaves, using Lime yarn. Backstitch the centers of the leaves as diagramed, using Leaf Green yarn.

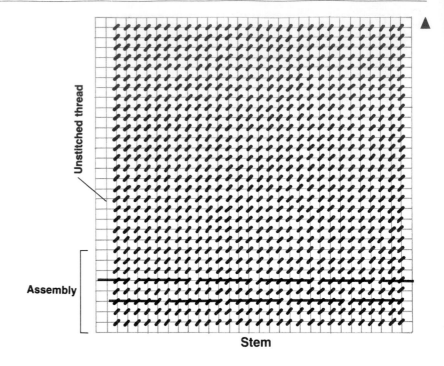

Stem

Color

▮	Red
▮	Yellow
▮	Lime
▰	Leaf Green

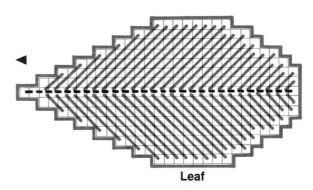

Leaf

Materials/Small Strawberry Basket

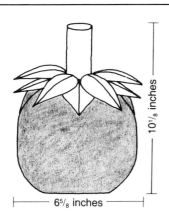

$6^5/_8$ inches · $10^1/_8$ inches

- Columbia-Minerva FashionEase clear 7-mesh plastic canvas: two sheets $10^1/_2''$ × $13^1/_2''$ (70 holes × 90 holes) one sheet $10^1/_2''$ × $13^1/_2''$ cut to 5″ × $13^1/_2''$ (34 holes × 90 holes)

- Columbia-Minerva FashionEase Yarn for Needlepoint:
#0014 Red	117 yards
#0007 Yellow	22 yards
#0015 Lime	33 yards
#0016 Leaf Green	26 yards

- Bernat 1–2–3 Ply Persian Type Yarn:
#N27–835 Lime	1 yard (or any Persian yarn that matches #0015 Lime)
#N21–896 Leaf Green	24 inches (or any Persian yarn that matches #0016 Leaf Green)

- no. 16 tapestry needle

- weaving needle

Cutout Diagrams/Small Strawberry Basket

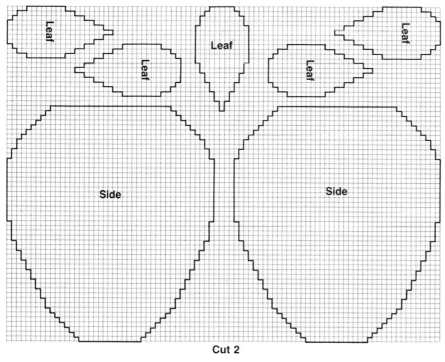

Pattern Pieces

Follow the cutting diagrams carefully, making sure to count the holes accurately and to cut the right number of pieces.

1. Base. Cut one piece
   13 holes wide × 13 holes high.
2. Sides. Cut four pieces
   43 holes wide × 49 holes high.
3. Lid. Cut one piece
   29 holes wide × 29 holes high.
4. Lid Rims. Cut four pieces
   21 holes wide × 5 holes high.
5. Stem. Cut one piece
   31 holes wide × 19 holes high.
6. Stem Cap. Cut one piece
   10 holes wide × 10 holes high.
7. Leaves. Cut ten pieces
   11 holes wide × 22 holes high

Cut 2

Cut 1

Stitching Diagrams/Small Strawberry Basket

Stitches Used

Tent stitch (see page 12)
Diagonal satin stitch (see page 14)
Brick stitch (see page 16)
Backstitch (see page 20)
Whip stitch (see page 21)

The Stitching

Work with one strand of FashionEase yarn and stitch the pieces as diagramed in the following order:

1. Work the base of the strawberry in tent stitch, using Red yarn.
2. Work the stem cap piece in tent stitch, using Leaf Green yarn.
3. Work the four pieces of the lid rim in tent stitch, using Red yarn; then overcast the bottom edge of each piece as diagramed.

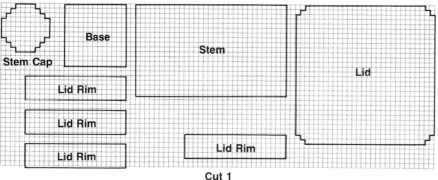

Lid Rim

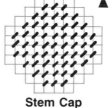

Stem Cap

Base

4. Work the four sides of the strawberry in brick stitch. Following the diagram carefully, put in the markings first with Yellow yarn, then do the background with Red yarn. Overcast the edge of each piece with Red yarn as diagramed.

5. Work the piece for the lid in tent stitch. Stitch the center first, using Leaf Green yarn. Work the rest in Red yarn. Overcast the edges, using Red yarn. (The unstitched plastic threads will be used in the assembly.)

6. Work the piece for the stem in tent stitch, using Leaf Green yarn. (The unstitched plastic thread will be used in the assembly.)

7. Work the leaves in diagonal satin stitch, using Lime yarn. Overcast the edges of the leaves, using Lime yarn. Backstitch the centers of the leaves as diagramed, using Leaf Green yarn.

Color

	Red
	Yellow
	Lime
	Leaf Green

Side

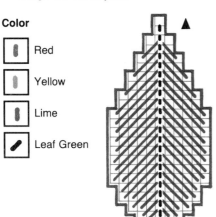

Leaf

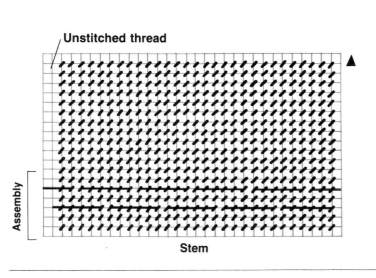

Unstitched thread

Assembly

Stem

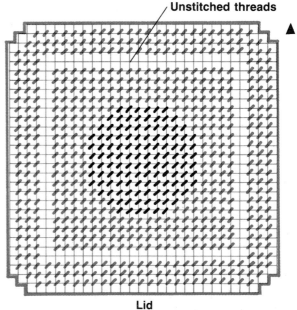

Unstitched threads

Lid

Assembly/Strawberry Baskets

Do all overcasting and joining using one strand of FashionEase yarn. Do all tacking using one strand of 1–2–3 Ply yarn.

Basket

1. With right sides up and in consecutive order, flush join the edges of the base of the strawberry to the bottom edges of the four sides, using Red yarn.

2. With right sides out and in consecutive order, flush join the adjacent edges of each two side pieces, using Red yarn.

Lid

3. The four lid rim pieces are attached to the wrong side of the lid piece, to create an open box. The wrong sides of two opposite lid rim pieces face each other and the center of the box. Using Red yarn, flush join the unovercast edge of one lid rim piece to one unstitched horizontal or vertical plastic thread on the lid piece, duplicating the direction of the tent stitch on the right side of the lid.

4. In the same way, using Red yarn, flush join in order each of the remaining three lid rim pieces.

5. Complete the box by flush joining the adjacent edges of the lid rim pieces using Red yarn.

Stem

6. Place the stem piece wrong side up. Curve the edges of the piece upward, placing the unovercast edge on the left side over the unstitched interior plastic thread on the right. Using the weaving needle and Leaf Green yarn, join the two overlapped plastic threads, matching the direction of the tent stitch on the right side of the piece. Complete by overcasting the bottom edge of the stem with Leaf Green yarn.

7. The bottom edges of the leaf pattern pieces are tacked to the stitched horizontal threads at the bottom of the stem cylinder with Lime yarn. The leaves are tacked in two rows. Placement lines for the tacking of leaves are shown on the stem stitch diagram.

   With right sides up, attach the top row of five leaves, tacking one leaf at a time in consecutive order. Attach the bottom row of leaves the same way.

8. Flush join the stem cap right side up to the top edge of the stem cylinder, using Leaf Green yarn.

9. Tack the bottom of the stem cylinder to the right side center of the lid, using Leaf Green yarn.

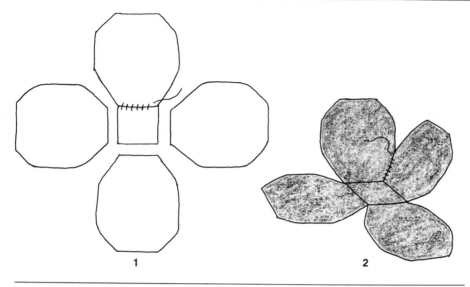

1 2

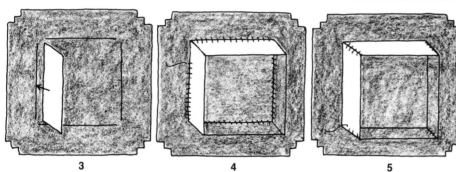

3 4 5

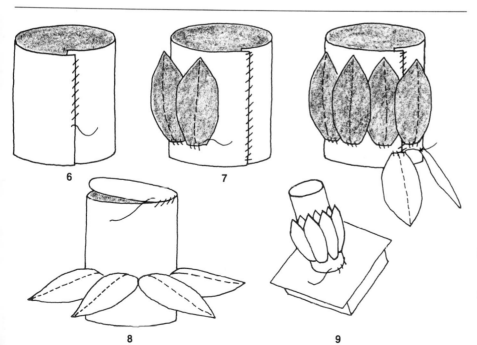

6 7

8 9

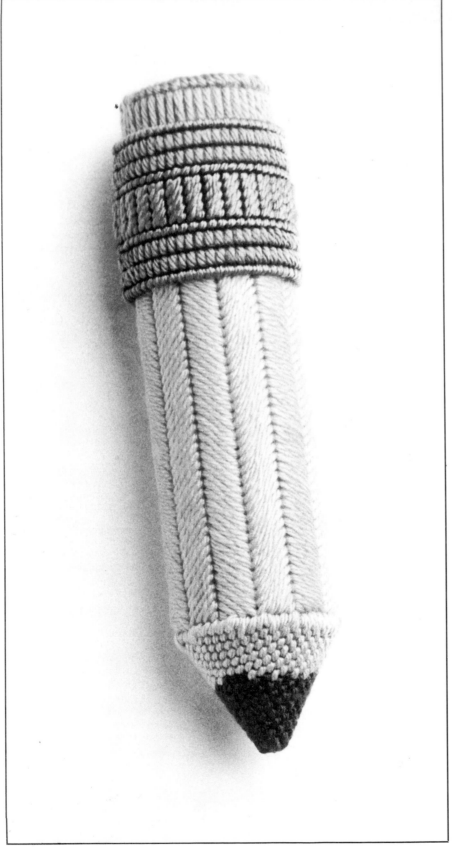

Pencil Case
Beginner

Any child will delight in this oversize pencil, which can be used to hold pencils, ruler, and eraser for school, to keep crayons close at hand, or even as a container for pieces of a jigsaw puzzle. It's easy to stitch and to assemble.

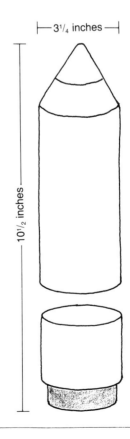

3¼ inches

10½ inches

Materials

- Boye E-Z Count clear 7-mesh plastic canvas: one sheet 10½″ × 13½″ (70 holes × 90 holes)
- Bernat 1-2-3 Ply Persian Type Yarn: #N04-942 Black   5 yards
- Bernat Tabriz Needle Art Yarn: #5854 Gun Metal   3 yards
  #5889 Sea Shell   6 yards
  #5875 Amber   35 yards
- #5852 Gray   15 yards
  #5821 Shocking Pink   19 yards
- no. 16 tapestry needle

Cutout Diagrams

Pattern Pieces

Follow the cutting diagrams carefully, making sure to count the holes accurately and to cut the right number of pieces.

1. Point. Cut one piece
   32 holes wide × 17 holes high.
2. Stem. Cut one piece
   50 holes wide × 46 holes high.
3. Metal Band. Cut one piece
   58 holes wide × 16 holes high.
4. Eraser Band. Cut one piece
   50 holes wide × 9 holes high.
5. Eraser Top. Cut one piece
   15 holes wide × 15 holes high.

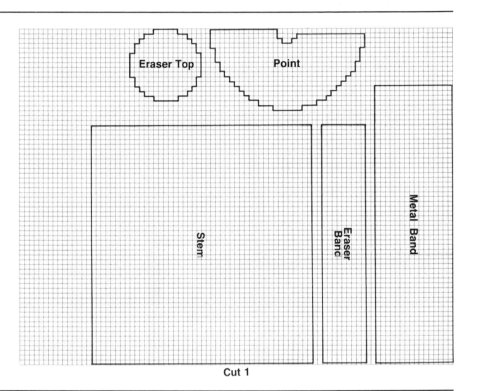

Cut 1

Stitching Diagrams

Stitches Used

Tent stitch (see page 12)
Slanted gobelin stitch (see page 13)
Diagonal satin stitch (see page 14)
Gobelin stitch (see page 15)
Backstitch (see page 20)
Whip stitch (see page 21)

The Stitching

Work all the stitches with one strand of Tabriz yarn. Stitch the pieces as diagramed in the following order:

1. Work the point of the pencil in tent stitch. Stitch the lead tip first, using Gun Metal yarn, then work the rest in Sea Shell yarn. (The unstitched plastic thread will be used in the assembly.)

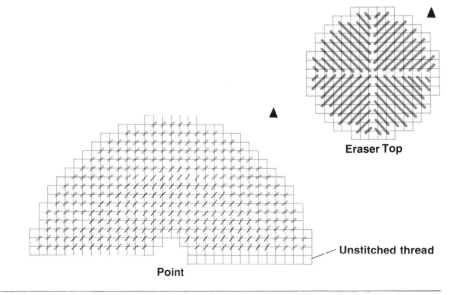

Eraser Top

Point

Unstitched thread

2. Work the top of the eraser in diagonal satin stitch, using Shocking Pink yarn.

3. Work the stem in slanted gobelin stitch, using Amber yarn. (The unstitched plastic thread will be used in the assembly.)

4. Work the background of the metal band, using Gray yarn. First work the four rows of gobelin stitch at the top and bottom of the band. Next work the two rows of tent stitch, as diagramed, above

and below the rows of gobelin stitch. Then work the center columns in slanted gobelin stitch. (The backstitch outlines will be put in during assembly. The unstitched plastic thread will be used in the assembly.)

5. Work the eraser band in gobelin stitch, using Shocking Pink yarn. (The unstitched plastic thread will be used in the assembly.)

Color

/	Gun Metal
/	Sea Shell
/	Amber
/	Gray
/	Shocking Pink
/	Black

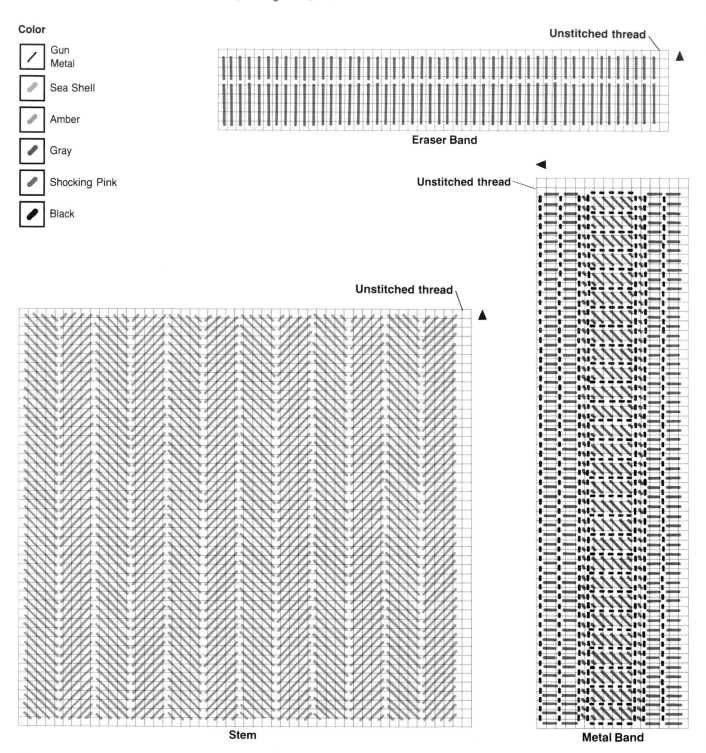

Unstitched thread

Eraser Band

Unstitched thread

Unstitched thread

Stem

Metal Band

Assembly

Do all overcasting and joining using one strand of Tabriz yarn. Work backstitch and do all tacking using one strand of 1−2−3 Ply yarn.

Pencil

1. Place the point piece wrong side up. The straight bottom edge on the left side has an unovercast edge and an unstitched horizontal interior plastic thread. Curve the bottom edges of the piece upward,

placing the unovercast edge on the right side over the unstitched interior thread on the left. Join the two overlapped plastic threads, matching the direction of the tent stitch on the right side. Start the join at the tip of the cone. Use Gun Metal yarn and Sea Shell yarn. Complete by overcasting the top edge of the cone with Gun Metal yarn.

2. Place the stem piece wrong side up. The left side of the piece has an unovercast

edge and an unstitched vertical interior plastic thread. Curve the edges of the piece upward, placing the unovercast edge on the right side over the unstitched interior thread on the left. Using Amber yarn, join the two overlapped plastic threads. Complete by overcasting the bottom edge of the stem with Amber yarn.

3. Place the bottom edge of the point cone against the top edge of the stem. Flush join the edges, using Sea Shell yarn.

Eraser

4. Place the metal band piece wrong side up. The left side of the piece has an unovercast edge and an unstitched vertical interior plastic thread. Curve the edges upward, placing the unovercast edge on the right side over the unstitched interior thread on the left. Using Gray yarn, join the two overlapped plastic threads, matching the direction of the tent stitch on the right side of the piece. Overcast the top and bottom edges with Gray yarn.

   Following the stitch diagram carefully, using Black yarn, work the outlines on the metal band in backstitch, so it goes across the join seam, forming continuous rings around the band.

5. Place the eraser band piece wrong side up. The left side has an unovercast edge and an unstitched vertical interior plastic thread. Curve the edges of the piece upward, placing the unovercast edge on the right side over the unstitched interior thread on the left. Using Shocking Pink yarn, join the two overlapped plastic threads. Complete by overcasting the top edge with Shocking Pink yarn.

6. Place the top edge of the eraser band inside the bottom edge of the metal band. Match the horizontal line of holes separating the two rows of gobelin stitch on the eraser band to the horizontal line of holes separating the overcast edge and the first row of gobelin stitches on the metal band. Tack these two pieces together along these matched hole lines, using Black yarn. Tack by working backstitch on the right side of the metal band, duplicating the horizontal row of backstitch along the top row of the band.

7. With right side out, place the top of the eraser against the bottom edge of the eraser band. Flush join the adjacent edges, using Shocking Pink yarn.

Point

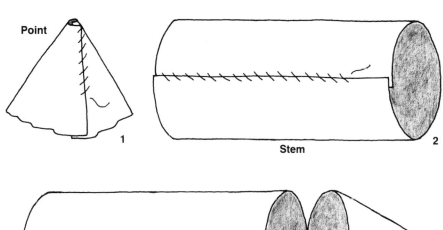

Stem

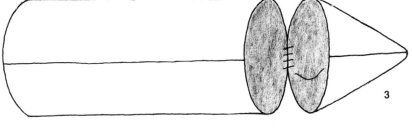

Eraser Band

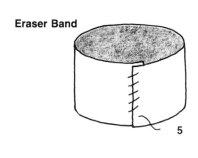

Metal Band

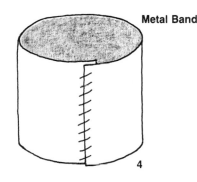

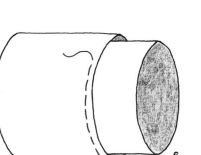

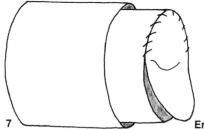

Eraser Top

Butterfly Table Setting
Beginner

Place mats, napkin rings, trivet, coasters and carrier—these beautiful butterflies will brighten your dining table and make an occasion of any meal at which you use them. You can work the butterflies in cotton or acrylic yarn. Both yarns are washable, but the cotton gives a more delicate effect. The assembly is simple, but the stitching is a bit more difficult because the stitching charts must be followed very carefully and nine colors of yarn are used.

Materials/Place Mat

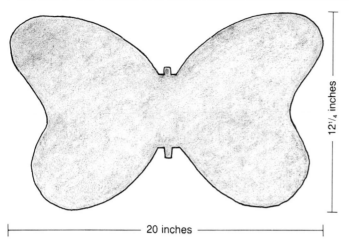

The materials listed are sufficient for one place mat.

- Boye E-Z Count clear 7-mesh plastic canvas: two sheets 10½" × 13½" (70 holes × 90 holes)
- DMC Size 3 Pearl Cotton:

Snow White	272 yards
#797 Light Blue	66 yards
#796 Dark Blue	50 yards
#739 Ecru	16 yards
#437 Light Tan	33 yards
#436 Medium Tan	33 yards
#434 Dark Tan	33 yards
#433 Light Brown	33 yards
#801 Dark Brown	33 yards

- no. 16 tapestry needle

12¼ inches

20 inches

Cutout Diagrams/Place Mat

Pattern Pieces

Follow the cutting diagrams carefully, making sure to count the holes accurately.

1. Right Wing. Cut one piece 63 holes wide × 82 holes high.
2. Left Wing. Cut one piece 63 holes wide × 82 holes high.
3. Center. Cut one piece 5 holes wide × 41 holes high.

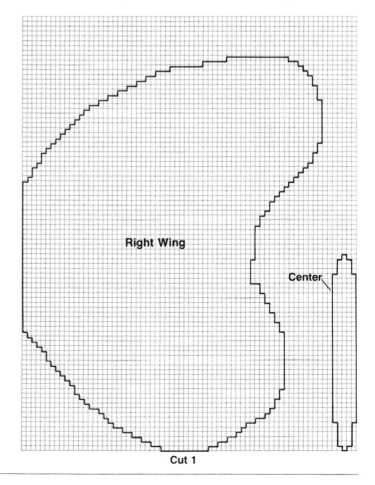

Left Wing

Cut 1

Right Wing

Center

Cut 1

Stitching Diagrams/Place Mat

The Stitching

The right and left wings are worked in the same way except that the left wing is reversed. Work with two strands of yarn, and stitch the pieces as diagramed in the following order:

1. Begin with the right wing. Work the outlines first in cross stitch, using White yarn.

Stitches Used

Tent stitch (see page 12)
Cross stitch (see page 18)
Backstitch (see page 20)
Whip stitch (see page 21)

Color

X		Snow White
/	X	Lt. Blue
X	/	Dk. Blue
/		Ecru
/		Lt. Tan
/		Med. Tan
/		Dk. Tan
/		Lt. Brown
/		Dk. Brown

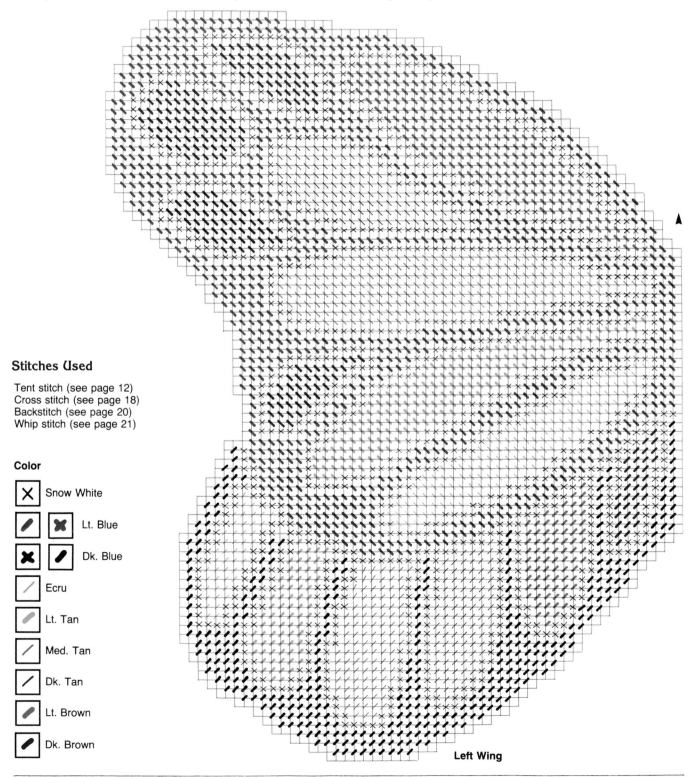

Left Wing

2. Fill in the outlined areas, working in tent stitch and using Dark Brown, Light Brown, Dark Tan, Medium Tan, Light Tan, and Ecru yarn, as indicated on the stitch diagram.

3. Work the background of the lower wing in tent stitch, using Dark Blue yarn. Work the background of the upper wing in tent stitch, using Light Blue yarn.

4. Now stitch the left wing.

5. Work the center piece in cross stitch, using Dark Blue yarn.

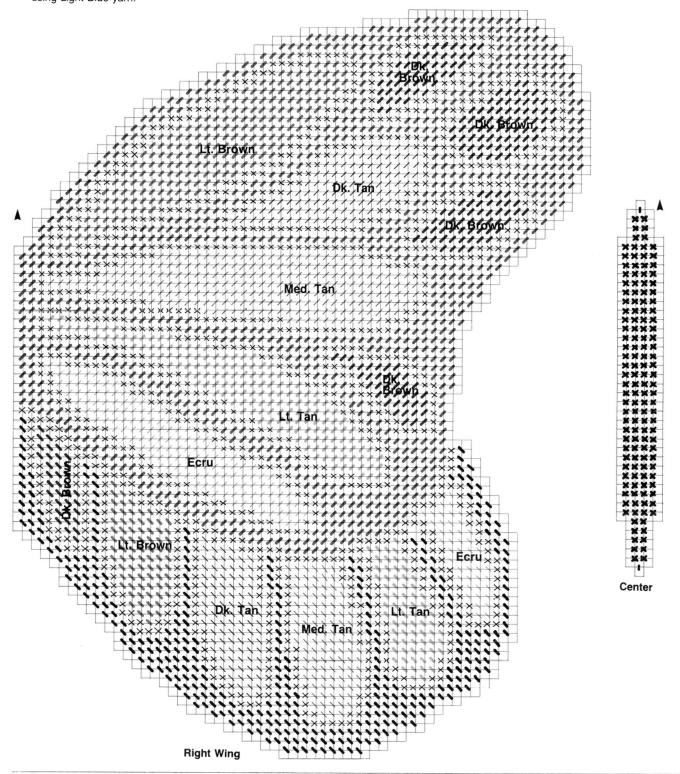

Dk. Brown

Dk. Brown

Lt. Brown

Dk. Tan

Dk. Brown

Med. Tan

Dk. Brown

Lt. Tan

Ecru

Dk. Brown

Lt. Brown

Dk. Tan

Med. Tan

Lt. Tan

Ecru

Right Wing

Center

Assembly/Place Mat

With right sides up, flush join the right edge of the center piece to the left edge of the right wing. Work blind cross stitch and use one strand of White yarn. Work over the joined edges in cross stitch, using two strands of White yarn.

With right sides up, flush join the left edge of the center to the right edge of the left wing. Work blind cross stitch and use one strand of White yarn. Work cross stitch over the joined edges, using two strands of White yarn.

Using whip stitch, overcast all the edges of the completed butterfly, using four strands of White yarn.

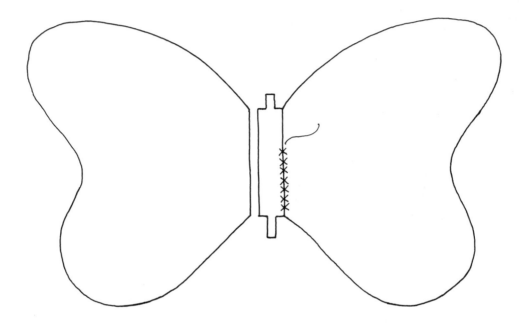

Materials/Coasters and Carrier

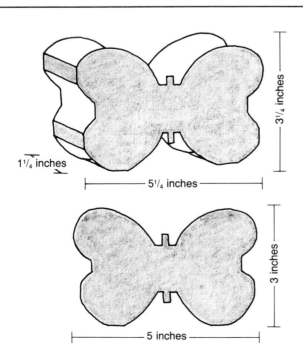

The materials listed will make four coasters and one carrier.

- Boye E-Z Count clear 10-mesh plastic canvas: one sheet 11″ × 14″ cut to 10³/₄″ × 11″ (108 holes × 110 holes)

- DMC Size 3 Pearl Cotton:

Snow White	26 yards
#799 Light Blue	18 yards
#796 Dark Blue	15 yards
#739 Ecru	7 yards
#437 Light Tan	7 yards
#436 Medium Tan	4 yards
#434 Dark Tan	7 yards
#433 Light Brown	7 yards
#801 Dark Brown	7 yards

- no. 18 and no. 20 tapestry needles

Cutout Diagrams/Coasters and Carrier

Pattern Pieces

Follow the cutting diagrams carefully, making sure to count the holes accurately and to cut the right number of pieces.

1. Coasters. Cut four pieces 51 holes wide × 32 holes high.
2. Carrier Front and Back. Cut two pieces 53 holes wide × 33 holes high.
3. Carrier Bands 1. Cut two pieces 15 holes wide × 4 holes high.
4. Carrier Bands 2. Cut two pieces 15 holes wide × 4 holes high.
5. Carrier Bands 3. Cut two pieces 4 holes wide × 15 holes high.

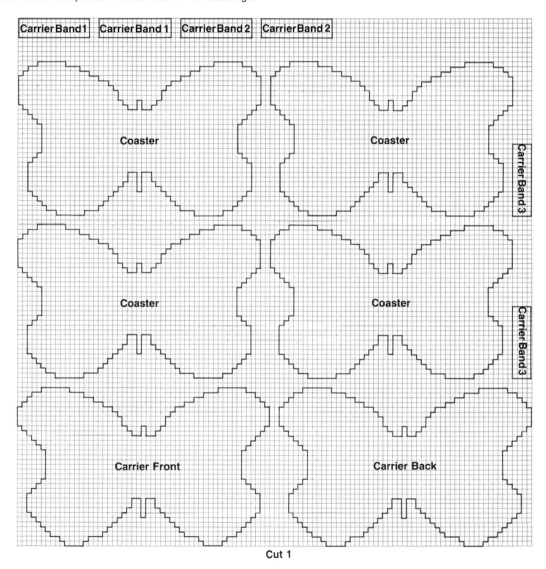

Cut 1

Stitching Diagrams/Coasters and Carrier

Stitches Used

Tent stitch (see page 12)
Cross stitch (see page 18)
Backstitch (see page 20)
Whip stitch (see page 21)

The Stitching

The coasters and the front and back of the carrier are stitched in the same way. It is recommended, however, that you work one butterfly at a time. Work with one strand of yarn and the no. 18 tapestry needle.

1. Work the center in cross stitch, using Dark Blue yarn, then work the backstitches, using Dark Blue yarn. Outline the center in cross stitch, using White yarn.

2. Work the wing center outlines in cross stitch, using White yarn.

3. Fill in the outlined areas, working in tent stitch and using Dark Brown, Light Brown, Dark Tan, Medium Tan, Light Tan, and Ecru yarn as indicated on the stitch diagram.

4. Work the background of the lower wing in tent stitch, using Dark Blue yarn. Work the background of the upper wing in tent stitch and cross stitch, using Light Blue yarn.

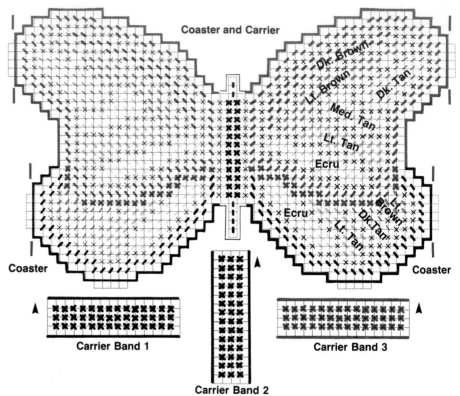

5. Use whip stitch to overcast the edges, using White, Light Blue, and Dark Blue yarn as indicated. (Note that the six outermost edges on the right, left, and bottom of each carrier piece are not overcast.)

6. Work carrier bands 1 and 2 in cross stitch, using Dark Blue yarn.

Use whip stitch to overcast the two long edges of each band, using Dark Blue yarn.

7. Work the two carrier bands 3 in cross stitch, using Light Blue yarn. Use whip stitch to overcast the two long edges of each band, using Light Blue yarn.

Assembly/Carrier

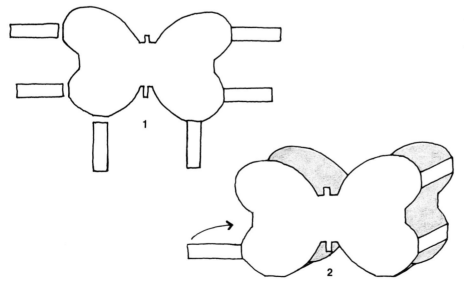

Carrier

Do all joining using two strands of yarn and the no. 20 tapestry needle.

1. The outermost right, left, and bottom edges of the carrier pieces are not overcast. With right sides up, match the right and left edges of carrier bands 1 and 2 and the top edges of carrier bands 3 to the unovercast edges of the front of the carrier. Flush join the matched carrier and band edges, using Light Blue yarn to join bands 1 and Dark Blue yarn to join bands 2 and 3. When complete, turn the piece wrong side up.

2. With wrong sides together, join the unovercast edges on the back of the carrier to the band edges in the same way you joined the first carrier piece.

Materials/Trivet

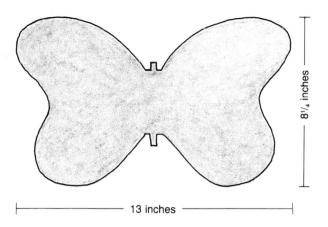

13 inches

8¹/₄ inches

The materials listed are sufficient for one trivet.

- Boye E-Z Count clear 10-mesh plastic canvas: one sheet 11″ × 14″ cut to 8¹/₄″ × 14″ (82 holes × 140 holes)
- DMC Size 3 Pearl Cotton:

Snow White	75 yards
#799 Light Blue	23 yards
#796 Dark Blue	16 yards
#739 Ecru	6 yards
#437 Light Tan	7 yards
#436 Medium Tan	10 yards
#434 Dark Tan	6 yards
#433 Light Brown	9 yards
#801 Dark Brown	9 yards

- no. 18 tapestry needle

Cutout Diagram/Trivet

Pattern Pieces

1. Trivet. Cut one piece 131 holes wide × 82 holes high.

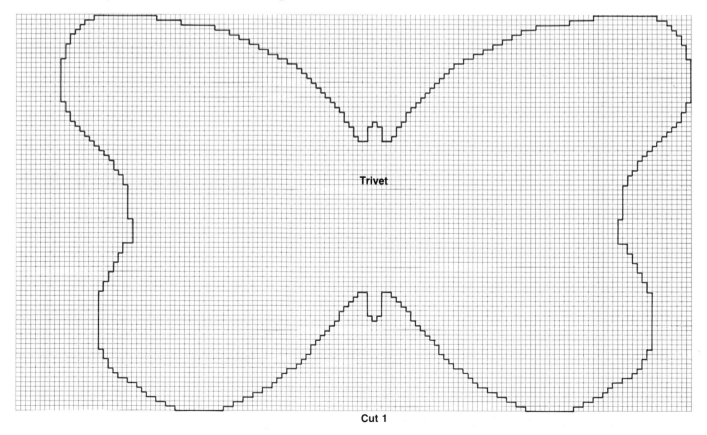

Trivet

Cut 1

Stitching Diagram/Trivet

Stitches Used

Tent stitch (see page 12)
Cross stitch (see page 18)
Backstitch (see page 20)
Whip stitch (see page 21)

Color

X	Snow White
/	Lt. Blue
✖ /	Dk. Blue
/	Ecru
/	Lt. Tan
/	Med. Tan
/	Dk. Tan
/	Lt. Brown
/	Dk. Brown

The Stitching

Work with one strand of yarn and stitch the trivet in the following order:

1. Work the center of the trivet in cross stitch, using Dark Blue yarn. Work backstitch at the top and bottom, using Dark Blue yarn.

2. Work the outlines of the center of the wings, and the markings of the wings in cross stitch, using White yarn.

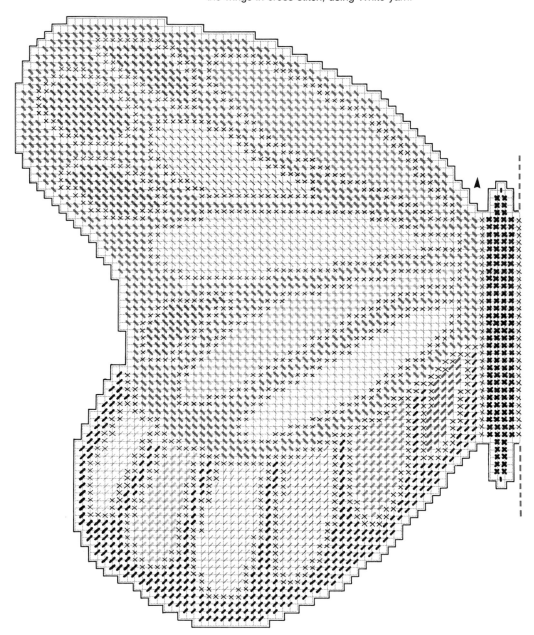

3. Fill in the outlined areas, working in tent stitch and using Dark Brown, Light Brown, Dark Tan, Medium Tan, Light Tan, and Ecru yarn, as indicated on the stitch diagram.

4. Work the background of the upper wings in tent stitch, using Light Blue yarn. Work the background of the lower wings in tent stitch, using Dark Blue yarn.

5. To complete, work whip stitch to overcast all the edges, using White yarn.

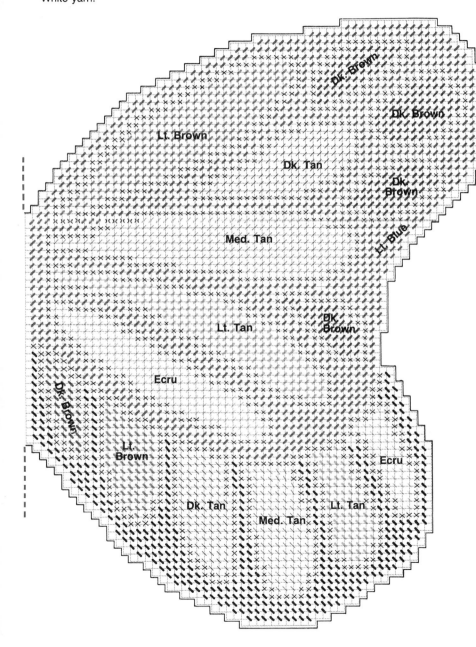

Butterfly Table Setting

To work the place mat in an acrylic yarn, substitute the following Brunswick Windrush yarn colors for the DMC colors.

#9010	White	Snow White
#9011	Powder Blue	Light Blue
#90131	Light Navy	Dark Blue
#9030	Parchment	Ecru
#90341	Brown	Light Tan
#90731	Caramel	Medium Tan
#90292	Coffee	Dark Tan
#90293	Dark Coffee	Light Brown
#90343	Dark Brown	Dark Brown

Since one strand of Windrush is larger in diameter than one strand of Size 3 Pearl Cotton, you will need approximately half the yarn quantities listed to work one place mat. Work tent stitch and cross stitch using one strand of yarn. Overcast using two strands of yarn.

To work the trivet, coasters and carrier, and napkin rings in an acrylic yarn, substitute the following Bernat 1–2–3 Ply Persian Type yarn colors for the DMC colors.

#N10–428	Snow White
#N12–657	Light Blue
#N12–652	Dark Blue
#N10–422	Ecru
#N00–206	Light Tan
#N26–188	Medium Tan
#N26–186	Dark Tan
#N26–184	Light Brown
#N26–182	Dark Brown

Since one strand of 1–2–3 Ply yarn is smaller in diameter than one strand of Size 3 Pearl Cotton, you will need approximately double the yarn quantities listed to work these pieces. Work tent stitch and cross stitch using two strands of yarn. Overcast using three strands of yarn.

Materials/Napkin Rings

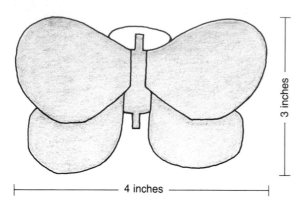

3 inches

4 inches

The materials listed will make four napkin rings.

- Boye E-Z Count clear 10-mesh plastic canvas: one sheet 11″ × 14″ cut to $7^3/_4$″ × $12^1/_4$″ (78 holes × 122 holes)
- DMC Size 3 Pearl Cotton:

Snow White	16 yards
#799 Light Blue	14 yards
#796 Dark Blue	18 yards
#739 Ecru	5 yards
#437 Light Tan	5 yards
#434 Dark Tan	7 yards
#433 Light Brown	7 yards

- no. 18 and no. 20 tapestry needles

Cutout Diagrams/Napkin Rings

Pattern Pieces

Follow the cutting diagrams carefully, making sure to count the holes accurately and to cut the right number of pieces.

1. Upper Right Wings. Cut four pieces 20 holes wide × 18 holes high.
2. Upper Left Wings. Cut four pieces 20 holes wide × 18 holes high.
3. Lower Right Wings. Cut four pieces 17 holes wide × 15 holes high.
4. Lower Left Wings. Cut four pieces 17 holes wide × 15 holes high.
5. Rings. Cut four pieces 40 holes wide × 17 holes high.

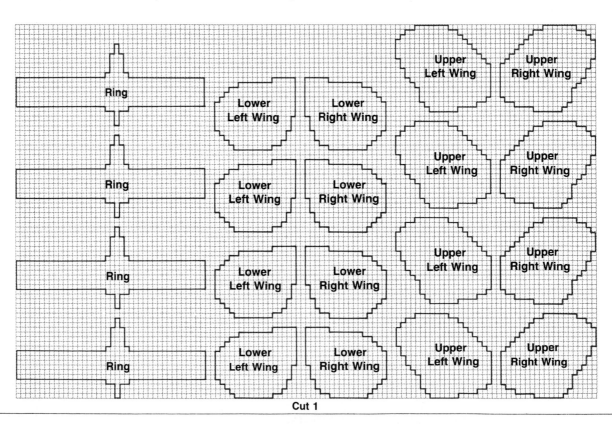

Cut 1

Stitching Diagrams/Napkin Rings

Stitches Used

Tent stitch (see page 12)
Cross stitch (see page 18)
Backstitch (see page 20)
Whip stitch (see page 21)

The Stitching

Work with one strand of yarn and the no. 18 tapestry needle. Stitch the pieces as diagramed in the following order:

1. First stitch each upper wing. Work the outlines in cross stitch, using White yarn.

2. Fill in the outlined areas in tent stitch, using Light Brown, Dark Tan, Light Tan, and Ecru yarn as indicated on the stitch diagram.

3. Work the background in tent stitch, using Light Blue yarn.

4. Work whip stitch to overcast the edges as indicated, using Light Blue yarn.

5. Stitch the lower wings in the same way as the upper wings, except using Dark Blue yarn for the background and overcasting.

6. Work the rings in cross stitch, using Dark Blue yarn. Work backstitch, using Dark Blue yarn. Work whip stitch to overcast as indicated, using White yarn. (The unstitched plastic threads are used in the assembly.)

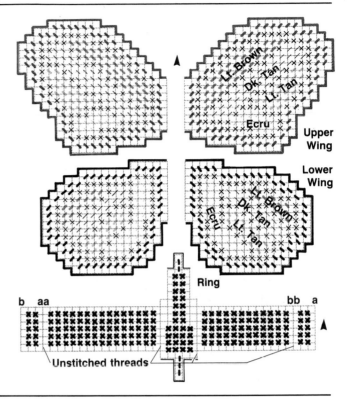

Assembly/Napkin Rings

Instructions are for one napkin ring. Repeat for each additional napkin ring. Do all joining and overcasting using one strand of yarn and the no. 20 tapestry needle.

Butterfly

1. The ring pattern piece is divided into three parts: a center sided by a short band and a long band. The ring center has two symmetrical sets of vertical threads that are combinations of edge threads and unstitched threads. There is an inside set and an outside set.
With right sides up, place the unovercast edges of the lower wings above the outside set of unstitched vertical threads on the ring. The wing edges match the height of the threads on the ring. Flush join the wing edges to the outside set of unstitched vertical threads on the ring, using White yarn.

2. With right sides up, place the unovercast edges of the upper wings above the inside set of unstitched threads on the ring. The wing edges match the height of the threads on the ring. Flush join the wing edges to the inside set of unstitched vertical threads on the ring, using White yarn.

Ring

3. Place the ring wrong side up. Curve the bands upward. Referring to the cutout diagram, place the longer band over the shorter band and match edge **a** to unstitched interior thread **aa** and edge **b** to unstitched interior thread **bb**. Flush join **a** to **aa** and **b** to **bb**, working cross stitch and using Dark Blue yarn. Using Dark Blue yarn, work whip stitch to overcast the top and bottom edges of the band, starting and stopping where the lower wings are joined to the center of the ring.

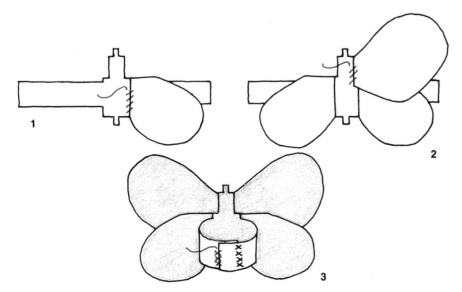

Zinnia Candlesticks

Beginner

Now you can have zinnias blooming in your home all through the year. These candlesticks would enhance a dining table or add a distinctive touch to a mantelpiece. Or use a single one in the bedroom or on a coffee table. There are directions here for making the candlesticks in two sizes. And, of course, you can change the colors to suit your fancy and your decor. Metal candle cups are available in craft and party shops, and you'll find glass candle caps, called bobeches, in the candle departments of department stores and large specialty shops.

Materials/Large Candlestick

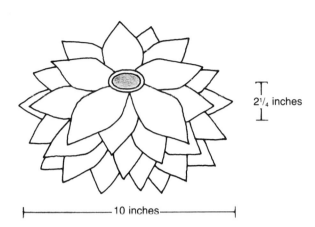

- 10 inches

2 1/4 inches

- Columbia-Minerva FashionEase clear 7-mesh plastic canvas: one sheet 10 1/2" × 13 1/2" (70 holes × 90 holes) one sheet 10 1/2" × 13 1/2" cut to 7 1/2" × 10 1/2" (53 holes × 70 holes)

- Bernat Berella "4" Yarn:
  #8922 Arbutus   31 yards
  #8927 Burgundy   63 yards
  #8865 Medium Leaf Green 19 yards
  #8864 Deep Leaf Green   25 yards
  #8909 Old Gold   1 yard

- Bernat 1–2–3 Ply Persian Type Yarn:
  #N22–262 Burgundy   1 1/2 yards (or any Persian yarn that matches #8927 Burgundy)

- one 12"-tall tapered candle with a 1"-diameter base

- one 7/8"-tall metal candle cup with a 1"-diameter center

- one glass candle cap (bobeche)

Cutout Diagrams/Large Candlestick

Pattern Pieces

1. Base. Cut one piece
   57 holes wide × 57 holes high.
2. Center. Cut one piece
   26 holes wide × 12 holes high.
3. Petal 1. Cut five pieces
   9 holes wide × 16 holes high.
4. Petal 2. Cut five pieces
   9 holes wide × 18 holes high.
5. Petal 3. Cut five pieces
   11 holes wide × 20 holes high.
6. Petal 4. Cut five pieces
   11 holes wide × 22 holes high.
7. Petal 5. Cut five pieces
   11 holes wide × 24 holes high.

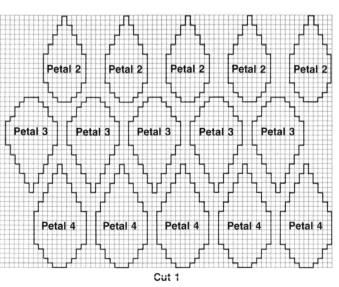

Cut 1

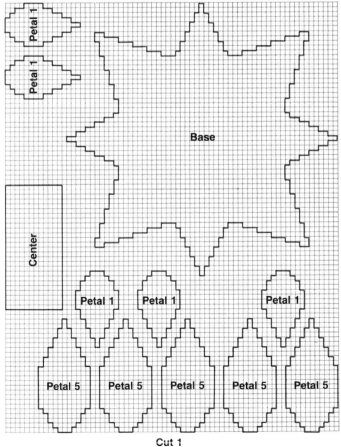

Cut 1

Stitching Diagrams/Large Candlestick

Stitches Used

Tent stitch (see page 12)
Diagonal satin stitch (see page 14)
Diagonal satin variation (see page 15)
Backstitch (see page 20)
Whip stitch (see page 21)
Edging stitch (see page 22)

Color

Arbutus

Burgundy

Med. Leaf
Green

Deep Leaf
Green

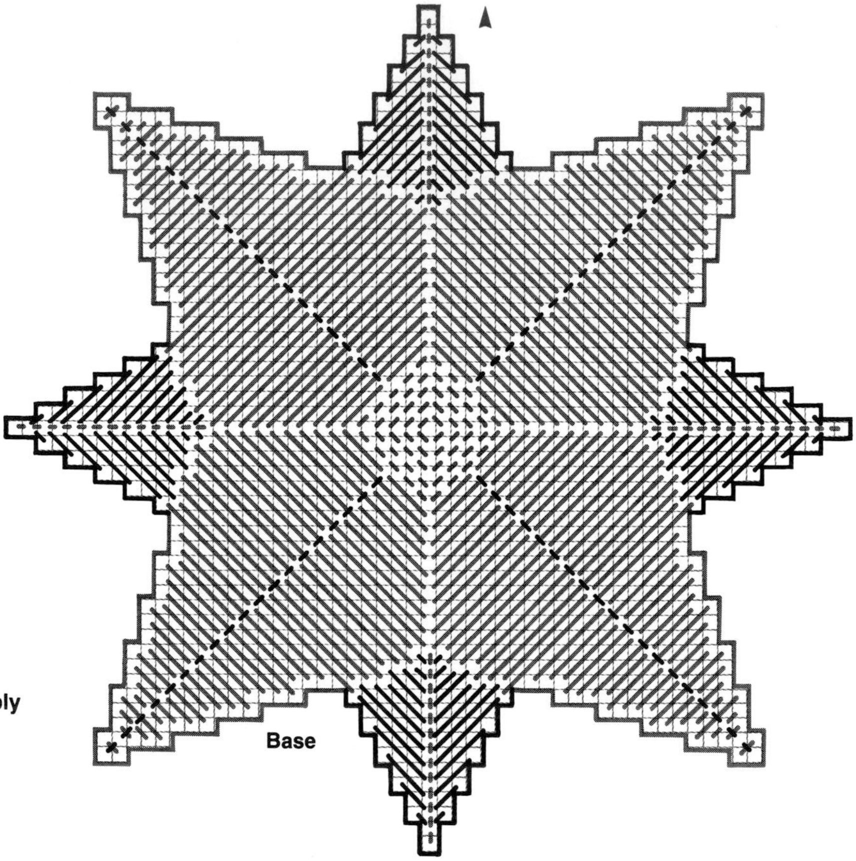

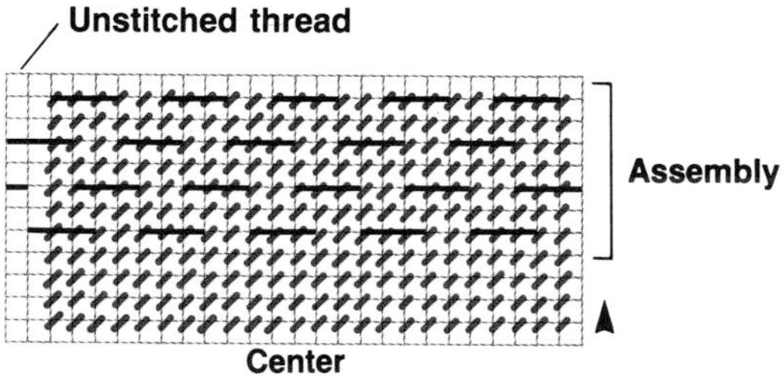

Unstitched thread

Assembly

Center

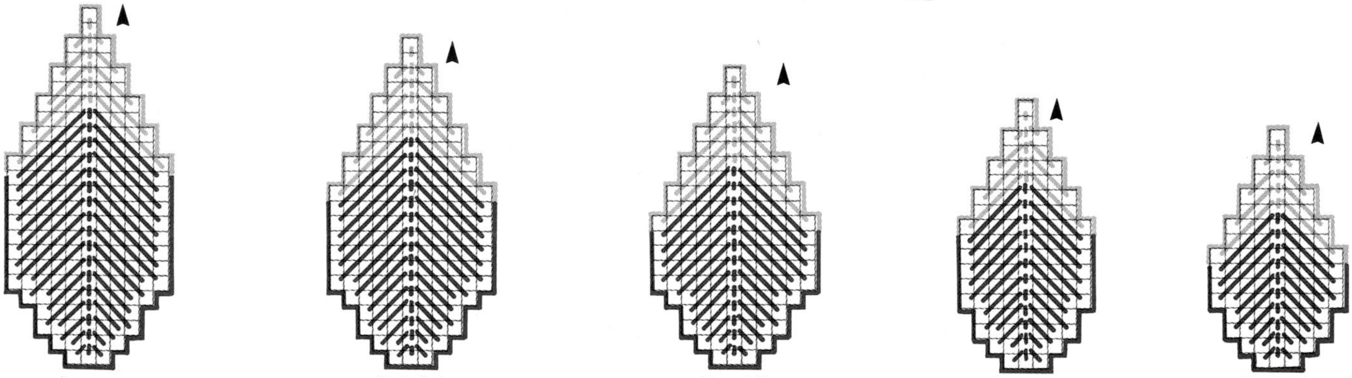

Base

Petal 5

Petal 4

Petal 3

Petal 2

Petal 1

The Stitching

Work with one strand of Berella "4" yarn and stitch the pieces as diagramed in the following order:

1. Work the center of the candlestick in tent stitch, using Burgundy yarn. (The unstitched vertical plastic thread will be used for assembly.)
2. Work the petals in diagonal satin stitch. Do the areas as diagramed with Burgundy yarn, then with Arbutus yarn. Then work whip stitch to overcast the edges, using Burgundy yarn and Arbutus yarn as indicated. Finish the center of each petal in backstitch as diagramed, using Burgundy yarn and Arbutus yarn.

3. Stitch the base of the candlestick as diagramed. Work the center in tent stitch, using Burgundy yarn. Next work the four small leaves in diagonal satin stitch, using Deep Leaf Green yarn. Now work the four large leaves in diagonal satin variation, using Medium Leaf Green yarn. Work the center of each large leaf in backstitch, using Deep Leaf Green yarn. Work whip stitch to overcast the edges of each piece, using the Medium and Deep Leaf Green yarns as indicated. Work the centers of each small leaf in backstitch, using Medium Leaf Green Yarn.

Materials/Small Candlestick

- Columbia-Minerva FashionEase clear 7-mesh plastic canvas:
  one sheet 10½″ × 13½″ (70 holes × 90 holes)
  one sheet 10½″ × 13½″ cut to 3″ × 13½″ (22 holes × 90 holes)

- Bernat Berella "4" Yarn:
#8922 Arbutus	51 yards
#8927 Burgundy	21 yards
#8865 Medium Leaf Green	10 yards
#8864 Deep Leaf Green	20 yards
#8909 Old Gold	1 yard

- Bernat 1–2–3 Ply Persian Type Yarn:
  #N22–266 Arbutus   1½ yards (or any Persian yarn that matches #8922 Arbutus)

- one 10″-tall tapered candle with a ⅞″-diameter base

- one ⅞″-tall metal candle cup with a 1″-diameter center

- one glass candle cap (bobeche)

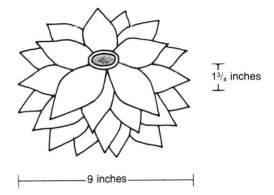

1¾ inches

9 inches

Cutout Diagrams/Small Candlestick

Pattern Pieces

Follow the cutting diagrams carefully, making sure to count the holes accurately and to cut the right number of pieces.

1. Base. Cut one piece
   53 holes wide × 53 holes high.
2. Center. Cut one piece
   26 holes wide × 10 holes high.
3. Petals 1. Cut five pieces
   9 holes wide × 16 holes high.
4. Petals 2. Cut five pieces
   9 holes wide × 18 holes high.
5. Petals 3. Cut five pieces
   11 holes wide × 20 holes high.
6. Petals 4. Cut five pieces
   11 holes wide × 22 holes high.

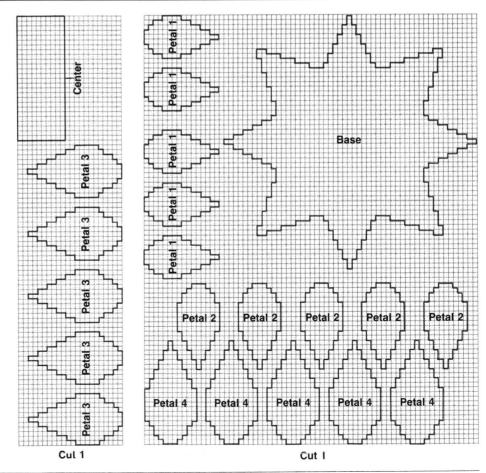

Cut 1   Cut 1

Stitching Diagrams/Small Candlestick

Stitches Used

Tent stitch (see page 12)
Diagonal satin stitch (see page 14)
Diagonal satin variation (see page 15)
Backstitch (see page 20)
Whip stitch (see page 21)
Edging stitch (see page 22)

Color

Arbutus

Burgundy

Med. Leaf Green

Deep Leaf Green

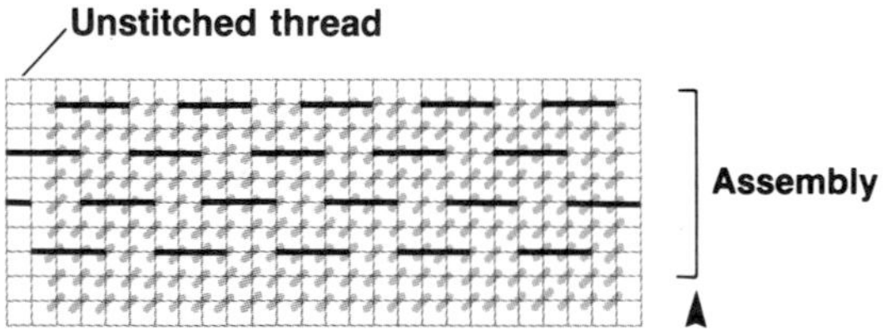

Unstitched thread

Assembly

Center

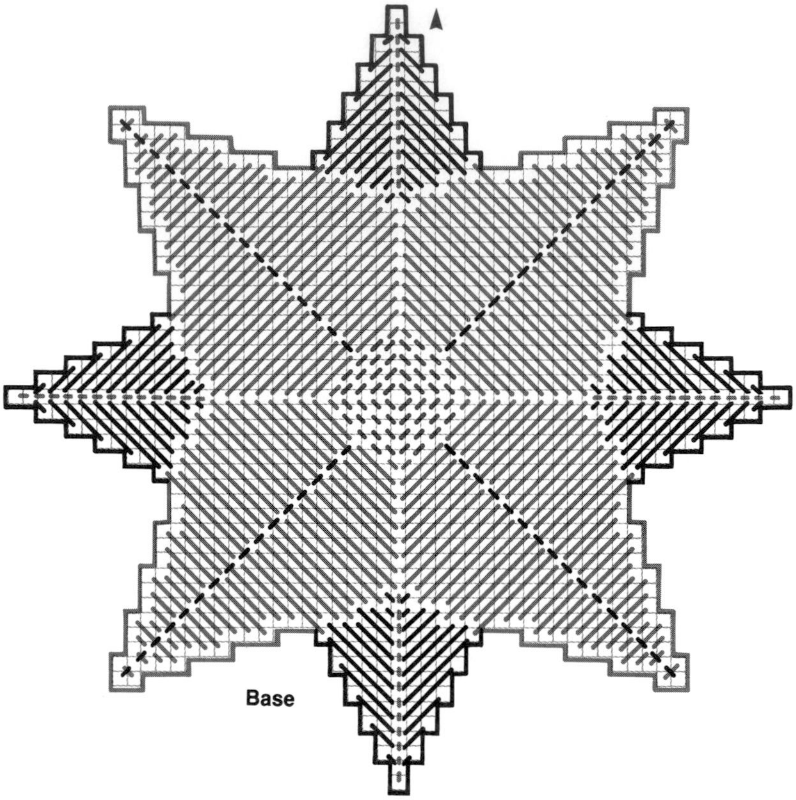

Base

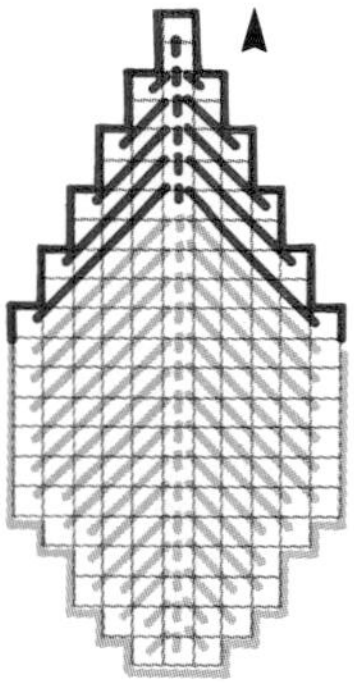

Petal 4 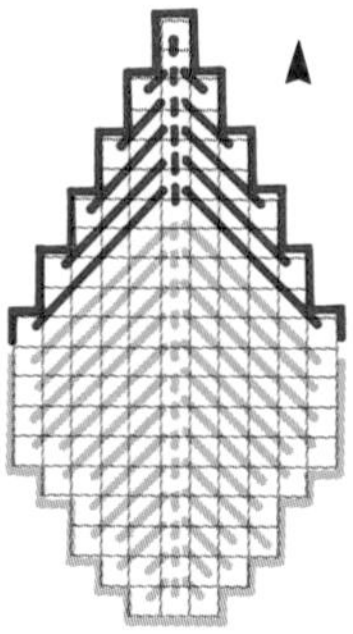   Petal 3 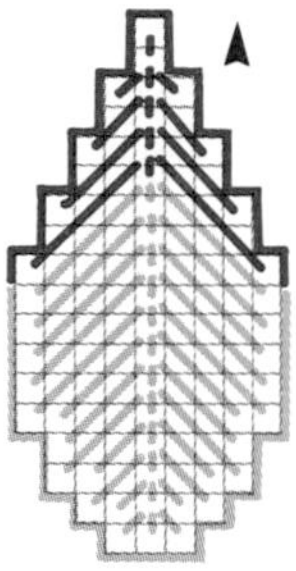   Petal 2 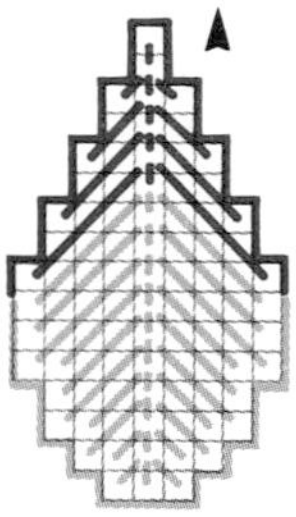   Petal 1

The Stitching

Work with one strand of Berella "4" yarn and stitch the pieces as diagramed in the following order:

1. Work the center of the candlestick in tent stitch, using Arbutus yarn. (The unstitched vertical plastic thread will be used for assembly.)

2. Work the petals in diagonal satin stitch. Do the areas as diagramed with Arbutus yarn, then with Burgundy. Then work whip stitch to overcast the edges, using Arbutus yarn and Burgundy yarn as indicated. Finish the center of each petal in backstitch along the unstitched center area as diagramed, using Arbutus yarn and Burgundy yarn.

3. Stitch the base of the candlestick as diagramed. Work the center in tent stitch, using Arbutus yarn. Next work the four small leaves in diagonal satin stitch, using Deep Leaf Green yarn. Now work the four large leaves in diagonal satin variation, using Medium Leaf Green yarn. Work the center of each large leaf in backstitch, using Deep Leaf Green yarn. Work whip stitch to overcast the edge of the piece, using the Medium and Deep Leaf Green yarns as indicated. Work the centers of each small leaf in backstitch, using Medium Leaf Green yarn.

Assembly/Candlesticks

Do all joining and overcasting using one strand of Berella "4" yarn. Do all tacking using one strand of 1–2–3 Ply yarn. The candlesticks are assembled in the same way, except where noted.

Centers

1. Place the center piece wrong side up so that the left side has an unovercast edge. The right side of the piece has an unovercast edge and an unstitched vertical interior plastic thread. To form the center cylinder, curve the edges of the piece upward, placing the unovercast edge of the left side over the unstitched interior plastic thread of the right side. Join the two overlapped plastic threads, matching the tent stitch direction on the right side of the piece. Use Arbutus yarn for the small candlestick and Burgundy yarn for the large candlestick. Using the same yarn color, complete by working whip stitch to overcast the bottom edge.

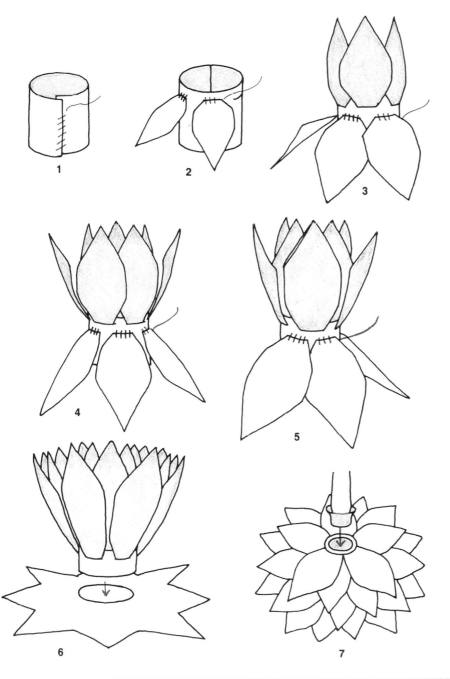

Petals

2. Tack the bottom edges of the petals to the stitched horizontal threads of the center cylinder, using 1–2–3 Ply yarn. Use Arbutus yarn for the small candlestick and Burgundy for the large. Tack the petals in four rows for the small candlestick and in five rows for the large candlestick. For clarity, placement lines for petal tacking are shown on the center stitch diagrams. Remember the columns of holes on the right and left of the flattened pieces overlap to form one column on the assembled cylinder.

   With right sides up and working along the top row, attach the five petal 1 pieces. Then bend the petals upward.

3. With right sides up and working along the second row from the top, attach the five petal 2 pieces. Then bend the petals upward.

4. With right sides up and working along the third row from the top, attach the five petal 3 pieces and bend them upward.

5. With right sides up and working along the fourth row from the top, attach the five petal 4 pieces. Assembly of the small candlestick petals is now complete.

   To complete the assembly of the large candlestick petals, bend the five petal 4 pieces upward. Then with right sides up and working along the fifth row from the top, attach the five petal 5 pieces.

   Finish the top edge of the center cylinder by working the edging stitch, using one strand of Old Gold yarn.

Base

6. With the base right side up, place the bottom edge of the center cylinder against it so that the center cylinder encircles the tent stitching in the center of the base. Tack the bottom edge of the cylinder to the base along this circle, using Arbutus yarn for the small candlestick and Burgundy yarn for the large candlestick.

Finishing

7. To curl the petals, bend each petal across its center width, curving the point downward. Hold for several seconds. Repeat as necessary until the curl is maintained.

   Place the candles in the candle cups and insert the cups into the center cylinders. Slip the bobeches over the candles and rest them against the top edge of the center cylinders of the candlesticks.

Owl Clock
Beginner

This owl is even wiser than most because he always knows what time it is. He's decorative, useful, and quite easy to stitch and to assemble. Addresses for suppliers of the clock movement and hands are given on page 191.

Materials

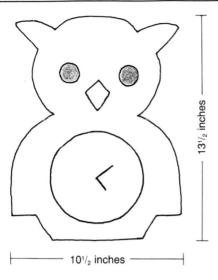

13¹/₂ inches

10¹/₂ inches

- Columbia-Minerva FashionEase clear 7-mesh plastic canvas: one sheet 10¹/₂″ × 13¹/₂″ (70 holes × 90 holes) one sheet 10¹/₂″ × 13¹/₂″ cut to 7¹/₂″ × 10¹/₂″ (52 holes × 70 holes)

- Columbia-Minerva Nantuk Yarn:
#5739 Gold	9 yards
#5709 Light Copperglo	33 yards

- Caron Sayelle Yarn:
#1042 Light Terra Cotta	15 yards
#1044 Terra Cotta	18 yards
#1046 Dark Rust	100 yards
#1002 Off White	24 yards

- National Artcraft Co. Ultra Thin-Ultra Small Quartz Clock Movement:
  #177–801–07 Clock movement with no second sweep hand
  or
  #177–802–07 Clock movement with a second sweep hand

Cutout Diagrams

Pattern Pieces

Follow the cutting diagrams carefully, making sure to count the holes accurately and to cut the right number of pieces.

1. Front. Cut one piece 69 holes wide × 90 holes high.
2. Body Bottom. Cut one piece 27 holes wide × 7 holes high.
3. Body Sides. Cut two pieces 7 holes wide × 11 holes high.
4. Wing Bottoms. Cut two pieces 11 holes wide × 7 holes high.
5. Wing Sides. Cut two pieces 7 holes wide × 50 holes high.
6. Head Sides. Cut two pieces 7 holes wide × 32 holes high.
7. Ear Bottoms. Cut two pieces 15 holes wide × 7 holes high.
8. Ear Tops. Cut two pieces 18 holes wide × 7 holes high.
9. Head Top. Cut one piece 37 holes wide × 7 holes high.

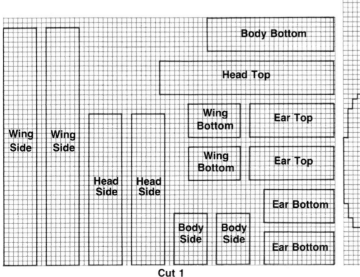

Cut 1

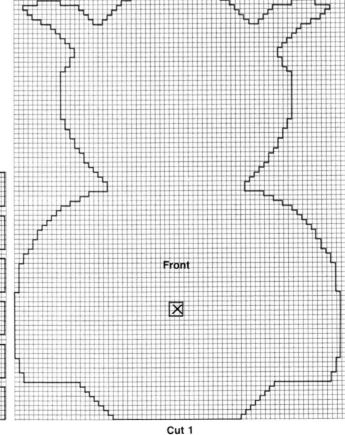

Cut 1

Stitching Diagrams

Stitches Used

Tent stitch (see page 12)
Gobelin stitch (see page 15)
Satin stitch (see page 16)
Brick stitch (see page 16)
Cross stitch (see page 18)
Whip stitch (see page 21)

The Stitching

Work tent stitch and cross stitch using one strand of yarn. Work brick stitch, satin stitch, and gobelin stitch using two strands of yarn. Overcast using two strands of yarn. Stitch the pieces as diagramed in the following order:

1. Begin by stitching the head of the owl. Work the satin stitches first, as diagramed, with Terra Cotta, Dark Rust, Light Terra Cotta, Light Copperglo, Off White, and Gold yarn. Start at the top edge of the head and work downward to the neck.

2. Work the outlines of the eyes in cross stitch, using Dark Rust yarn.

3. Work the outline of the clock in cross stitch, using Dark Rust yarn. Then work the numeral markings in cross stitch in Dark Rust and Terra Cotta yarn. Work the background of the clock face in tent stitch, using Off White yarn.

4. Work the wings in satin stitch, using Dark Rust, Terra Cotta, and Light Terra Cotta yarn.

5. Outline the clock face in brick stitch, using Light Copperglo yarn.

6. Work whip stitch to overcast the edges of the hole in the center of the clock, using Off White yarn.

7. Work the top of the head, the tops of the ears, the bottoms of the ears, the sides of the head, the sides of the wings, and the bottoms of the wings in gobelin stitch, using Dark Rust yarn. Use whip stitch to overcast the edges, as diagramed, using Dark Rust yarn.

8. Work the bottom of the body and the sides of the body in gobelin stitch, using Light Copperglo yarn. Use whip stitch to overcast the edges, as diagramed, using Light Copperglo yarn.

Color

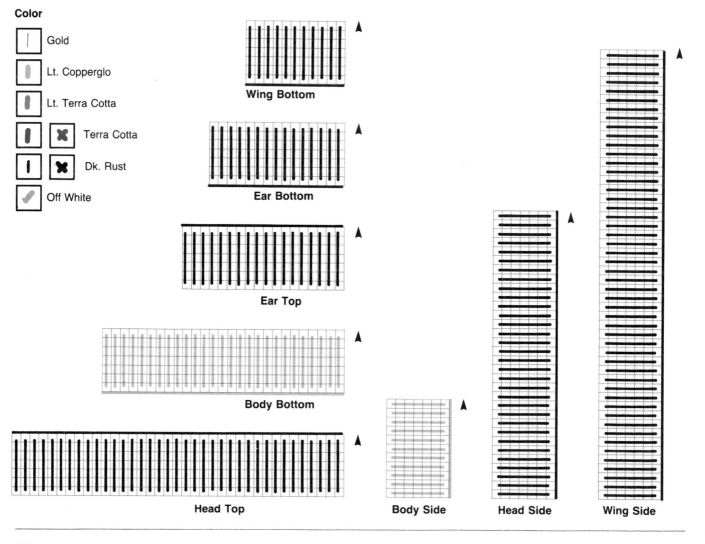

	Gold
	Lt. Copperglo
	Lt. Terra Cotta
	Terra Cotta
	Dk. Rust
	Off White

Wing Bottom

Ear Bottom

Ear Top

Body Bottom

Head Top

Body Side

Head Side

Wing Side

Ear Top

Head Top

Ear Top

Ear Bottom

Head Side

Head Side

Ear Bottom

Wing Side

Wing Side

Wing Bottom

Wing Bottom

Body Side

Body Side

Body Bottom

Assembly

Do all joining using two strands of yarn.

1. All the pieces are joined to the front piece and to each other, forming a band around the owl's head and body. The names of pattern pieces 2 through 9 refer to outline edges on the stitch diagram of the front of the owl.

   With right sides up, place the long unovercast edge of the body bottom against the bottom edge of the front piece. Flush join, using Light Copperglo.

   With right sides up, place the long unovercast edges of the bottoms of the wings against the bottom edges of the wings on the front pattern piece. The wing bottom pieces are each eleven holes wide. The wing bottom edges on the front piece are twelve holes wide. Match each wing bottom piece to the eleven outside holes on the front piece wing bottom edges. Flush join these, using Dark Rust yarn.

2. With right sides up, place the long unovercast edges of the body side pieces against the body side edges of the front piece. Flush join the adjacent edges of the body side and body bottom pieces, using Light Copperglo yarn. Flush join the adjacent short edges of the body side and wing bottom pieces, using Dark Rust yarn. Now flush join the long unovercast edges of the body side pieces to the body side edges of the front piece, using Light Copperglo yarn.

3. With right sides up, place the long unovercast edges of the wing side pieces against the wing side edges of the front piece. Using Dark Rust yarn, flush join the adjacent short edges of the wing side pieces and the wing bottom pieces. Starting at the top of the wings, flush join the long unovercast side edges of the wing side pieces to the wing side edges of the front piece, using Dark Rust yarn.

4. With right sides up, place the long unovercast edge of the head top piece against the head top edge of the front piece. The head top piece is twenty-two holes wider than the head top edge of the front piece. Center the head top piece so that eleven holes extend to the right and left of the front piece. Beginning at the left side of the head top edge on the front piece and working to the right, flush join the long unovercast edge of the head top piece to the head top edge of the front piece, using Dark Rust yarn. Complete by joining the edge of the remaining eleven-hole length of the head top piece to the left side of the head top edge of the front piece.

5. With right sides up, place the long unovercast edges of the ear top pieces against the ear top edges of the front piece. Using Dark Rust yarn, flush join the adjacent short edges of the head top and ear top pieces. Starting from this join and using Dark Rust yarn, flush join the long unovercast edges of the ear top pieces to the ear top edge of the front piece.

6. With right sides up, place the long unovercast edges of the ear bottom pieces against the ear bottom edges of the front piece. Using Dark Rust yarn, flush join the adjacent short edges of the ear top and ear bottom pieces. Starting from this join and using Dark Rust yarn, flush join the long unovercast edges of the ear bottom pieces to the ear bottom edges of the front piece.

7. With right sides up, place the long unovercast edges of the head side pieces against the head side edges of the front piece. Using Dark Rust yarn, flush join the adjacent short edges of the head side pieces and the wing side and ear bottom pieces. Now flush join the long unovercast edges of the head side pieces to the head side edges of the front piece, using Dark Rust yarn.

8. With the wrong side up, attach the hanger included with the clock movement to the wrong side of the front piece, using one strand of Light Copperglo yarn. Place the hanger in the center of the Light Copperglo stitching between the eyes and stitch to secure as diagramed.

   Following the manufacturer's instructions, attach the clock movement through the hole in the center of the clock face.

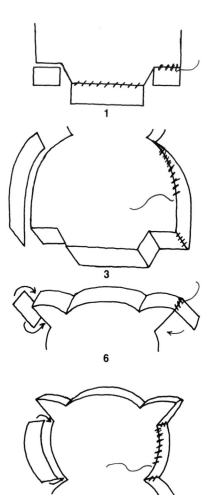

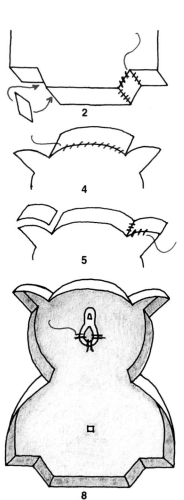

Old Woman's Shoe Photo Frame
Beginner

Mother Goose's rhyme about the old woman who lived in a shoe was the starting point for the design of this whimsical wall hanging, which will display six of your favorite photographs. The photo frame is fun to make. The assembly is simple, but the stitching is a bit more difficult because nine colors of yarn are used.

Materials

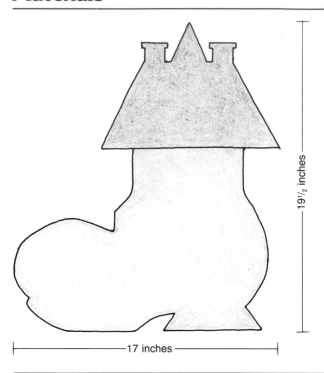

19½ inches

17 inches

- Boye E-Z Count clear 7-mesh plastic canvas:
  one sheet 12″ × 18″ (80 holes × 120 holes)
  one sheet 12″ × 18″ cut to 9″ × 12¼″ (61 holes × 81 holes)
- Columbia-Minerva Nantuk Yarn:
#5972 Cornflower	14 yards
#5776 Medium Blue	30 yards
#5977 Navy	55 yards
#5709 Light Copperglo	17 yards
#2907 Grey Flannel	9 yards
#5739 Gold	41 yards
- Caron Sayelle Yarn:
#1042 Light Terra Cotta	62 yards
#1044 Terra Cotta	12 yards
#1046 Dark Rust	15 yards
- Bernat 1–2–3 Ply Persian Type Yarn:
  | #N11–036 Gold | 1 yard (or any Persian yarn that matches #5739 Gold) |
- Six photographs with picture area in the dimensions listed. For secure mounting, each photograph should be at least ½ inch larger in each dimension.
  one photograph 3″ wide × 5″ high
  one photograph 3¾″ wide × 2¼″ high
  one photograph 2¾″ wide × 2¾″ high
  one photograph 2½″ wide × 2½″ high
  two photographs 1¾″ wide × 3″ high
- masking tape
- one white shoelace 48″ long

Cutout Diagrams

Pattern Pieces

Follow the cutting diagrams carefully, making sure to count the holes accurately.

1. Shoe. Cut one piece
   114 holes wide × 80 holes high.
2. Roof. Cut one piece
   81 holes wide × 61 holes high.

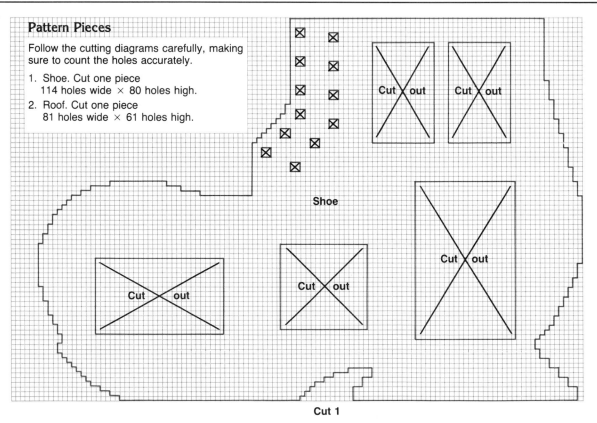

Shoe

Cut out

Cut out

Cut out

Cut out

Cut out

Cut out

Cut 1

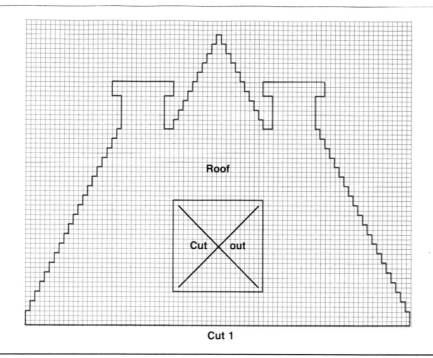

Roof

Cut out

Cut 1

Stitching Diagrams

Stitches Used

Tent stitch (see page 12)
Slanted gobelin stitch
(see page 13)
Gobelin stitch
(see page 15)
Satin stitch
(see page 16)
Brick stitch
(see page 16)
Parisian stitch
(see page 17)
Whip stitch
(see page 21)

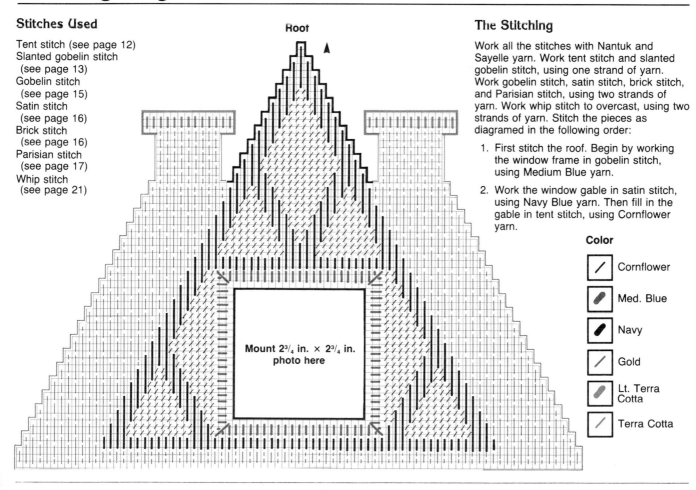

Roof

Mount 2³/₄ in. × 2³/₄ in. photo here

The Stitching

Work all the stitches with Nantuk and Sayelle yarn. Work tent stitch and slanted gobelin stitch, using one strand of yarn. Work gobelin stitch, satin stitch, brick stitch, and Parisian stitch, using two strands of yarn. Work whip stitch to overcast, using two strands of yarn. Stitch the pieces as diagramed in the following order:

1. First stitch the roof. Begin by working the window frame in gobelin stitch, using Medium Blue yarn.

2. Work the window gable in satin stitch, using Navy Blue yarn. Then fill in the gable in tent stitch, using Cornflower yarn.

Color

/	Cornflower
🖊	Med. Blue
🖊	Navy
/	Gold
🖊	Lt. Terra Cotta
/	Terra Cotta

Color

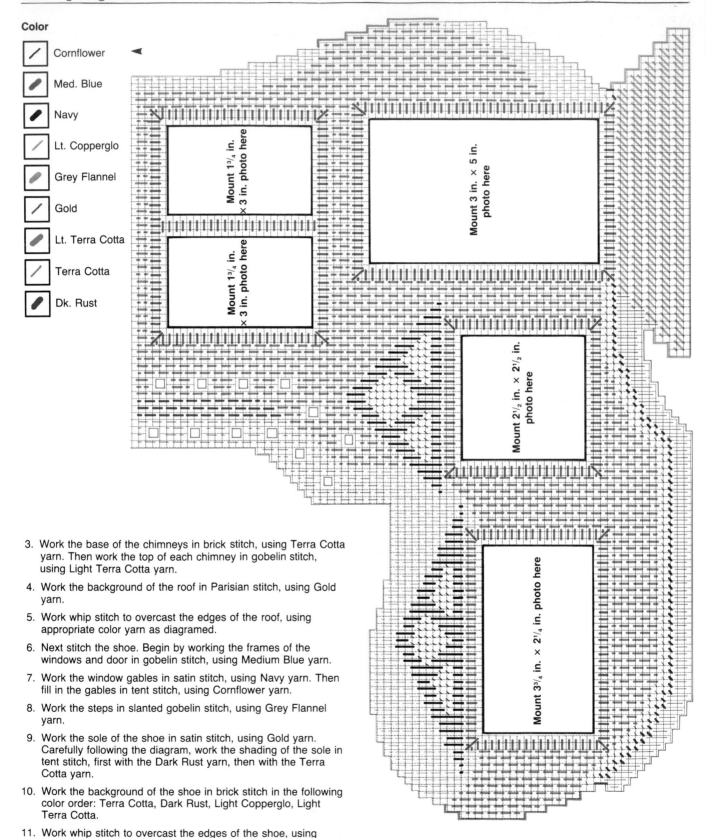

/	Cornflower ◄
/	Med. Blue
/	Navy
/	Lt. Copperglo
/	Grey Flannel
/	Gold
/	Lt. Terra Cotta
/	Terra Cotta
/	Dk. Rust

Mount 1³/₄ in. × 3 in. photo here

Mount 1³/₄ in. × 3 in. photo here

Mount 3 in. × 5 in. photo here

Mount 2¹/₂ in. × 2¹/₂ in. photo here

Mount 3³/₄ in. × 2¹/₄ in. photo here

3. Work the base of the chimneys in brick stitch, using Terra Cotta yarn. Then work the top of each chimney in gobelin stitch, using Light Terra Cotta yarn.

4. Work the background of the roof in Parisian stitch, using Gold yarn.

5. Work whip stitch to overcast the edges of the roof, using appropriate color yarn as diagramed.

6. Next stitch the shoe. Begin by working the frames of the windows and door in gobelin stitch, using Medium Blue yarn.

7. Work the window gables in satin stitch, using Navy yarn. Then fill in the gables in tent stitch, using Cornflower yarn.

8. Work the steps in slanted gobelin stitch, using Grey Flannel yarn.

9. Work the sole of the shoe in satin stitch, using Gold yarn. Carefully following the diagram, work the shading of the sole in tent stitch, first with the Dark Rust yarn, then with the Terra Cotta yarn.

10. Work the background of the shoe in brick stitch in the following color order: Terra Cotta, Dark Rust, Light Copperglo, Light Terra Cotta.

11. Work whip stitch to overcast the edges of the shoe, using appropriate color yarn as diagramed.

Assembly

1. With right sides up, flush join the unovercast areas on the bottom edge of the roof to the top edge of the shoe, using blind cross stitch and one strand of Gold Persian yarn. Using gobelin stitch and two strands of Gold Nantuk yarn, stitch over these joined edges to hide the cross stitching.

Trim the photographs as necessary and use masking tape to mount them on the wrong side of the frame, as indicated on the stitch diagrams.

2. Insert the shoelace and tie it as shown.

3. Using two strands of Terra Cotta yarn, tie a loop of yarn on the wrong side of each chimney for hanging. Leaving a 4-inch tail, start each loop by entering the yarn through the stitching at the base of each chimney and going upward $1/2$ inch. To complete, turn and take the yarn downward, again through the stitching at each chimney base. Tie the starting and ending tails of each loop in an overhand knot and trim tails to $1/4$ inch.

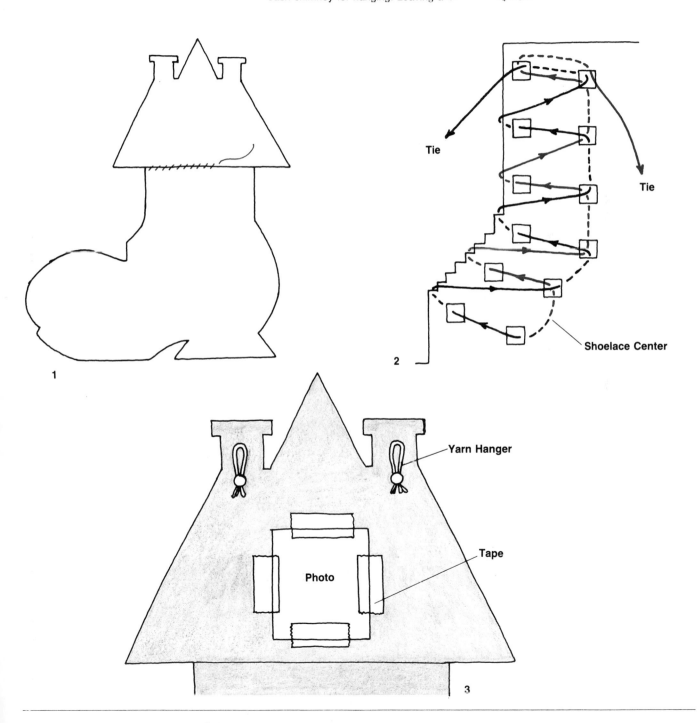

Gingerbread House Recipe Box
Intermediate

This charming gingerbread house is practical as well as decorative. It not only brightens your kitchen, it also keeps your favorite recipes neat and handy. It's fun to make.

Seven different stitches are required, and you must follow the stitch diagrams carefully, so you won't be bored. The assembly is fairly simple.

Materials

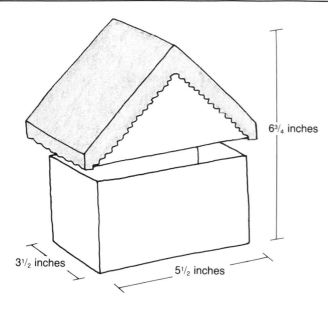

3½ inches

5½ inches

6¾ inches

- Columbia-Minerva FashionEase clear 7-mesh plastic canvas:
  one sheet 10½" × 13½" (70 holes × 90 holes)
  one sheet 10½" × 13½" cut to 7" × 13½" (48 holes × 90 holes)
- Bernat Tabriz Needle Art Yarn:

#5801	Straw	42 yards
#5802	Light Gold	19 yards
#5836	Ashes of Roses	41 yards
#5837	Gothic Red	33 yards
#5846	Gendarme Blue	5 yards
#5862	Medium Blue	6 yards
#5888	Emerald	15 yards
#5821	Shocking Pink	2 yards
#5825	Orange	2 yards

- no. 16 tapestry needle
- 3" × 5" recipe cards and dividers

Cutout Diagrams

Pattern Pieces

Follow the cutting diagrams carefully, making sure to count the holes accurately and to cut the right number of pieces.

1. House Base. Cut one piece 36 holes wide × 22 holes high.
2. House Front. Cut one piece 36 holes wide × 24 holes high.
3. House Back. Cut one piece 36 holes wide × 24 holes high.
4. House Side. Cut two pieces 22 holes wide × 24 holes high.
5. Roof Front and Back. Cut two pieces 39 holes wide × 24 holes high.
6. Roof Sides. Cut two pieces 25 holes wide × 5 holes high.
7. Gable Front and Back. Cut two pieces 43 holes wide × 24 holes high.
8. Gable Sides. Cut two pieces 4 holes wide × 22 holes high.
9. Roof. Cut two pieces 29 holes wide × 31 holes high.

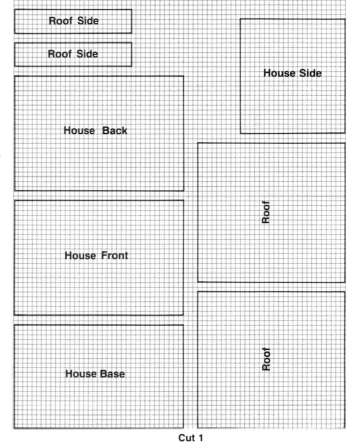

Cut 1

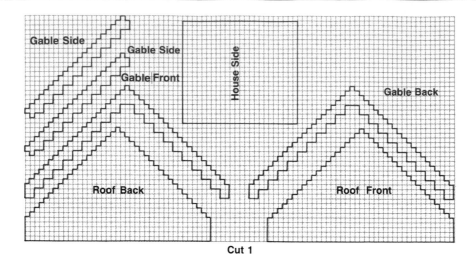

Cut 1

Stitching Diagrams

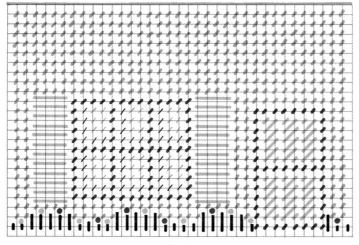

Front

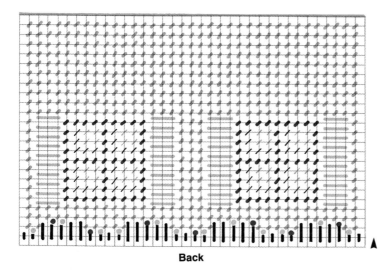

Back

Stitches Used

Tent stitch (see page 12)
Slanted gobelin stitch (see page 13)
Gobelin stitch (see page 15)
Satin stitch (see page 16)
Backstitch (see page 20)
French knot (see page 21)
Whip stitch (see page 21)

The Stitching

Do all the stitching and overcasting using one strand of yarn. Stitch the pieces as diagramed in the following order:

1. Work the base of the house in gobelin stitch, using Emerald yarn.

2. Stitch the front of the house. First work the grass in satin stitch, using Emerald yarn. Work the door frame and window frame in tent stitch, using Gothic Red yarn. Work the door panels in slanted gobelin stitch, using Ashes of Roses yarn. Work the shutters in gobelin stitch, using Ashes of Roses yarn. Work the shadows in the windowpanes in tent stitch, using Gendarme Blue yarn. Work tent stitch to fill the panes, using Medium Blue yarn. Work the background in tent stitch, using Straw yarn. Work the flowers in French knots, using Shocking Pink and Orange yarn. Work whip stitch to overcast the top edge, using Straw yarn.

Color

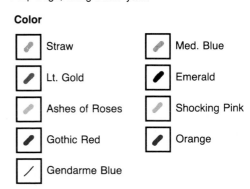

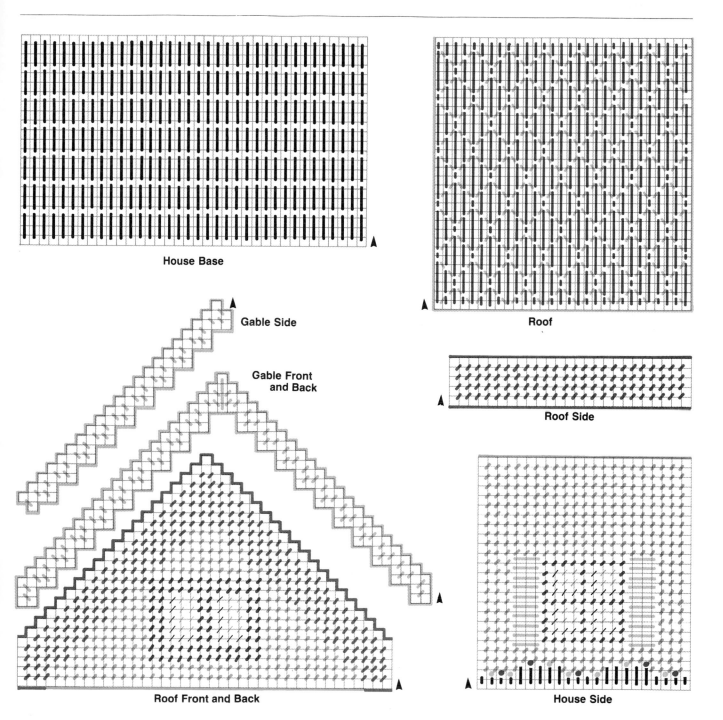

House Base

Roof

Gable Side

**Gable Front
and Back**

Roof Side

Roof Front and Back

House Side

3. Work the back of the house, using the same stitches and colors you used on the front.

4. Work the two sides of the house, using the same stitches and colors as the front.

5. Stitch the front and back of the roof next. First work the window frame in tent stitch, using Gothic Red yarn. Work the shadow of the windowpanes in tent stitch, using Gendarme Blue yarn. Fill in the windowpanes in tent stitch, using Medium Blue yarn. Work the upper roof area in tent stitch, using Straw and Light Gold yarn, as indicated. Work whip stitch to overcast the edges, using Straw and Light Gold yarn, to match the stitching.

6. Work the two roof side pieces in tent stitch, using Light Gold yarn. Work whip stitch to overcast the two long sides of each piece, using Light Gold yarn.

7. Work the two gable side pieces and the gable front and back pieces in tent stitch, using Ashes of Roses yarn. Work whip stitch to overcast the edges, using Ashes of Roses yarn.

8. Stitch the two roof pieces. First work the diamonds in satin stitch, using Gothic Red yarn. Then work the outline in backstitch, using Ashes of Roses yarn. Work whip stitch to overcast three sides, as diagramed, using Ashes of Roses yarn.

Assembly

A four-ply yarn is composed of four small individual yarn elements twisted together to form one strand. For tacking during assembly, untwist a four-ply strand and work with only a single ply that is 18 inches long. If the single ply softens and pulls apart while tacking, twist it tightly in one direction. You will find that twisting one way continues to weaken the strand, and twisting the opposite way will tighten it. For joining, use a complete four-ply strand.

Box

1. With right sides up and in consecutive order, flush join the edges of the base of the house to the bottom edges of the house front, back, and sides, using Emerald yarn.

2. With right sides out and in consecutive order, flush join the adjacent edges of the house pieces to create a box. Use Emerald and Straw yarn, matching the colors on the right sides.

Roof

3. With right sides out and in consecutive order, flush join the side bottom edges of the front and back of the roof to the adjacent edges of the two sides of the roof, using Light Gold yarn.

4. With right sides up and using Ashes of Roses yarn, flush join the top edges of the two roof pieces.

5. With right side up, place the joined roof pieces over the joined roof front, back, and sides. The right and left edges of the roof pieces will extend two holes beyond the edges of the roof front and back pieces.

6. Using Gothic Red yarn, tack the top edges of the roof front, back, and side pieces to the roof. Use blind tent stitch to tack the front and back pieces. Place the stitches along the second interior plastic thread inward from each of the roof side edges. Use blind gobelin stitch to tack the roof side pieces. Place the stitches along the fourth interior plastic thread inward from each of the roof bottom edges.

Gables

7. With right side out, place the top edge of one gable front and back piece along the outside edge of one side of the angled roof pieces, matching the center point of the gable to the point of the roof. Starting at the center point of the angle and working downward to the base, tack these edges, using Ashes of Roses yarn and the figure-eight stitch. Now tack the second gable front and back piece in the same way.

8. With right side out, place the top edge of one gable side along the bottom edge of one roof piece. Tack these edges, using Ashes of Roses yarn and the figure-eight stitch. Tack the adjacent edges of the gable side and the two front and back gable pieces in the same way. Now tack the second side gable to the bottom of the other roof piece the same way.

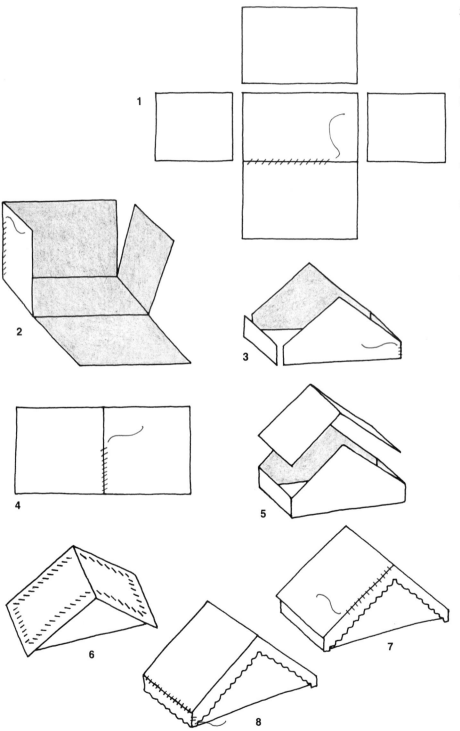

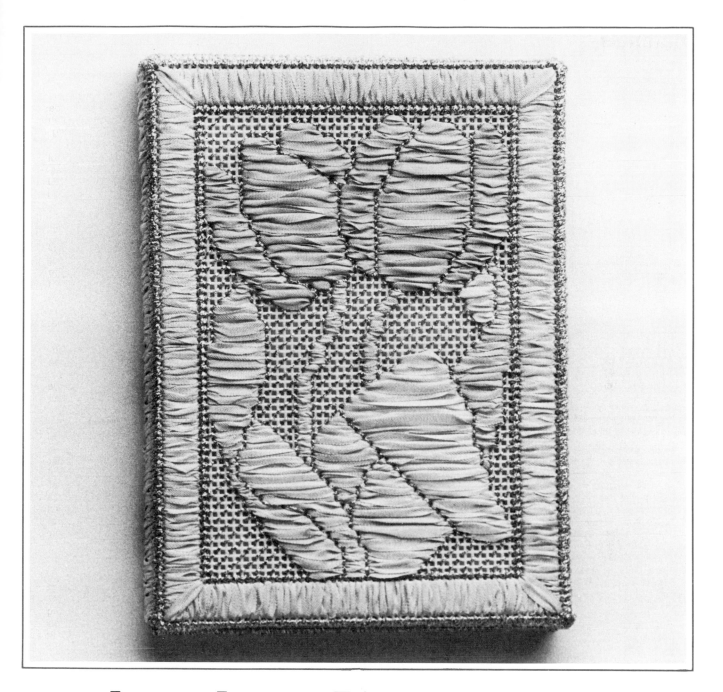

Lace-Look Picture Frame
Intermediate

This elegant picture frame is stitched with ribbon rather than yarn, which accounts for its delicate silky look. The basic stitching and assembly are not difficult, but it takes a bit of practice to work comfortably with the ribbon. Ribbons yarn is available only on 100-yard spools. You will therefore have enough ribbon to make two frames. You can make additional frames with the ribbon that's left by doing all the stitching in one color. This is subtle and effective, since the metallic yarn sets off the border and delineates the shapes of the leaves and the flowers.

Materials

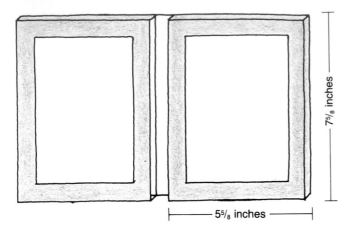

- Westex Industries opaque white 10-mesh plastic canvas: four sheets 8″ × 10″ (80 holes × 100 holes)
- Gemini ¼″ Ribbons Yarn:

#4 Pale Blue	50 yards
#5 Soft Pink	8½ yards
#6 Pastel Peach	10 yards
#7 Orchid	15 yards

- Phildar Sunset 330 Yarn:

#72 Or Metallic	136 yards

- nos. 18 and 20 tapestry needles
- two 5″ × 7″ photographs
- two white unruled 5″ × 8″ index cards
- transparent tape

7⅝ inches

5⅝ inches

Cutout Diagrams

Pattern Pieces

Follow the cutting diagrams carefully, making sure to count the holes accurately and to cut the right number of pieces.

1. Front. Cut two pieces
   54 holes wide × 74 holes high.
2. Back 1. Cut one piece
   54 holes wide × 74 holes high.
3. Back 2. Cut one piece
   54 holes wide × 74 holes high.
4. Top/Bottom Seams. Cut four pieces
   54 holes wide × 3 holes high.
5. Side Seams. Cut two pieces
   3 holes wide × 74 holes high.
6. Spine. Cut one piece
   6 holes wide × 74 holes high.

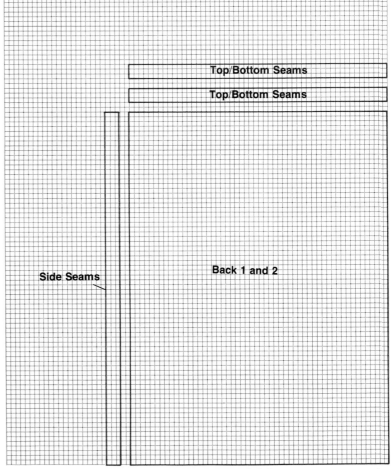

Top/Bottom Seams

Top/Bottom Seams

Side Seams

Back 1 and 2

Cut 2

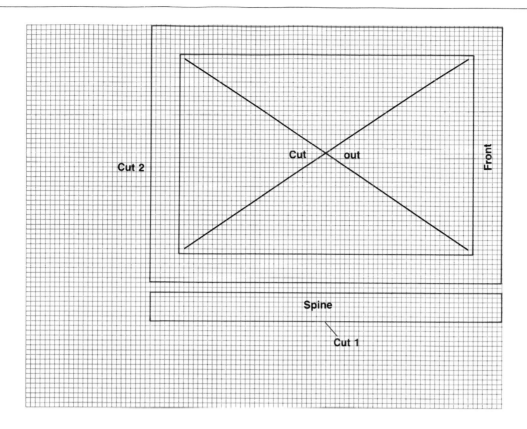

Cut 2

Cut out

Front

Spine

Cut 1

Stitching Diagrams

Stitches Used

Tent stitch (see page 12)
Gobelin stitch (see page 15)
Satin stitch (see page 16)
Backstitch (see page 20)
Whip stitch (see page 21)

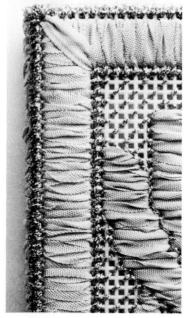

Detail (Actual Size)

The Stitching

All gobelin and satin stitching is done with Ribbons yarn. When working with the ribbon, use one strand and a no. 18 tapestry needle. Cut the ribbon in 1-yard lengths to work, unless specified otherwise. Since ribbon that is doubled through the needle eye is crushed while stitching, work the ribbon with only a 3-inch tail through the needle eye. The two strands of ribbon through the needle eye will create a snug fit in the holes of the plastic canvas. Tug gently when pulling the needle through to prevent splitting the canvas. Ribbon will twist while stitching, so be sure to straighten it as you work, to avoid a crinkled surface. The cut ends of the ribbon may unravel while you are stitching. Trim the threads as necessary to prevent them from catching. The ribbon is slippery, so you will have to leave a 1- to 1½-inch starting and ending tail to secure each strand.

Work tent stitch, backstitch, and whip stitch with Or metallic yarn and a no. 20 tapestry needle. Use three strands of yarn for tent stitch. Work backstitch with one strand of yarn. When overcasting, use four strands of yarn. Cut the yarn in 1-yard lengths to work. The tails may untwist while stitching, because the yarn is slippery. The stitching must be done with tightly twisted strands of yarn so that it is even. As with the ribbon, leave a 1- to 1½-inch starting and ending tail to secure the yarn.

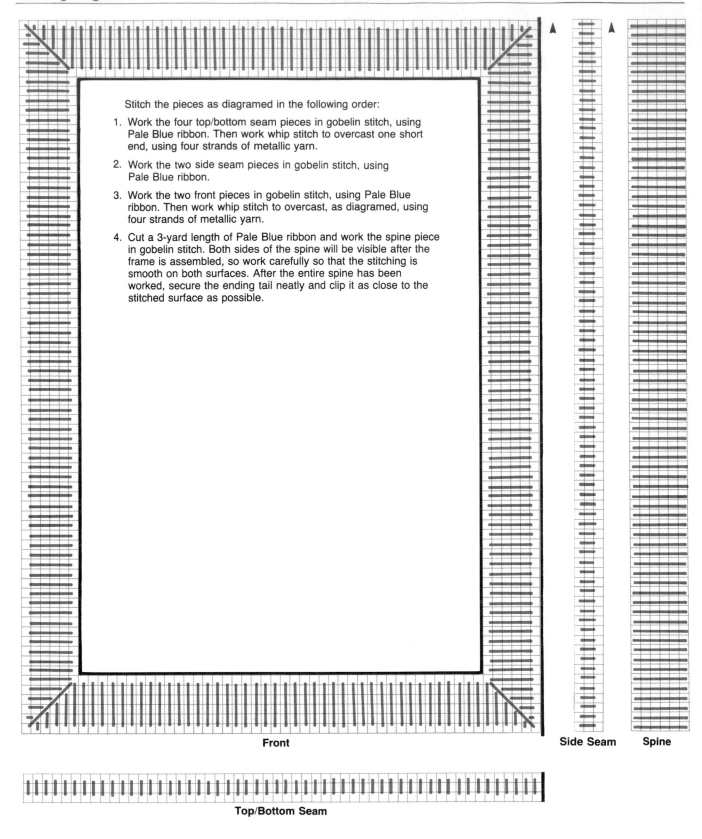

Stitch the pieces as diagramed in the following order:

1. Work the four top/bottom seam pieces in gobelin stitch, using Pale Blue ribbon. Then work whip stitch to overcast one short end, using four strands of metallic yarn.

2. Work the two side seam pieces in gobelin stitch, using Pale Blue ribbon.

3. Work the two front pieces in gobelin stitch, using Pale Blue ribbon. Then work whip stitch to overcast, as diagramed, using four strands of metallic yarn.

4. Cut a 3-yard length of Pale Blue ribbon and work the spine piece in gobelin stitch. Both sides of the spine will be visible after the frame is assembled, so work carefully so that the stitching is smooth on both surfaces. After the entire spine has been worked, secure the ending tail neatly and clip it as close to the stitched surface as possible.

Front

Side Seam

Spine

Top/Bottom Seam

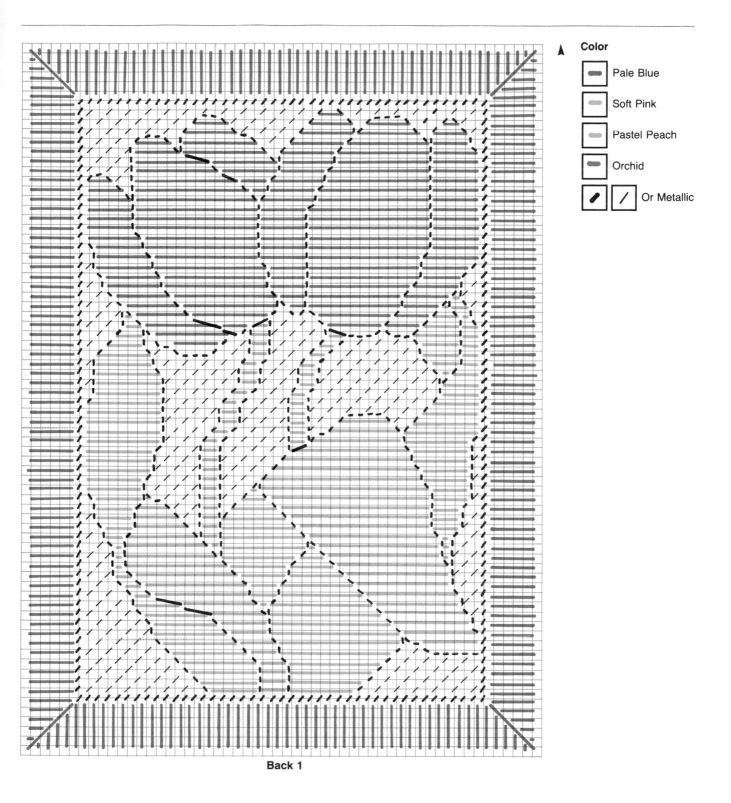

Back 1

5. Now stitch the two back pieces. First work the frame in gobelin stitch, using Pale Blue ribbon. Work one row of tent stitch around the inner edge of the border, using three strands of metallic yarn. Work the leaves and stems in satin stitch, using Soft Pink and Pastel Peach ribbon as diagramed. Work the petals in satin stitch, using Orchid ribbon. Work the outlines of the leaves and flowers in backstitch, using one strand of metallic yarn. Work the background in a diagonal backstitch, using one strand of metallic yarn.

Color

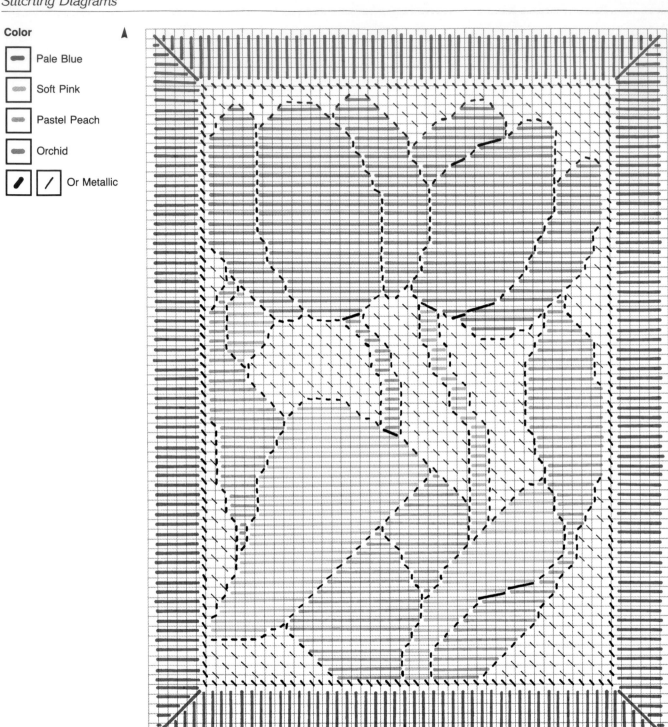

Pale Blue

Soft Pink

Pastel Peach

Orchid

Or Metallic

Back 2

Assembly

Do all joining using four strands of metallic yarn and a no. 20 tapestry needle.

1. With right sides up, flush join the edges of the two back pieces to the edges of the spine.

2. With right sides up, flush join the edges of the four top/bottom seam pieces to the edges of the two back pieces. Align the pieces so the one overcast side edge on each seam is near the spine. Working across the top of the frame first and then across the bottom, work whip stitch to overcast the top and bottom edges of the spine piece while joining the seam pattern pieces. Both the right side and the wrong side of the spine will be visible on the completed frame; therefore, start and end only on the wrong sides of the back and seam pieces.

With right sides up, flush join the edges of the two side seam pieces to the edges of the back pieces.

3. To complete the seam assembly, turn the joined back, spine, and seam pieces wrong side up. Turning the seam pieces upward, flush join the adjacent edges of each two top/bottom seam and side seam pieces.

4. With wrong sides together, flush join the edges of the two front pieces to the edges of the top/bottom seam and side seam pieces.

5. Trim the two 5-inch × 8-inch index cards to 5 inches × $7\frac{3}{8}$ inches. Center one photograph on each card. Tape along the edges to secure. Insert the photographs in the frame through the sleeve openings on the right and left of the front.

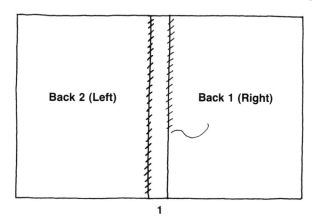

Back 2 (Left)   Back 1 (Right)

1

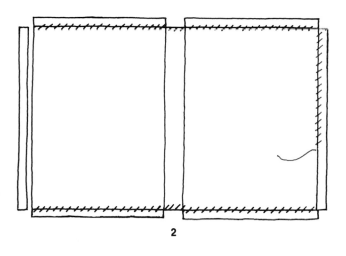

2

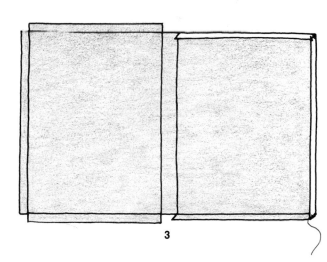

3

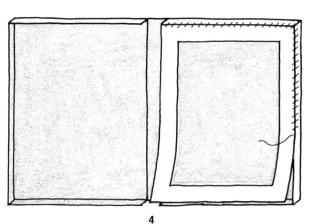

4

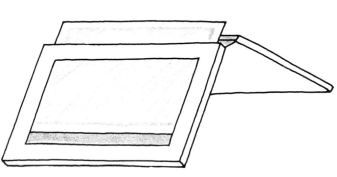

5

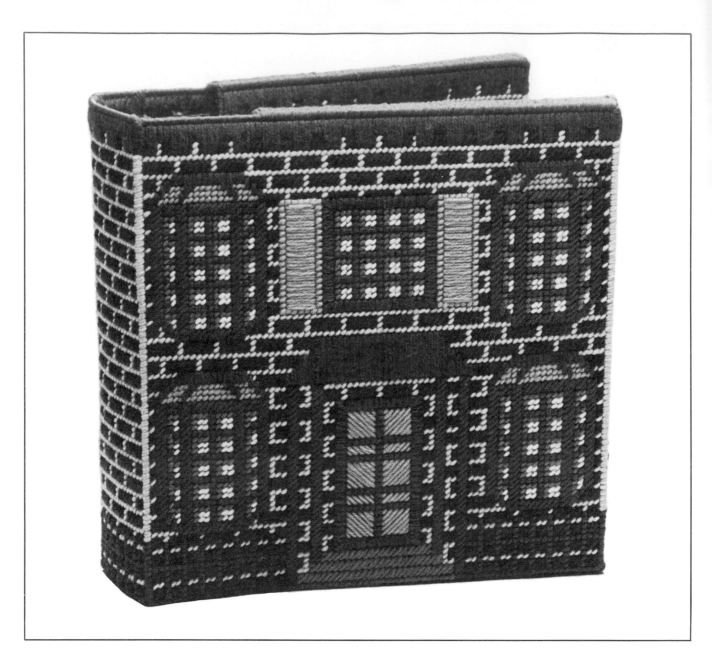

Victorian Town House
Photo Album Cover
Intermediate

With this wonderful cover on your photograph album, you will want always to keep it on display. If you prefer you can use other colors or adapt the design to create a picture of your own house. When you are working on this project, you must follow the stitching chart very carefully because it is quite complicated. The assembly, however, is fairly simple.

Materials

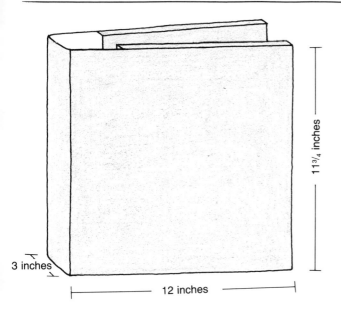

3 inches

11¾ inches

12 inches

- Boye E-Z Count clear 7-mesh plastic canvas:
  one sheet 12″ × 18″ (80 holes × 120 holes)
  three sheets 12″ × 18″ cut to 12″ × 12¼″ (80 holes × 81 holes)
- Coats and Clark Red Heart 4-Ply Handknitting Yarn:

#286 Bronze	112 yards
#246 Sea Coral	68 yards
#849 Olympic Blue	255 yards
#814 Robin Blue	65 yards
#001 White	48 yards
#404 Grey	27 yards

- one #2040 Magic Mount Jumbo Photo Album with 3-Ring Binder

Cutout Diagrams

Pattern Pieces

Follow the cutting diagrams carefully, making sure to count the holes accurately and to cut the right number of pieces.

1. Front and Back Covers. Cut two pieces 78 holes wide × 81 holes high.

2. Spine. Cut one piece 18 holes wide × 81 holes high.

3. Front Cover Sleeve. Cut one piece 58 holes wide × 81 holes high.

4. Back Cover Sleeve. Cut one piece 58 holes wide × 81 holes high.

5. Side Sleeve Seams. Cut two pieces 4 holes wide × 81 holes high.

6. Top Sleeve Seams. Cut two pieces 58 holes wide × 4 holes high.

7. Bottom Sleeve Seams. Cut two pieces 58 holes wide × 4 holes high.

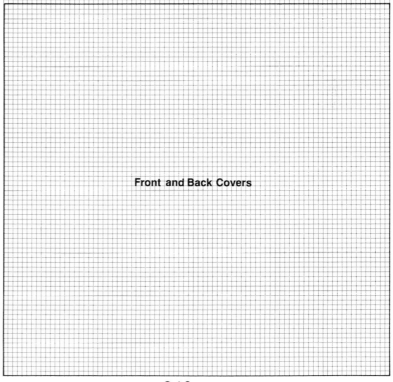

Front and Back Covers

Cut 2

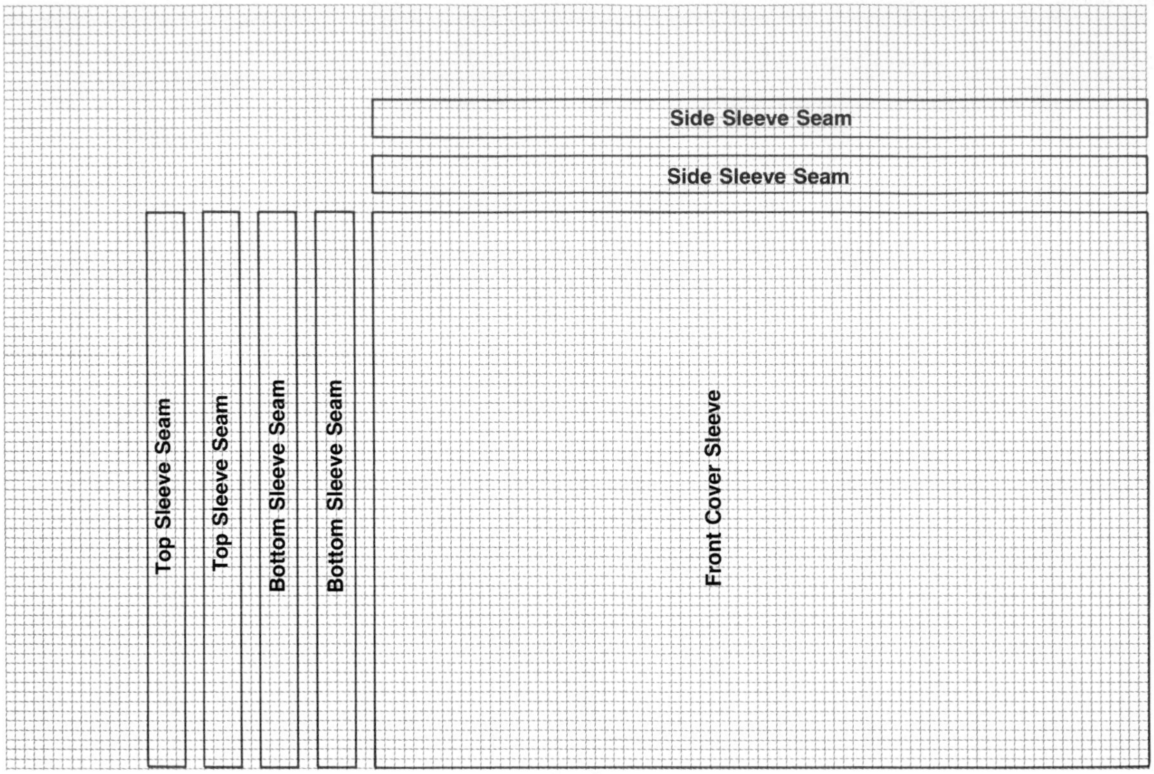

Side Sleeve Seam

Side Sleeve Seam

Top Sleeve Seam

Top Sleeve Seam

Bottom Sleeve Seam

Bottom Sleeve Seam

Front Cover Sleeve

Cut 1

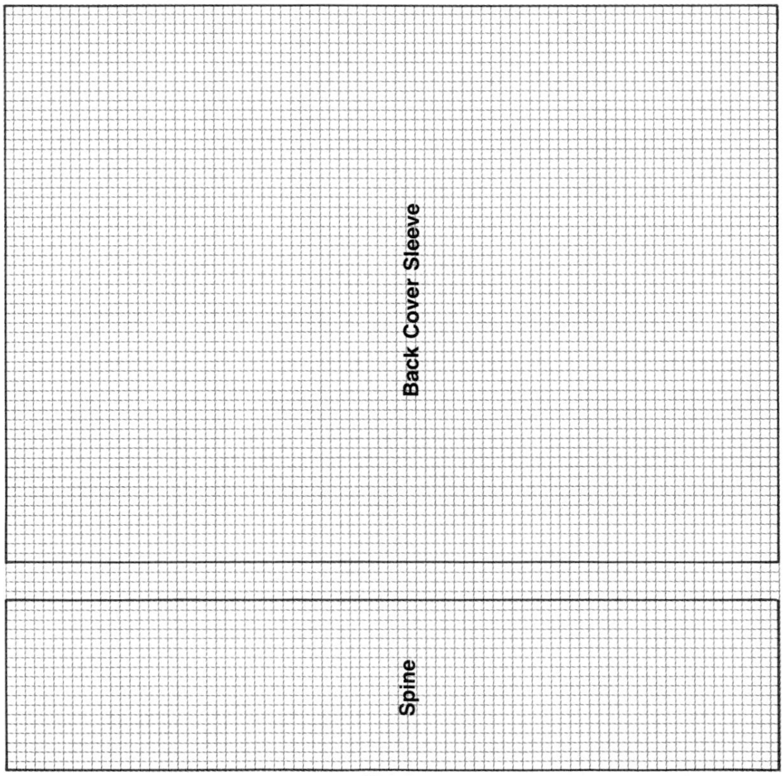

Back Cover Sleeve

Spine

Cut 1

Stitching Diagrams

Stitches Used

Tent stitch (see page 12)
Slanted gobelin stitch
 (see page 13)
Gobelin stitch (see page 15)
Satin stitch (see page 16)
Cross stitch (see page 18)
Whip stitch (see page 21)

Color

Bronze

White

Grey

Sea Coral

Olympic Blue

Robin Blue

The Stitching

Work cross stitch, slanted gobelin stitch, and tent stitch using one strand of yarn. Work gobelin stitch and satin stitch using two strands of yarn. Work whip stitch to overcast, using two strands of yarn. When overcasting, be sure to duplicate the direction of the tent stitch and the slanted gobelin stitch on the right sides of the pieces.
 Stitch the pieces as diagramed in the following order:

1. The front and back covers and the two sleeves are worked in the same way. Begin by working the fence in cross stitch, using Olympic Blue yarn.

2. Work the stairs in slanted gobelin stitch, using Grey yarn.

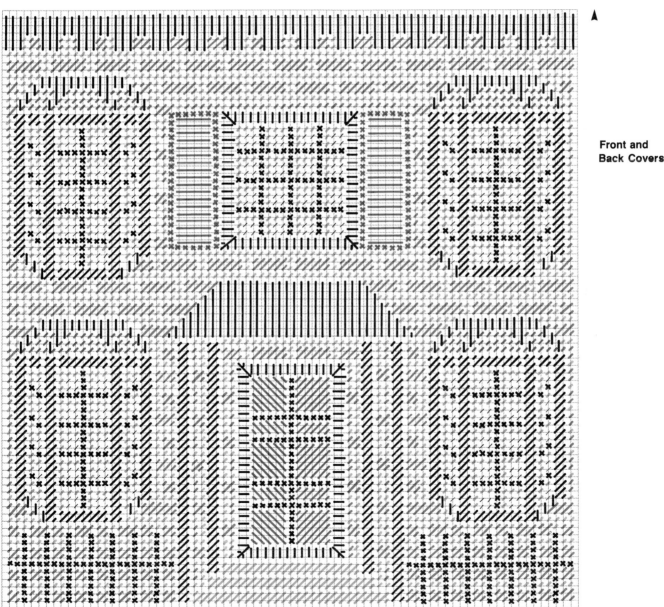

Front and Back Covers

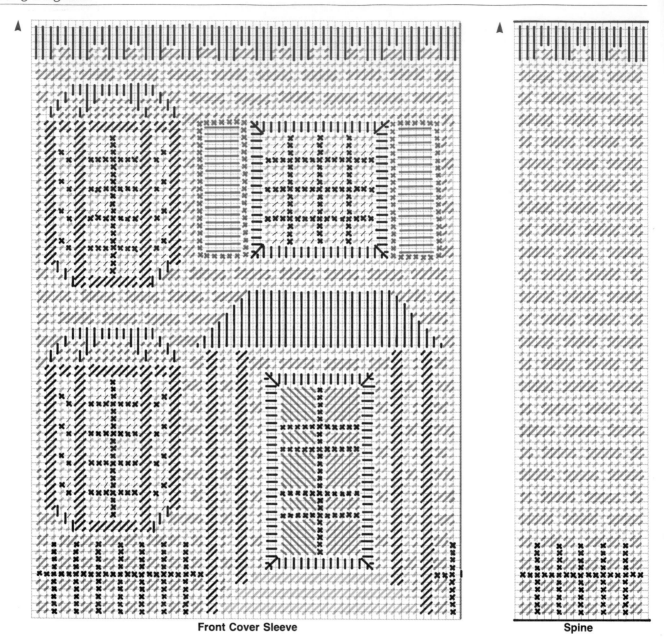

Front Cover Sleeve

Spine

3. Next work the door. Work the door frame in gobelin stitch, using Olympic Blue yarn; then work the interior detail in cross stitch, using Olympic Blue yarn. Fill in the panels of the door in slanted gobelin stitch, using Robin Blue yarn.

4. Work the porch next. Work the uprights in slanted gobelin stitch, using Olympic Blue yarn. Work the porch roof in satin stitch, using Olympic Blue yarn.

5. Work the window above the door next. Work the outer window frame in gobelin stitch, using Olympic Blue yarn. Work the inner window frame in cross stitch, using Olympic Blue yarn. Work the glass panes in tent stitch. Put in the shadows first, using Grey yarn; then fill in the panes, using White yarn. Work the outline of the shutters in cross stitch, using Robin Blue yarn. Work the inner area of the shutters in gobelin stitch, using Robin Blue yarn.

6. Stitch the bay windows next, working one window at a time. First work the outer window frame in slanted gobelin stitch, using Olympic Blue yarn. Work the outline of the gable and the lower sides of the window frame in satin stitch, using Olympic Blue yarn. Work the interior of the gable in tent stitch, using Robin Blue yarn. Work the inner window frame in cross stitch, using Olympic Blue yarn. Work the glass panes in tent stitch. Put in the shadows first, using Grey yarn; then fill in the panes, using White.

7. Work the roof in satin stitch, using Olympic Blue yarn.

8. Work the bricks in slanted gobelin stitch and tent stitch, using Bronze yarn.

9. Work the mortar in tent stitch, using Sea Coral yarn.

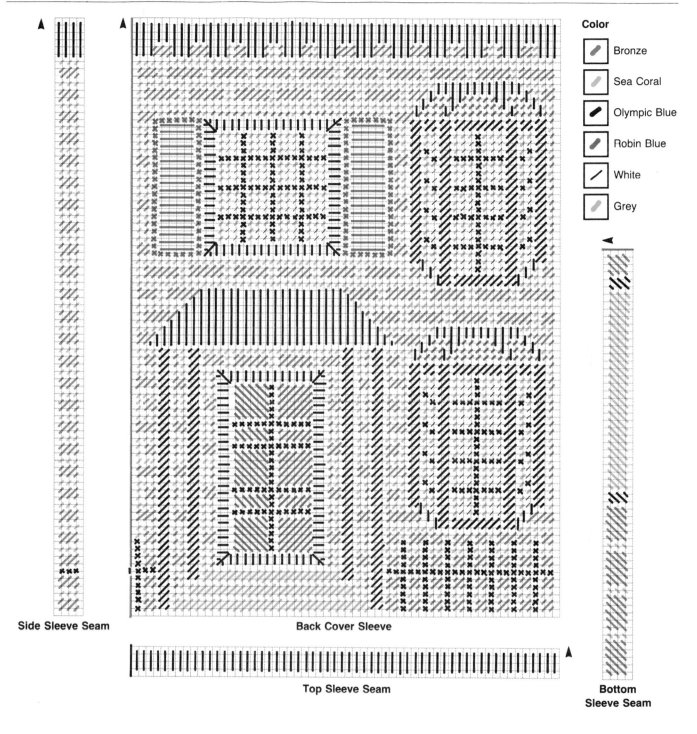

Color

	Bronze
	Sea Coral
	Olympic Blue
	Robin Blue
	White
	Grey

Side Sleeve Seam

Back Cover Sleeve

Top Sleeve Seam

Bottom Sleeve Seam

10. Stitch the spine piece of the album next. Work the fence in cross stitch, using Olympic Blue yarn. Work the roof in satin stitch, using Olympic Blue yarn. Work the bricks in slanted gobelin stitch, using Bronze yarn. Work the mortar in tent stitch, using Sea Coral yarn.

11. Stitch the two side sleeve seams, working one seam at a time. First put in the cross stitches, using Olympic Blue yarn. Then work the continuation of the roof in gobelin stitch, using Olympic Blue yarn. Work the bricks in slanted gobelin stitch, using

Bronze yarn. Work the mortar in tent stitch, using Sea Coral yarn.

12. Work the top sleeve seams in gobelin stitch, using Olympic Blue yarn.

13. Work the bottom sleeve seams in slanted gobelin stitch, using Bronze, Olympic Blue, and Grey yarn, as diagrammed. Add the three rows of tent stitch, using Sea Coral yarn.

Assembly

Do all overcasting and joining using two strands of yarn. Be sure to duplicate the direction of the tent stitch and the slanted gobelin stitch on the right sides of the pieces when you overcast and join.

1. With right sides up, flush join the edges of the front cover to the edges of the spine. Then join the edges of the back cover to the spine. Align the three pieces so the roof edge on each one is at the top. Working from the bottom edge of the spine to the top, start the join using Olympic Blue yarn to the top of the fence posts. Continue the join with Sea Coral yarn, until you reach the lower edge of the roof. Complete the join using Olympic Blue yarn.

With right sides up and working one seam at a time, flush join the edges of the two side seam pieces to the front and back covers, duplicating the yarn color order and placement of the spine join at the front and back covers as described above. Align the four pieces so the roof edge on each one is at the top.

With right sides up and working one seam at a time, flush join the edges of the two bottom sleeve seam pieces to the bottom edges of the front and back covers. Align the pieces so the one overcast side edge on each seam is in the center of the covers. Working from the outside edge of the cover to the spine, join, using Olympic Blue yarn, to the steps. Then join the step area, using Grey yarn. Complete, using Olympic Blue yarn.

With right sides up and working one seam at a time, flush join the edges of the two top sleeve seam pieces to the top edges of the front and back covers, using Olympic Blue yarn. Align the pieces so the one overcast side edge on each seam is in the center of the covers.

With right side up and using Olympic Blue yarn, overcast the top and bottom edges of the front and back covers between the top and bottom sleeve seam joins and the spine.

2. Place the joined covers wrong side up. Turning the seam pieces upward and using Olympic Blue yarn, flush join the adjacent edges of the top and bottom sleeve seams and the side seams.

Working one cover sleeve at a time, wrong sides together, flush join the edges of the two front and back cover sleeve pieces to the edges of the top and bottom sleeve seam and the side sleeve seam pieces. Work the joins, duplicating the yarn color order and placement used to join the edges of the front and back covers to the edges of the seam pieces.

3. Place the stitched album cover sleeve side up. Remove the photo mounting sheets from the Magic Mount Album. Holding the binder by the rings, fold the cover downward. Insert the two sides of the binder cover into the front and back sleeves of the stitched album cover. Lay the binder and album flat and replace the photo mounting sheets.

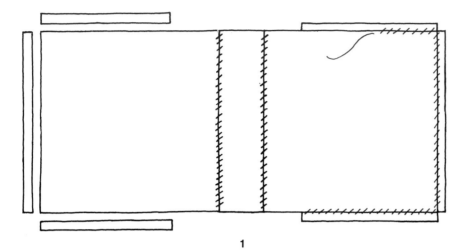

1

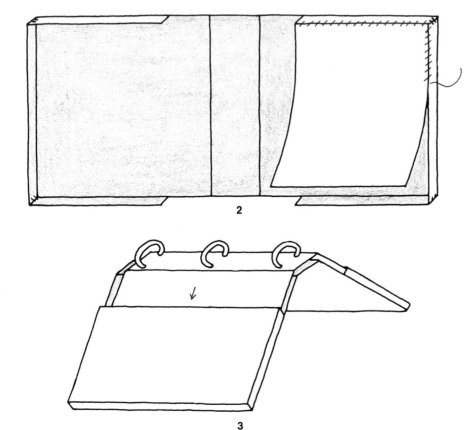

2

3

Scallop Shell Box

Intermediate

What could be nicer than a pretty scallop shell box in which you can keep treasured baubles? This is three-dimensional needlepoint at its most elegant. The stitching is done in ribbon to create a silken, woven effect. The box is not difficult to make—only three different stitches are used—although the construction is rather complicated.

Materials

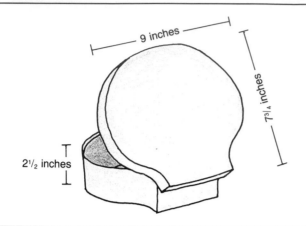

9 inches

7³/₄ inches

2¹/₂ inches

- Boye E-Z Count clear 10-mesh plastic canvas: two sheets 11″ × 14″ (110 holes × 140 holes)
- Gemini ¹/₄″ Ribbons Yarn:

#3 Ecru	12 yards
#6 Pastel Peach	82 yards
#10 Silver Grey	8 yards
#13 Copper	68 yards

- DMC Size 3 Pearl Cotton:

#434 Copper	2 yards

- nos. 18 and 20 tapestry needles
- 17″ × 22″ sheet of velour paper matching one color of the ribbon
- fabric glue
- 24″ ruler

Cutout Diagrams

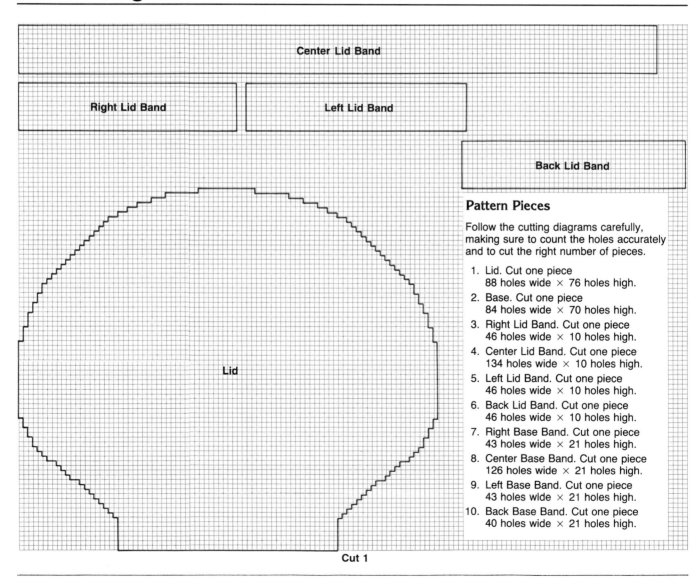

Center Lid Band

Right Lid Band

Left Lid Band

Back Lid Band

Lid

Cut 1

Pattern Pieces

Follow the cutting diagrams carefully, making sure to count the holes accurately and to cut the right number of pieces.

1. Lid. Cut one piece
   88 holes wide × 76 holes high.
2. Base. Cut one piece
   84 holes wide × 70 holes high.
3. Right Lid Band. Cut one piece
   46 holes wide × 10 holes high.
4. Center Lid Band. Cut one piece
   134 holes wide × 10 holes high.
5. Left Lid Band. Cut one piece
   46 holes wide × 10 holes high.
6. Back Lid Band. Cut one piece
   46 holes wide × 10 holes high.
7. Right Base Band. Cut one piece
   43 holes wide × 21 holes high.
8. Center Base Band. Cut one piece
   126 holes wide × 21 holes high.
9. Left Base Band. Cut one piece
   43 holes wlde × 21 holes high.
10. Back Base Band. Cut one piece
    40 holes wide × 21 holes high.

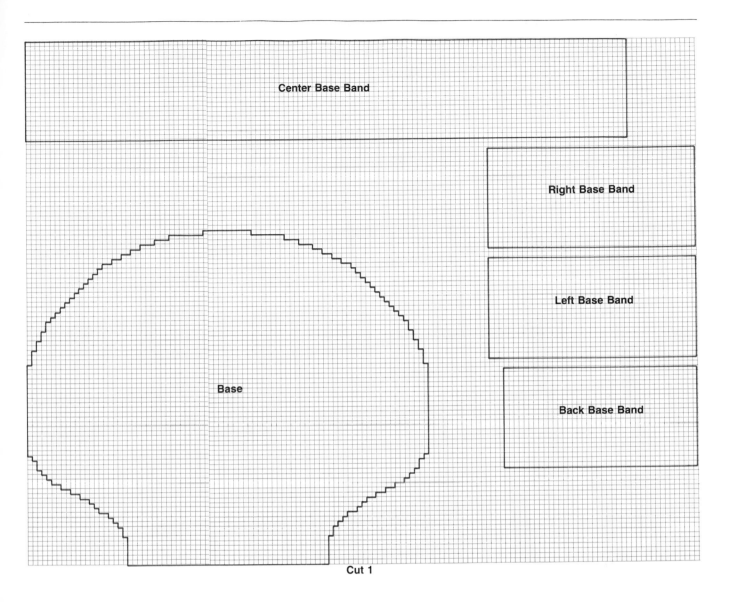

Center Base Band

Right Base Band

Left Base Band

Base

Back Base Band

Cut 1

Stitching Diagrams

Stitches Used

Gobelin stitch (see page 15)
Satin stitch (see page 16)
Whip stitch (see page 21)

The Stitching

Work gobelin and satin stitches with Ribbons yarn. Work ribbon using one strand and a no. 18 tapestry needle. Cut ribbon in 1-yard lengths to work, unless specified otherwise. Ribbon that is doubled through the needle eye is crushed when stitching; therefore, work with only a 3-inch tail through the needle eye. The two strands of ribbon through the needle eye will fit snugly in the canvas holes. Tug gently when pulling the needle through, to prevent splitting the canvas. The cut ends of the ribbon may unravel; if they do, trim the threads as necessary to prevent them from catching. Because the ribbon is slippery, leave a 1- to 1½-inch starting and ending tail on each strand to secure it. Stitch the pieces as diagramed in the following order:

1. Work the lid of the box in satin stitch. Begin with Copper ribbon, then work Silver Grey and then Ecru. Then fill in the background areas with Pastel Peach ribbon.

2. Work the center lid band and the center base band in gobelin stitch. Begin with Copper ribbon and then work the Pastel Peach areas. Add the Silver Grey lines, then complete by filling in the Ecru lines. (The unstitched ends of these pieces will be stitched when the box is assembled.)

3. Work the pieces for the left lid band, the left base band, the right lid band, and the right base band in gobelin stitch. Work first with Copper ribbon, then with Pastel Peach. (The unstitched ends of these pieces will be stitched when the box is assembled.)

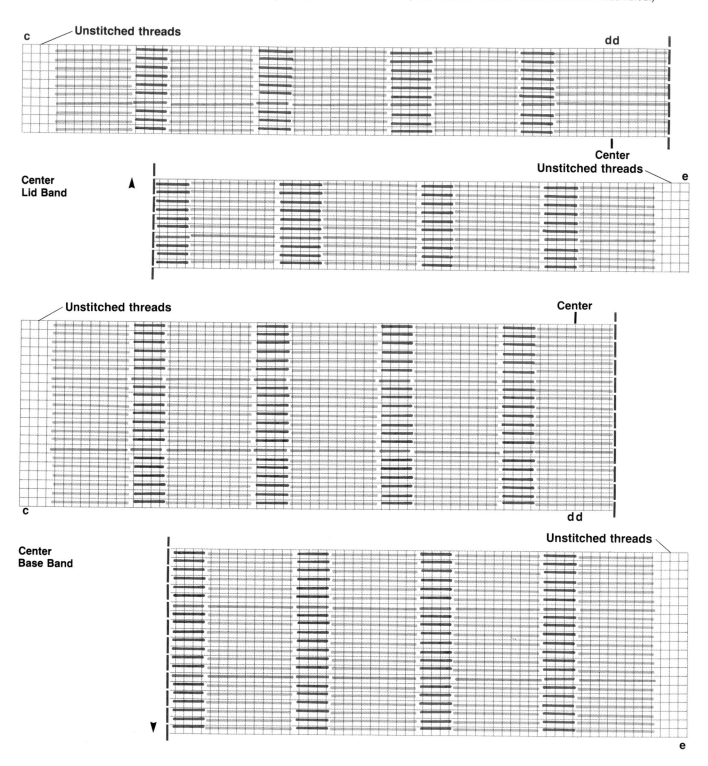

Color

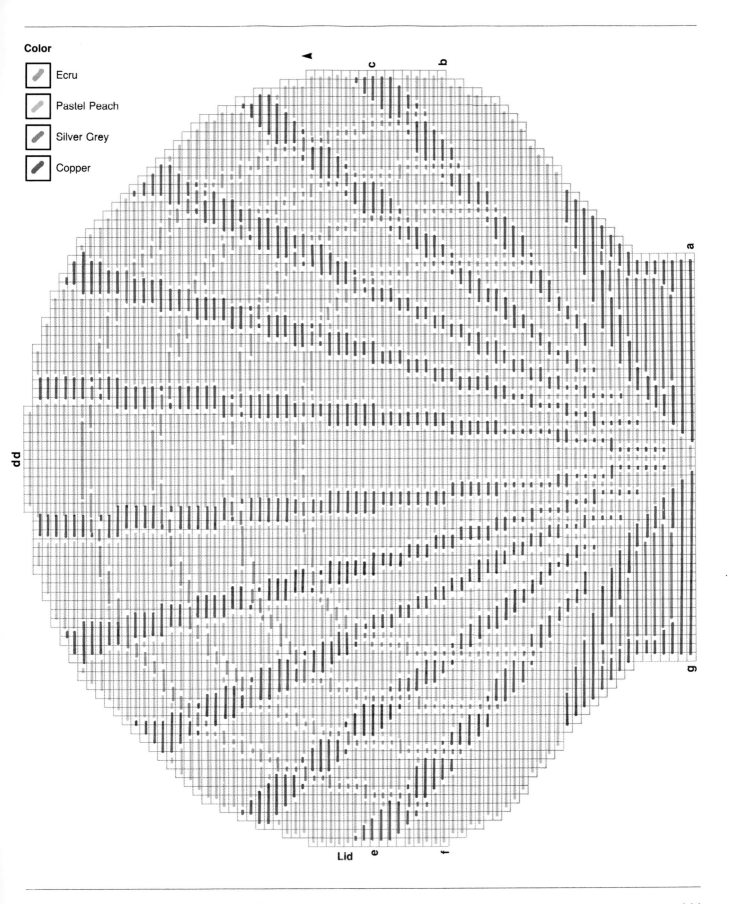 Ecru	
Pastel Peach	
Silver Grey	
Copper	

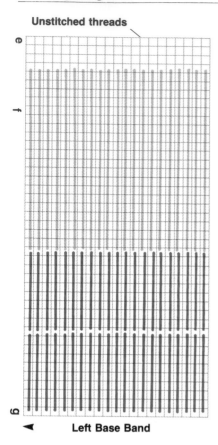

Unstitched threads

e

f

g

Left Base Band ◄

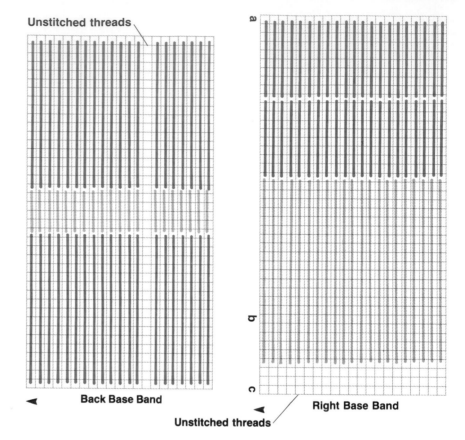

Unstitched threads

a

b

c

Back Base Band ◄

Right Base Band ◄

Unstitched threads

4. Work the base of the box in satin stitch. Begin with Copper ribbon, then work Silver Grey and then Ecru. Then fill in the background areas with Pastel Peach ribbon.

5. Work the back band of the lid and the back band of the base in gobelin stitch. Work first with Pastel Peach ribbon and then with Copper ribbon. (The unstitched plastic thread on the back base band will be used in the assembly.)

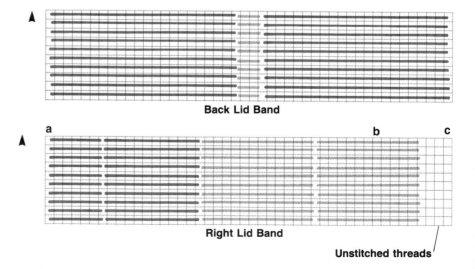

e   f   g

Left Lid Band

Unstitched threads

Back Lid Band

a   b   c

Right Lid Band

Unstitched threads

Color

⟋	Ecru
⟋	Pastel Peach
⟋	Silver Grey
⟋	Copper

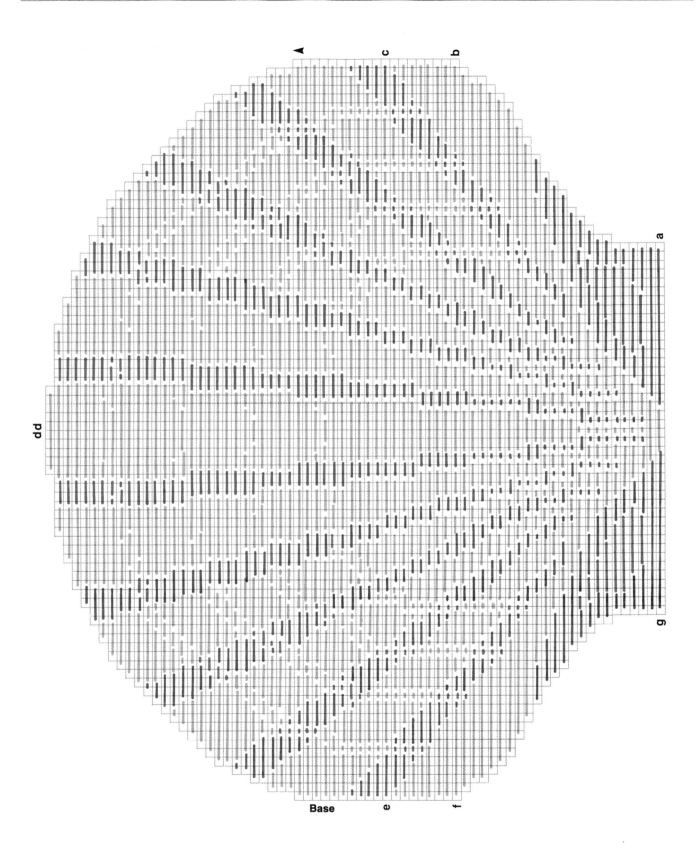

Assembly

Do all joining and overcasting using the no. 20 tapestry needle and Copper ribbon unless otherwise indicated. To avoid splitting the canvas while joining, stitch through the holes to be joined on adjacent pattern piece edges separately, going up through the hole on one edge and down through the hole on the second edge.

Lining Preparation

On the wrong side of the velour paper, trace the outline of the base of the box. Then add a second outline 1/4 inch outside the first. This is the cutting line.
On the wrong side of the paper, trace the outline of the lid. On the wrong side of the paper, measure and outline a 2 1/2-inch × 21-inch strip.
On the wrong side of the paper, measure and outline a 2 1/2-inch × 4-inch strip.

Preassembly

1. With right sides up, lay the right edge of the right lid band over the left edge of the center lid band, matching the outside holes and creating a five-hole column. Overlap join the matched holes, using pearl cotton and the blind backstitch method. Repeat with left lid bands.

   Using ribbon and working the gobelin stitch, fill in the joined columns, covering the blind backstitch, matching the Copper and Silver Grey on the center lid band.

2. Join the right and left base bands to the center base band in the same way the right and left lid bands were joined to the center lid band. Then stitch in the same way.

Base and Lid

3. Place the base wrong side up. Using 4-inch lengths of waste ribbon, temporarily but securely tack the top edge of the assembled base band to the edge of the base, at the matched points indicated on the stitch diagrams of these pieces.

   Turn the tacked pieces so the base is right side up. Flush join the tacked pieces by stitching up through the base and down through the band, removing each tacking ribbon piece as the joining reaches each match point. Starting at match point **a,** work around the base to point **b,** easing the band to fit the curve. Continue to **c.** Work around to **d** and continue to **e,** easing the band to fit the curve. Then work from **e** to **f.** Complete by starting at **g** and joining back to **f,** easing the band to fit the inward curve. Join the top edge of the assembled lid band to the lid, in the same way that the base band was attached to the base, matching the points indicated on the stitch diagram.

4. With right sides up, place the top edge of the back base band against the bottom edge of the base. The back base band is two holes narrower. Center the base band edge so one hole of the bottom edge of the base extends on either side. Flush join the matched edges.

   Join the top edge of the back lid band to the bottom edge of the lid, matching the edges exactly.

5. To complete the base assembly, flush join the adjacent edges of the back base band and the right and left base bands. Flush join the adjacent edges of the back lid band and the right and left lid bands, to complete the lid assembly.
   Finish the base by working whip stitch to overcast the bottom edges of all the base band pieces.

6. Placing the lid wrong side up, work whip stitch to overcast the bottom edges of the right, left, and center lid band pieces. Start and end the overcasting by joining the three holes on each side of the back

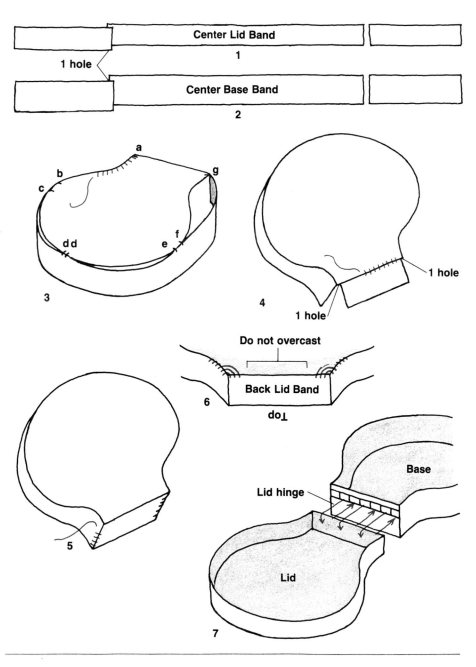

114

of the lid to the three holes of the adjacent right and left lid band pieces. This joining will slightly bow the back lid. Do not overcast the remaining holes in the center of the back lid band.

Lid Hinge

7. Form the lid hinge by placing the open lid and the open base back to back on a flat surface. Join the unovercast bottom edge of the back lid band to the unstitched row of the back base band, using the wrapping stitch diagramed. The wrap stitching should be even and reasonably loose, so that the lid opens

and closes easily. Do two or three stitches to test the tension. Adjust, tighter or looser, if necessary.

Lid Hinge Catches

The lid hinge catches are small pieces of ribbon tied between the back base band and the lid, to hold the lid upright when it is opened. To make the catches, work with two 18-inch lengths of Copper ribbon, one length for each catch.

8. Working one side at a time, insert the needle into the second hole in from the right side of the back base band, six holes down from the top, leaving an 8-

inch tail of ribbon inside the bottom. Now insert the needle into a hole in the wrong side of the lid, covered by Copper ribbon when previously stitched, directly level with the needle entry in the back. Insert the needle carefully, so the ribbon on the right side of the lid is not split.

From the right side of the lid, insert the needle one hole above the previous lid entry hole. Complete the catch stitching by going through the right side of the back base band, entering the needle one hole above the previous entry. Stitch the catch on the left side the same way.

Place the right side of the open lid against a vertical surface. Tie the starting and ending tails of each catch together, leaving approximately 1 inch of ribbon on each side between the back base band and the lid. Adjust the lengths as necessary so that the lid remains vertical when open. Then securely knot the yarn tails of each catch. Dab the knots with glue to strengthen. Trim the tails close to the knots when the glue is dry.

Lining

9. Cut out the four pattern pieces outlined on the velour paper.

   Place the paper base right side up inside the base of the box. Center the paper and gently score the surface along the edge, folding the edges of the paper upward.

   Remove the paper and clip the edges to the score line where necessary, so the center of the paper remains flat.

   Place the paper right side up in the box. Apply glue sparingly to the back of the paper that goes against the base bands.

10. Place the 21-inch paper band right side out inside the box, starting and stopping approximately $\frac{1}{2}$ inch on the right and left sides of the back base band pattern piece. Fold the band under at the top, wrong sides together, so that the folded edge is level with the top edge of the base bands. Glue to secure.

11. Place the 4-inch paper band right side out inside the box against the back band. Trim the right and left edges as necessary so the paper lies flat against the back of the box. Fold the paper band under at the top, wrong sides together, so that the folded edge is level with the top edge of the base band. Glue to secure.

   Wrong side up, place the paper lid piece inside the lid. Center the paper pattern piece and outline the edge of the lid. Remove the paper and trim along the outlined edge. Place the paper right side up inside the lid. Trim the right and left side bottom edges as necessary to accommodate the lid hinge catches. Glue to secure.

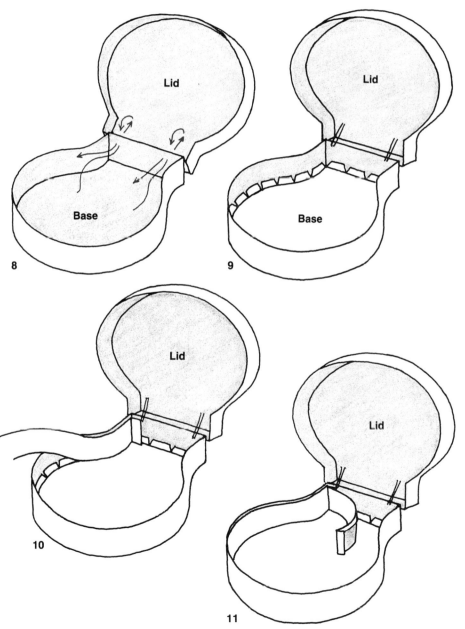

Grand Piano Container
Intermediate

This miniature grand piano can hold a note pad and pencil, serve as a receptacle for paper clips, rubber bands, or hairpins, or as an unusual candy dish full of tiny jelly beans. You can make the piano in a wood tone, as suggested here, but it will be equally effective in sophisticated black or in a bright color to match your decor. The stitching is simple—only four stitches are used. But the assembly is complicated and requires patience and dexterity.

Materials

- Boye E-Z Count clear 10-mesh plastic canvas:
  one sheet 11″ × 14″ (110 holes × 140 holes)
  one sheet 11″ × 14″ cut to 7″ × 14″ (70 holes × 140 holes)
  one sheet 11″ × 14″ cut to 7½″ × 11″ (76 holes × 110 holes)

- Bernat 1–2–3 Ply Persian Type Yarn.
  #N26–184 Brown   215 yards
  #N04–942 Black   3 yards
  #N10–428 White   2 yards
  #N04–944 Grey   4 yards

- nos. 18 and 20 tapestry needles

- 1 ounce pastina or birdseed

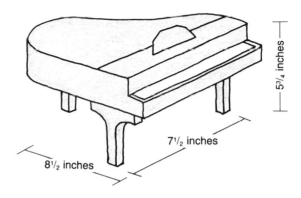

Cutout Diagrams

Pattern Pieces

Follow the cutting diagrams carefully, making sure to count the holes accurately and to cut the right number of pieces.

1. Piano Bottom. Cut one piece
   72 holes wide × 80 holes high.
2. Piano Lid. Cut one piece
   76 holes wide × 65 holes high.
3. Piano Lid Rim. Cut one piece
   70 holes wide × 59 holes high.
4. Piano False Bottom. Cut one piece
   70 holes wide × 78 holes high.
5. Keyboard. Cut one piece
   72 holes wide × 8 holes high.
6. Keyboard Front. Cut one piece
   72 holes wide × 6 holes high.
7. Keyboard Back. Cut one piece
   72 holes wide × 9 holes high.
8. Keyboard Top. Cut one piece
   76 holes wide × 9 holes high.
9. Keyboard Top Brace. Cut one piece
   70 holes wide × 6 holes high.
10. Piano Side 1. Cut one piece
    63 holes wide × 15 holes high.
11. Piano Side 2. Cut one piece
    35 holes wide × 15 holes high.
12. Piano Side 3. Cut one piece
    14 holes wide × 15 holes high.
13. Piano Side 4. Cut one piece
    25 holes wide × 15 holes high.
14. Piano Side 5. Cut one piece
    61 holes wide × 15 holes high.

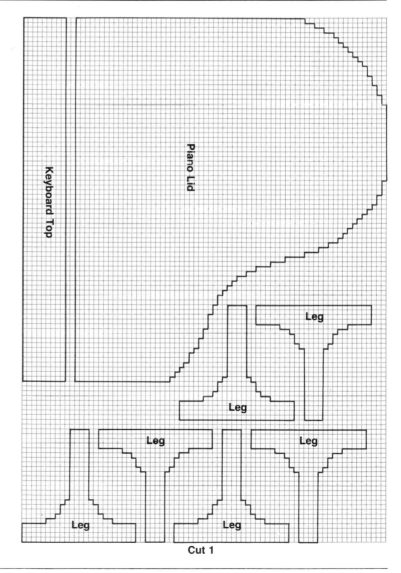

15. Music Stand. Cut one piece 20 holes wide × 10 holes high.
16. Lid Support 1. Cut one piece 3 holes wide × 50 holes high.
17. Lid Support 2. Cut one piece 3 holes wide × 52 holes high.
18. Catch 1. Cut two pieces 4 holes wide × 3 holes high.
19. Catch 2. Cut two pieces 5 holes wide × 3 holes high.

20. Leg. Cut six pieces 24 holes wide × 24 holes high.
21. Leg Front 1. Cut six pieces 4 holes wide × 28 holes high.
22. Leg Front 2. Cut six pieces 4 holes wide × 4 holes high.
23. Leg Bottom. Cut three pieces 4 holes wide × 4 holes high.

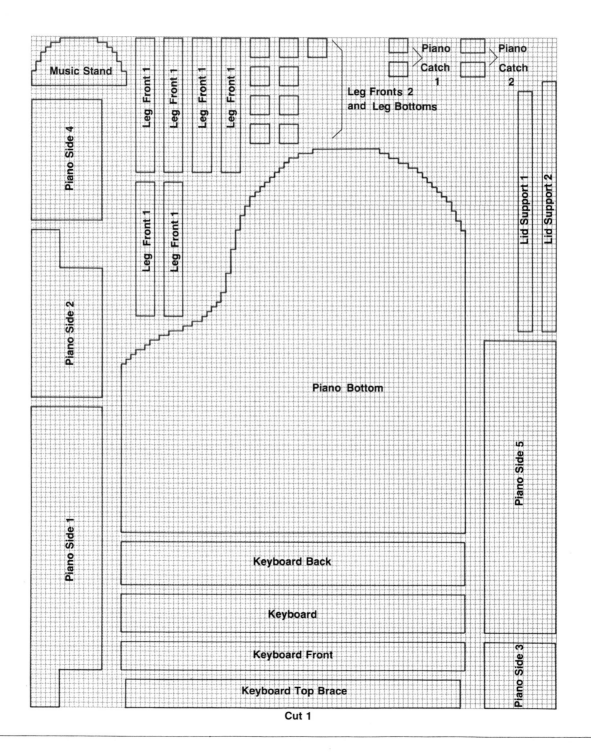

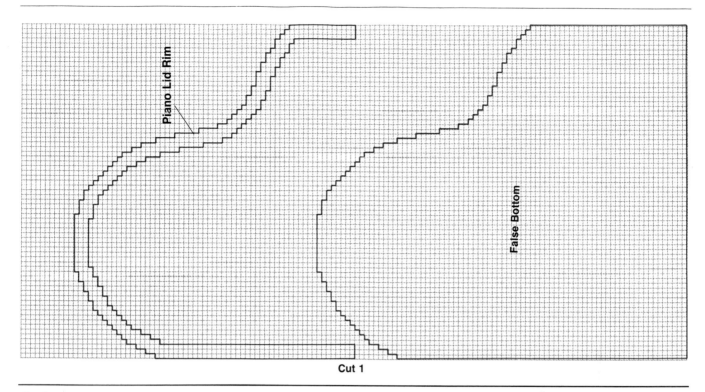

Cut 1

Stitching Diagrams

Stitches Used

Tent stitch (see page 12)
Gobelin stitch (see page 15)
Backstitch (see page 20)
Whip stitch (see page 21)

The Stitching

Work tent stitch using two strands of yarn. Work gobelin stitch and whip stitch using three strands of yarn. Work backstitch using one strand of yarn. Do all stitching and overcasting using the no. 18 tapestry needle. When stitching the lid and side pieces, work as neatly as possible, since both sides will be visible after the piano is assembled. Stitch the pieces as diagramed in the following order:

1. Using tent stitch and Brown yarn, work the keyboard front, keyboard back, piano side 1, lid support 2, catch 1, catch 2, leg, leg front 1, leg front 2, and leg bottom pieces.

2. Using tent stitch and Brown yarn, work the piano lid rim, piano false bottom, piano side 3, piano side 4, piano side 5, music stand, and lid support 1 pieces. Use the whip stitch to overcast each piece, as diagramed, using Brown yarn.

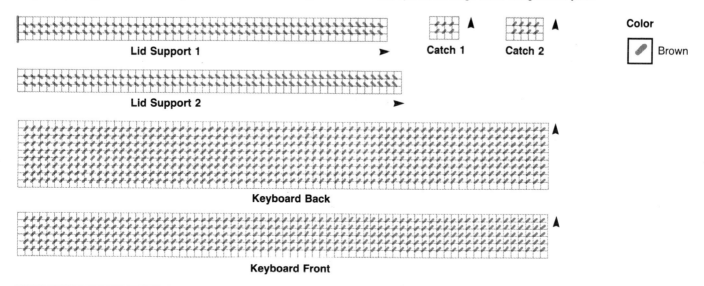

Lid Support 1 ▶

Lid Support 2 ▶

Catch 1 ▲   **Catch 2** ▲

Color

Brown

Keyboard Back ▲

Keyboard Front ▲

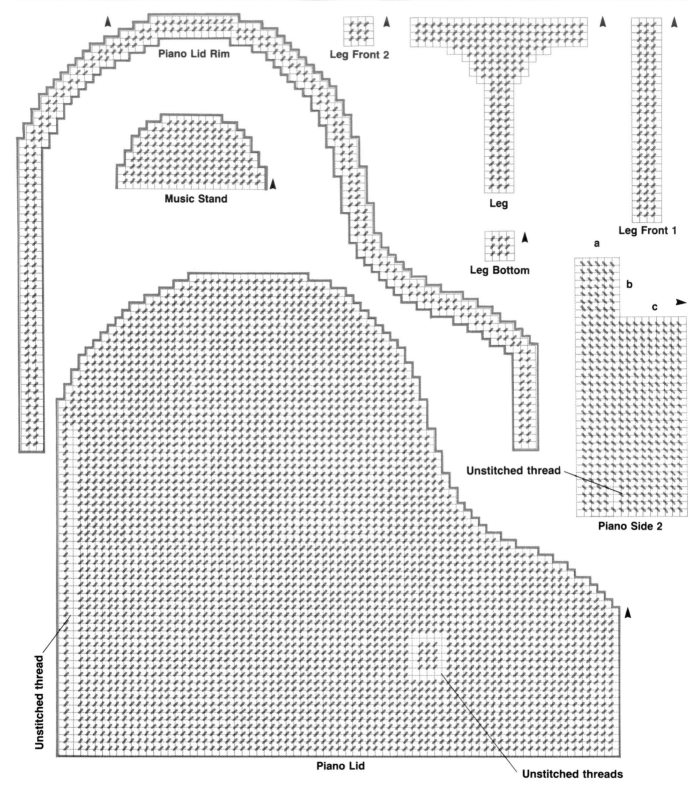

Piano Lid Rim

Leg Front 2

Leg

Leg Front 1

Music Stand

Leg Bottom

a

b

c

Unstitched thread

Piano Side 2

Unstitched thread

Piano Lid

Unstitched threads

3. Work the piano lid, keyboard top, and keyboard top brace in tent stitch, using Brown yarn. Then work the whip stitch to overcast, as diagramed, using Brown yarn. (The unstitched plastic threads on these pieces are assembly points.)

4. Work the piano bottom and piano side 2 pieces in tent stitch with Brown yarn. (The unstitched plastic threads on these pieces are assembly points.)

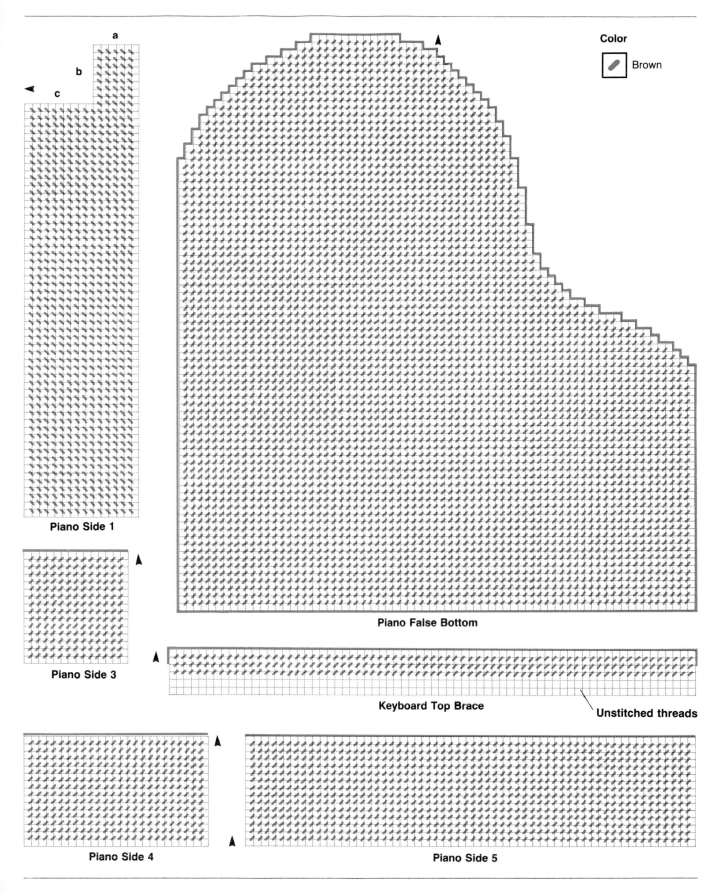

a

b

c

Piano Side 1

Piano Side 3

Piano Side 4

Piano False Bottom

Keyboard Top Brace

Unstitched threads

Piano Side 5

Color

Brown

5. Work the keyboard, doing the tent stitch first in Brown yarn. Then, using White yarn, work the gobelin stitch as diagramed. Work the gobelin stitch next with Black yarn. Finally, work the backstitch in Grey yarn.

Color

Brown

Black

White

Grey

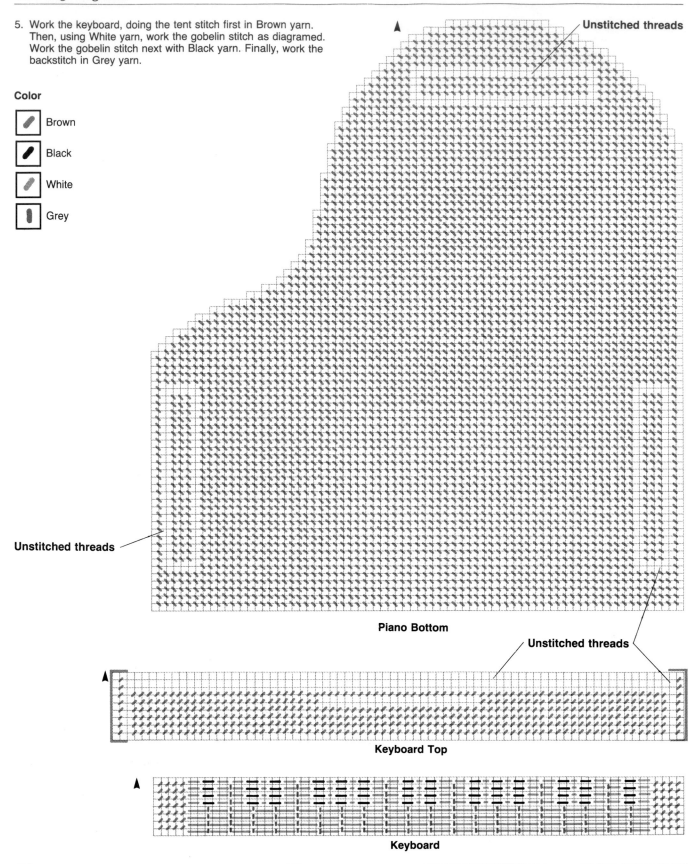

Unstitched threads

Unstitched threads

Piano Bottom

Unstitched threads

Keyboard Top

Keyboard

Assembly

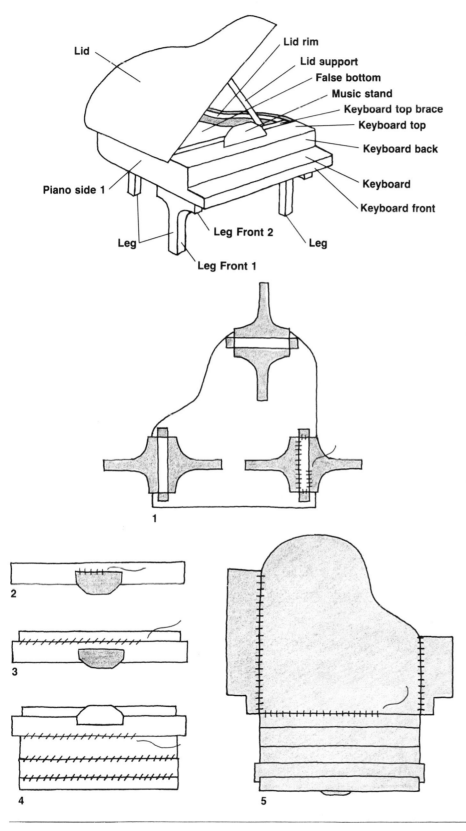

Lid
Lid rim
Lid support
False bottom
Music stand
Keyboard top brace
Keyboard top
Keyboard back
Piano side 1
Keyboard
Keyboard front
Leg Front 2
Leg
Leg
Leg Front 1

1

2

3

4

5

Use three strands of yarn for all joining. Use one strand of yarn for tacking. Use three strands of yarn to overcast. Join, tack, and overcast using Brown yarn and a no. 20 tapestry needle. When joining, be sure to duplicate the direction of the tent stitch on the right side of each piece.

Preassembly

1. The three rectangular areas of unstitched threads on the bottom of the piano are for the leg assembly. First, partially assemble the legs by flush joining the top edges of two leg pieces and two leg front 2 pieces to each rectangle. To join, place the right sides of the pieces together and stitch. Work one leg at a time, joining the four pieces for each leg in consecutive order.

2. With right sides together, match the bottom edge of the music stand to the unstitched thread in the center of the top of the keyboard. Flush join these two pieces.

3. With the pieces right side up, place the bottom edge of the keyboard top brace under the top edge of the keyboard, matching the three unstitched horizontal rows of threads on each piece. The keyboard top brace is six holes narrower in width than the keyboard top. Center the keyboard top brace so that three holes of the keyboard top extend beyond it on each side. Join the three overlapped rows of threads on these pieces, using tent stitch.

4. With right sides up, flush join the top edge of the front of the keyboard to the bottom edge of the keyboard.

   With right sides up, flush join the top edge of the keyboard to the bottom edge of the back of the keyboard.

   With right sides up, flush join the top edge of the keyboard back to the bottom edge of the keyboard top. The keyboard back is four holes narrower than the keyboard top. Center the keyboard back so two holes of the keyboard top extend beyond it on either side.

Keyboard

5. With wrong sides together, flush join the bottom edge of the piano side 1 piece to the left edge of the piano bottom piece.

   With wrong sides together, flush join the bottom edge of the piano side 2 piece to the right edge of the piano bottom.

   With wrong sides together, flush join the bottom edge of the keyboard front to the bottom edge of the piano bottom.

6. Refer to the stitch diagrams of piano sides 1 and 2. Bend the joined keyboard pieces to form a stair step, matching the stepped edge of the piano side 1 and 2 pieces. Flush join the right edge of the keyboard front piece to edge **a** of piano side 2. Continue, joining the right edge of the keyboard piece to edge **b** of piano side 2. Complete by joining the right edge of the keyboard back piece to edge **c** of piano side 2. Repeat this assembly, joining the left side of the three keyboard pattern pieces to the stepped edge of piano side 1.

   Match the unstitched interior vertical threads on the right and left of the keyboard top to the top edges of piano sides 1 and 2. Flush join the pieces along these threads.

   Work whip stitch to overcast the top edge of piano side 2. Starting at the edge of the keyboard top piece and stopping three holes beyond the edge of the keyboard top brace piece, overcast the top edge of piano side 1. The remaining unovercast top edge of piano side 1 is the assembly point for the lid.

   To secure the keyboard top brace to piano sides 1 and 2, tack the right and left edges of the brace to the adjacent top edges of the piano sides, using the figure-eight stitch.

Bed

7. With wrong sides together, flush join the unovercast bottom edge of piano side 3 to the top edge of the piano bottom.

   Place piano side 4, with the unovercast bottom edge down and the wrong side facing the wrong side of the piano bottom, between piano sides 3 and 1. Flush join the two edges of piano side 4 to the adjacent edges of piano side 3 and piano side 1.

   Flush join the bottom edge of piano side 4 to the adjacent edge of the piano bottom, easing the side into position to conform to the piano bottom's outward curve.

   Place the piano side 5 piece, with the unovercast bottom edge down and the wrong side facing the wrong side of the piano bottom, between piano sides 2 and 3. Flush join the two edges of piano side 5 to the adjacent edges of piano side 2 and piano side 3.

   Flush join the bottom edge of piano side 5 to the adjacent edge of the piano bottom, easing the piano side into position to conform to the piano bottom's inward curve.

   Right side up, insert the piano false bottom piece into the assembled piano bed.

Lid Rim

8. The lid rim piece is required to hold the piano side pieces upright and stable. To assemble, place the lid rim piece right side up in the piano bed. Place the last horizontal column of three holes on the right and left sides of the lid rim, under the first three holes on the right and left of the top edge of the keyboard brace.

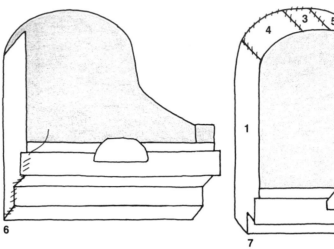

6

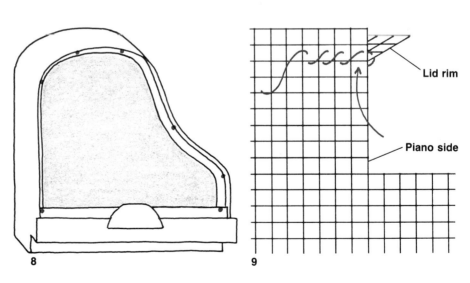

8

Tack these two pattern pieces together along these matched holes, duplicating the tent stitch direction on the right side of the keyboard top brace pattern piece.

Using a temporary tack, attach the lid rim to the piano sides at their four edge joins and at the innermost curve of the lid rim and piano side 5. Tack, matching the outside edge of the lid rim to the

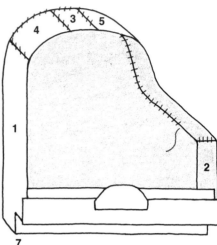

7

Lid rim

Piano side

9

10

horizontal thread covered by the second row of tent stitching from the top edge of each of the piano sides.

9. Tack the lid rim to the horizontal thread covered by the second row of tent stitching from the top edge of each of the piano sides, duplicating the direction of the tent stitching on the right side of the piano sides. Starting at piano side 1, tack by entering the piano side from the right side, under the thread with the second row of tent stitching. Go up through the outside edge of the lid rim, entering through the wrong side of the pattern piece and exiting from the right side. Go over the outside edge of the lid rim and back through the wrong side of the piano side over the second row of tent stitching, entering the hole directly above the previous entry. Continue this way, completing the tacking of piano side 1. Work around the lid, joining piano sides 4, 3, 5, and 2 to complete.

Lid

10. With wrong sides together, place lid support 1 over lid support 2, matching the top edges. Starting at the bottom right edge, working upward to the top, across the top, and then down to the bottom left edge, overcast join the two pieces. At the bottom, the unovercast bottom edge of lid support 2 should extend two holes beyond the edge of lid support 1.

11. Place the joined lid support inside the piano bed, with the lid support 2 side down and the unovercast edge facing piano side 2. Flush join the bottom edge of lid support 2 to the unstitched horizontal thread in piano side 2.

12. To form the lid support catch, match the bottom edges of the two catch 1 pieces and the two catch 2 pieces to the rectangle of unstitched threads on the piano lid. Place the pieces so that the right sides of the catches are facing the wrong side of the piano lid. Flush join.

    Flush join the adjacent edges of the four catch pieces, forming a box. To complete, overcast the top edges of the catch pieces.

13. With right side up, match the unstitched vertical thread on the piano lid to the top edge of piano side 1. Flush join the piano lid to the piano side along this line. The bottom edge of the piano lid goes over the keyboard top brace, but does not meet the edge of the keyboard top.

Legs

Directions are for one leg. Assemble three, working one at a time.

14. Flush join the adjacent edges of the leg front 2 and the leg pieces.

    With right sides out, flush join the top edges of two leg front 1 pieces to the bottom edges of two leg front 2 pieces.

    Flush join the adjacent sides of one leg front 1 piece and one leg piece. Start the join at the top of the leg stem (the bottom edge of the pieces) and work downward, easing the leg side piece into position. Repeat this join along the remaining three adjacent sides of the leg front 1 and leg pieces. To strengthen, tightly stuff the assembled leg stem with pastina or birdseed.

15. To complete the leg assembly, place the leg bottom piece right side up over the leg stem, matching the edges of both pieces. Flush join the edges in consecutive order.

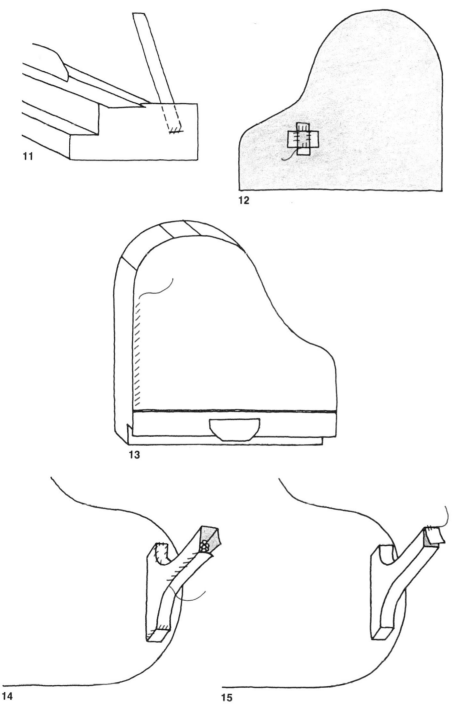

The Dinosaur Trio
Intermediate

These three tame dinosaurs—Tyrannosaurus, Stegosaurus, and Dimetrodon—will delight any child. Make one or all three. Although the stitch diagrams must be followed carefully, the stitching is easy—no more than seven different stitches are used for each dinosaur. The assembly is rather complicated because of all the small pieces involved in the construction. Nevertheless, these unusual and sturdy pets are worth the effort.

Materials/Tyrannosaurus

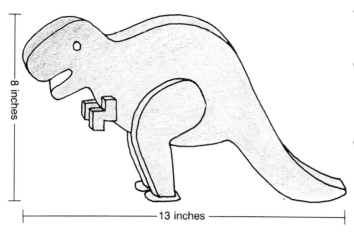

8 inches

13 inches

- W. T. Rogers Quick-Count clear 7-mesh plastic canvas: two sheets 10½″ × 13½″ (70 holes × 90 holes) one sheet 10½″ × 13½″ cut to 1½″ × 13½″ (10 holes × 90 holes)
- Brunswick Windrush Yarn:

#9044 Dark Green	3 yards
#9095 Dark Lime	210 yards
#9093 Lime	80 yards
#9008 Saffron	2 yards
#9025 Scarlet	2 yards

- no. 16 tapestry needle

Cutout Diagrams/Tyrannosaurus

Pattern Pieces

Follow the cutting diagrams carefully, making sure to count the holes accurately and to cut the right number of pieces.

1. Side 1. Cut one piece 86 holes wide × 49 holes high.
2. Side 2. Cut one piece 86 holes wide × 49 holes high.
3. Front Leg 1. Cut one piece 7 holes wide × 8 holes high.
4. Front Leg 2. Cut one piece 7 holes wide × 8 holes high.
5. Front Leg Band 1. Cut eight pieces 5 holes wide × 2 holes high.
6. Front Leg Band 2. Cut four pieces 2 holes wide × 3 holes high.
7. Front Leg Band 3. Cut four pieces 2 holes wide × 2 holes high.
8. Back Leg 1. Cut one piece 22 holes wide × 37 holes high.
9. Back Leg 2. Cut one piece 22 holes wide × 37 holes high.
10. Back Leg Band 1. Cut two pieces 4 holes wide × 79 holes high.
11. Back Leg Band 2. Cut two pieces 4 holes wide × 18 holes high.
12. Feet. Cut two pieces 10 holes wide × 11 holes high.
13. Head Band. Cut one piece 10 holes wide × 42 holes high.
14. Spine Band. Cut one piece 10 holes wide × 90 holes high.
15. Jaw Band. Cut one piece 10 holes wide × 20 holes high.
16. Underbelly Band. Cut one piece 10 holes wide × 47 holes high.
17. Lower Tail Band. Cut one piece 10 holes wide × 42 holes high.

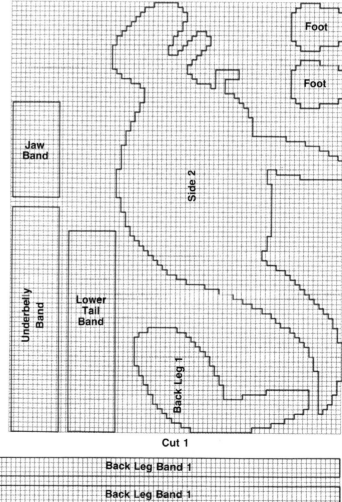

Foot

Foot

Jaw Band

Side 2

Underbelly Band

Lower Tail Band

Back Leg 1

Cut 1

Back Leg Band 1

Back Leg Band 1

Cut 1

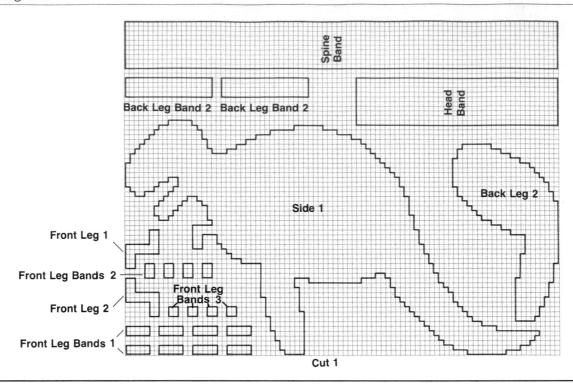

Spine Band

Back Leg Band 2   Back Leg Band 2

Head Band

Back Leg 2

Side 1

Front Leg 1

Front Leg Bands 2

Front Leg Bands 3

Front Leg 2

Front Leg Bands 1

Cut 1

Stitching Diagrams/Tyrannosaurus

Stitches Used

Gobelin stitch (see page 15)
Satin stitch (see page 16)
Parisian stitch (see page 17)
Rhodes stitch (see page 18)
Whip stitch (see page 21)

The Stitching

Work Rhodes stitch using one strand of yarn. Work Parisian stitch, gobelin stitch, satin stitch, and whip stitch using two strands of yarn. Stitch the pieces as diagramed in the following order:

1. Work the two sides of the tyrannosaurus in Parisian stitch, working one side at a time. Work the long stitches first, using Dark Lime yarn, then work the short lines, using Lime yarn. Add the eye in Rhodes stitch, using Saffron yarn. Then, stitching on the wrong side, work the lower back legs in Parisian stitch, using Dark Lime and Lime yarn. Alternating Dark Lime and Lime yarn, work the gobelin stitches of the lower front legs. (The unstitched plastic threads will be used in assembly.)

2. Work the two front leg pieces in gobelin stitch, alternating Dark Lime yarn and Lime yarn. Work with Dark Lime yarn first, then with Lime.

3. Work the sixteen front leg band pieces in gobelin stitch, alternating Dark Lime and Lime yarn. Work the Dark Lime stitches first, then the Lime.

4. Work the two back leg pieces in Parisian stitch. Work the long stitches first with Dark Lime yarn, then work the short stitches with Lime yarn.

5. Work the four back leg band pieces in Parisian stitch. Work the short stitches first with Lime yarn. Then add the long stitches, using Dark Lime yarn.

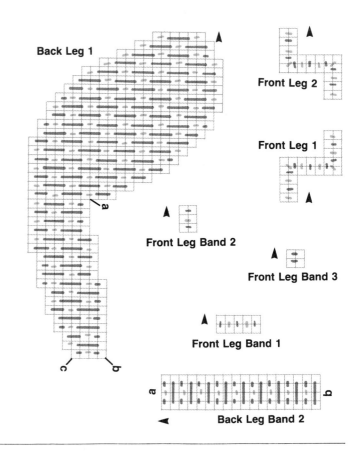

Back Leg 1

Front Leg 2

Front Leg 1

Front Leg Band 2

Front Leg Band 3

Front Leg Band 1

Back Leg Band 2

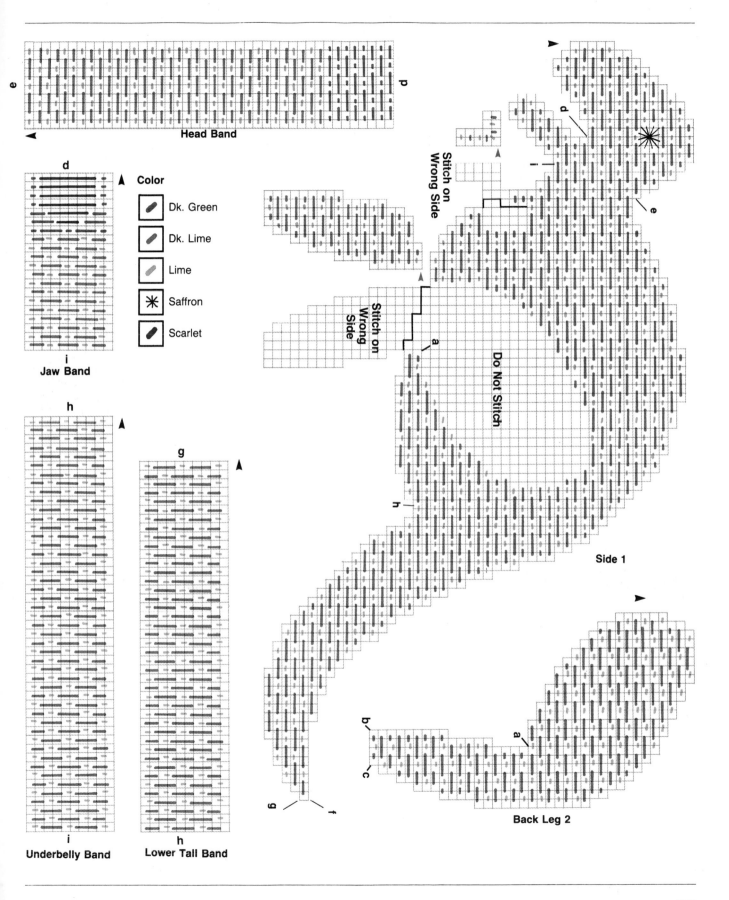

Head Band

d

Color

	Dk. Green
	Dk. Lime
	Lime
✳	Saffron
	Scarlet

i
Jaw Band

h

g

i
Underbelly Band

h
Lower Tail Band

Stitch on Wrong Side

Stitch on Wrong Side

Do Not Stitch

Side 1

Back Leg 2

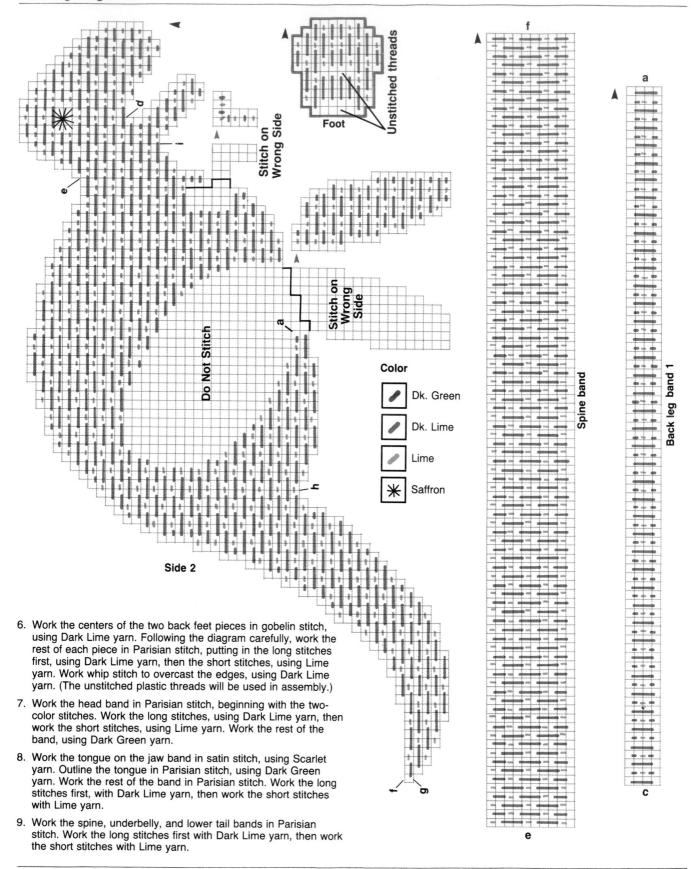

Stitch on Wrong Side

Foot

Unstitched threads

Stitch on Wrong Side

Do Not Stitch

Side 2

Spine band

f

e

Back leg band 1

a

c

Color

Dk. Green

Dk. Lime

Lime

Saffron

6. Work the centers of the two back feet pieces in gobelin stitch, using Dark Lime yarn. Following the diagram carefully, work the rest of each piece in Parisian stitch, putting in the long stitches first, using Dark Lime yarn, then the short stitches, using Lime yarn. Work whip stitch to overcast the edges, using Dark Lime yarn. (The unstitched plastic threads will be used in assembly.)

7. Work the head band in Parisian stitch, beginning with the two-color stitches. Work the long stitches, using Dark Lime yarn, then work the short stitches, using Lime yarn. Work the rest of the band, using Dark Green yarn.

8. Work the tongue on the jaw band in satin stitch, using Scarlet yarn. Outline the tongue in Parisian stitch, using Dark Green yarn. Work the rest of the band in Parisian stitch. Work the long stitches first, with Dark Lime yarn, then work the short stitches with Lime yarn.

9. Work the spine, underbelly, and lower tail bands in Parisian stitch. Work the long stitches first with Dark Lime yarn, then work the short stitches with Lime yarn.

Assembly/Tyrannosaurus

Do all joining using two strands of Dark Lime yarn unless otherwise indicated.

Front Leg Preassembly

Place side 1 right side up and refer to the stitch diagram. The angled shape of the front leg has four edges that are five holes long. With wrong sides up, match one five-hole edge of each of the four front leg band 1 pieces to each of the five-hole edges of the front leg. Flush join each of these four matched edges.

The angled shape of the front leg has two edges that are three holes long. With wrong sides up, match one three-hole edge of each of two front leg band 2 pieces to each of the three-hole edges of the front leg. Flush join each of these two matched edges.

The angled shape of the front leg has two edges that are two holes long. With wrong sides up, match one two-hole edge of each of two front leg band 3 pieces to each of the two-hole edges of the front leg. Flush join each of these two matched edges.

Turn the eight joined band pieces upward so their wrong sides face each other and the center of the leg. Flush join the adjacent edges of each two band pieces, forming an open angled box.

Join the eight remaining front leg band pieces to the right side of side 2 the same way the first set of eight pieces was joined to side 1.

Back Leg Preassembly

The two back leg bands are joined on their long sides to the outline edge of the back leg on the right side of side 1 and to each other on one of their short sides, forming

an open box the shape of the back leg. Refer to the stitch diagrams of these pieces for the join placement points of the bands along the edges of the back leg.

Place the side 1 piece right side up. Place one long side of one back leg band 2 piece wrong side up against the lower back edge of the back leg, matching the **b** end of the band to the **b** end of the leg and the **a** end of the band to the **a** point of the leg. Flush join these two matched edges.

With wrong sides up, flush join the **a** end of one back leg band 1 piece to the **a** end of the previously joined back leg band 2 piece.

Curving the joined bands upward so the wrong sides face each other and the center of the leg, match the **c** end of back leg band 1 to the **c** end of the leg. Starting at this point, flush join the long side of back leg band 1 adjacent to side 1 to the remaining outline edge of the leg on the right side of side 1.

Join the remaining two back leg band pieces to the right side of side 2 and each other the same way the two back leg bands were joined to side 1.

Body

The five body bands, pieces 14 through 17, are joined on their long sides to the edges of side 1 and to each other on their short sides, forming an open box. Refer to the stitch diagrams of side 1 and of the bands for the join placement points.

Place the side 1 piece right side up. Place the **d** end of the head band right side up against the **d** join placement point on side 1. Starting at **d,** flush join the long edge of the head band to the adjacent edge of side 1, easing the band up and around the curve of the dinosaur's head, ending at join point **e**.

With right side up, flush join the **e** end of the spine band to the **e** end of the head band.

Starting at join point **e**, flush join the long edge of the spine band to the adjacent edge of side 1, easing the band around the upward curve of the dinosaur's back and the downward curve of the upper tail, ending at join point **f**.

Turn the side 1 piece wrong side up. Right sides together and using Dark Green yarn, flush join the **d** ends of the head and jaw bands.

Turn the side 1 piece right side up. Starting at join point **d** flush join the long edge of the jaw band to the adjacent edge of side 1, easing the band down and around the curve of the dinosaur's jaw, ending at join point **i**.

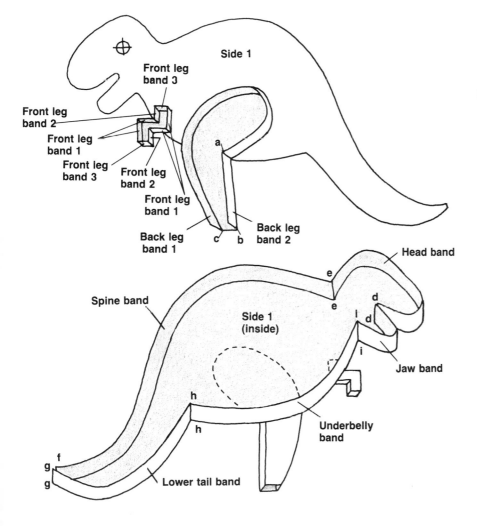

With right side up, flush join the **i** end of the jaw band to the **i** end of the underbelly band.

Starting at join point **i**, flush join the long edge of the underbelly band to the adjacent edge of side 1, easing the band around the outward curve of the dinosaur's belly, ending at join point **h**. When joining the band to the front and back legs, the outline edge of side 1 is the edge to the right of the reversed gobelin stitches on the front leg and the

edge above the reversed Parisian stitches on the back leg as indicated on the stitch diagrams.

With right side up, flush join the **h** end of the lower tail band to the **h** end of the underbelly band.

Starting at join point **h**, flush join the long edge of the lower tail band to the adjacent edge of side 1, easing the band around the outward curve of the dinosaur's lower tail, ending at join point **g**.

Turn the dinosaur's body wrong side up. Join the edges of the side 2 piece right side up to the second side of long edges on the bands. Start and stop the band joins on side 2 at the same join placement points as side 1, following the same order of joining as side 1.

To complete the dinosaur body, flush join the **f** end of the spine band to the **g** end of the lower tail band.

Leg Finishing

Place the dinosaur side 1 side up. Place front leg 1 right side up over the top edges of the assembled front leg bands. Flush join the top edges of the bands to the edges of front leg 1.

Place back leg 1 right side up over the top edges of the assembled back leg bands. Flush join the top edges of the bands to the edges of back leg 1. Start and stop the band joins at the same join placement points as the back leg preassembly, following the same order of joining.

Place one of the feet right side up below the back leg. Match the unstitched plastic thread at the back of the foot to the bottom edge of back leg band 2. Match the unstitched plastic thread at the center of the foot to the bottom edge of back leg band 1. These two unstitched plastic threads and the two perpendicular threads that join them form a square. Flush join this square to the square-shape bottom edge of the back leg.

Join the front leg 2 and back leg 2 pieces to side 2 of the dinosaur the same way the front leg 1 and back leg 1 pieces were joined to side 1.

Join the second foot to the bottom edge of back leg 2 the same way the first foot was joined to the bottom edge of back leg 1.

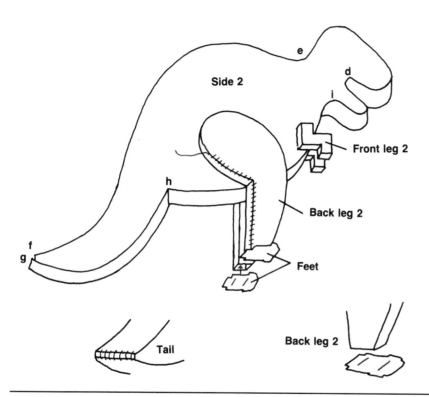

Materials/Stegosaurus

- W. T. Rogers Quick-Count clear 7-mesh plastic canvas: two sheets 10½″ × 13½″ (70 holes × 90 holes)
- Brunswick Windrush Yarn:

#9095	Dark Lime	225 yards
#9093	Lime	86 yards
#90921	Misty Lime	11 yards
#9008	Saffron	2 yards

- no. 16 tapestry needle

8¾ inches

14 inches

Cutout Diagrams/Stegosaurus

Pattern Pieces

Follow the cutting diagrams carefully, making sure to count the holes accurately and to cut the right number of pieces.

1. Side 1. Cut one piece 88 holes wide × 35 holes high.
2. Side 2. Cut one piece 88 holes wide × 35 holes high.
3. Front Leg 1. Cut two pieces 6 holes wide × 11 holes high.
4. Front Leg 2. Cut two pieces 6 holes wide × 11 holes high.
5. Front Leg Band 1. Cut two pieces 2 holes wide × 11 holes high.
6. Front Leg Band 2. Cut two pieces 2 holes wide × 9 holes high.
7. Front Leg Band 3. Cut two pieces 6 holes wide × 2 holes high.
8. Front Leg Band 4. Cut two pieces 4 holes wide × 2 holes high.
9. Back Leg 1. Cut one piece 14 holes wide × 29 holes high.
10. Back Leg 2. Cut one piece 14 holes wide × 29 holes high.
11. Back Leg Band 1. Cut two pieces 4 holes wide × 58 holes high.
12. Back Leg Band 2. Cut two pieces 4 holes wide × 10 holes high.
13. Front Feet. Cut two pieces 6 holes wide × 5 holes high.
14. Back Feet. Cut two pieces 8 holes wide × 9 holes high.
15. Spine Band. Cut one piece 10 holes wide × 63 holes high.
16. Upper Tail Band. Cut one piece 10 holes wide × 53 holes high.
17. Underbelly Band. Cut one piece 10 holes wide × 62 holes high.
18. Lower Tail Band. Cut one piece 10 holes wide × 36 holes high.
19. Scale 1. Cut two pieces 5 holes wide × 5 holes high.
20. Scale 2. Cut four pieces 7 holes wide × 7 holes high.
21. Scale 3. Cut four pieces 9 holes wide × 9 holes high.
22. Scale 4. Cut four pieces 11 holes wide × 11 holes high.
23. Scale 5. Cut four pieces 15 holes wide × 15 holes high.
24. Scale 6. Cut two pieces 17 holes wide × 17 holes high.

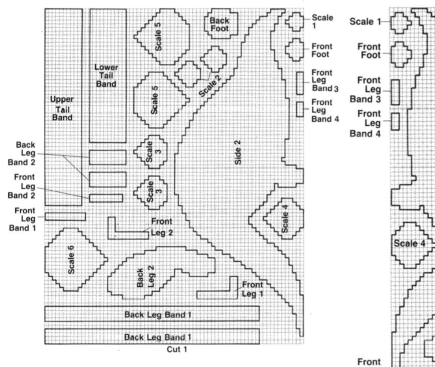

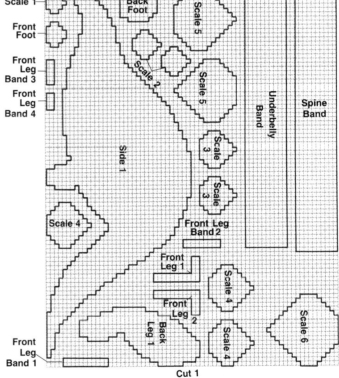

Stitching Diagrams/Stegosaurus

Stitches Used

Gobelin stitch (see page 15)
Parisian stitch (see page 17)
Double cross stitch (see page 18)
Backstitch (see page 20)
Whip stitch (see page 21)

(see page 15) (see page 17) (see page 18) (see page 20) (see page 21)

Color

✏ Dk. Lime	✏ Misty Lime
✏ Lime	✏ Saffron

The Stitching

Work double cross stitch and backstitch using one strand of yarn.
Work Parisian stitch, gobelin stitch, and whip stitch using two
strands of yarn. Stitch the pieces as diagramed in the following
order:

1. Work the two sides of the stegosaurus in Parisian stitch,
   working one side at a time. Following the diagram carefully, put
   in the long stitches first, using Dark Lime yarn, then work the
   short stitches, using Lime yarn. Add the eye in double cross
   stitch, using Saffron yarn. Then, stitching on the wrong side,
   work the lower back leg in Parisian stitch, using the Lime and
   Dark Lime yarn. (The unstitched plastic threads will be used in
   the assembly.)

2. Work the two front leg pieces in gobelin stitch, alternating Dark
   Lime yarn and Lime yarn as indicated. Work with Dark Lime
   yarn first, then with Lime.

3. Work the eight front leg band pieces in gobelin stitch,
   alternating Dark Lime yarn and Lime yarn. Work with Dark Lime
   yarn first, then with Lime.

4. Work the two back leg pieces in Parisian stitch. Following the
   diagram carefully, put in the longer stitches first, using Dark
   Lime yarn; then work the short stitches, using Lime yarn.

5. Work the four back leg band pieces in Parisian stitch. Following
   the diagram carefully, work the short stitches first, using Lime
   yarn. Then add the long stitches, using Dark Lime yarn.

6. Work the two front feet pieces in Parisian stitch, using Lime
   yarn. Work whip stitch to overcast the edges, using Dark Lime
   yarn. (The unstitched plastic threads will be used in the
   assembly.)

7. Work the centers of the two back feet in gobelin stitch, using
   Dark Lime yarn. Following the diagram carefully, work the rest
   of the pieces in Parisian stitch, putting in the long stitches first
   with Dark Lime yarn, then the short stitches with Lime yarn.
   Work whip stitch to overcast the edges, using Dark Lime yarn.
   (The unstitched plastic threads will be used in assembly.)

8. Work the twenty scale pieces in backstitch. Following the
   diagram carefully, work the alternating diagonal lines, using
   Lime yarn. Alternating Dark Lime yarn and Misty Lime yarn,
   work the lines between the Lime yarn lines. Stitch the centers,
   using Dark Lime yarn. Overcast the edge of each piece with
   Dark Lime yarn as diagramed.

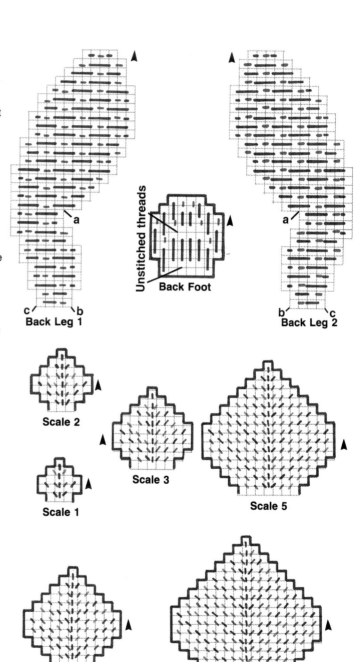

Back Leg 1

Back Leg 2

Unstitched threads

Back Foot

Scale 1

Scale 2

Scale 3

Scale 4

Scale 5

Scale 6

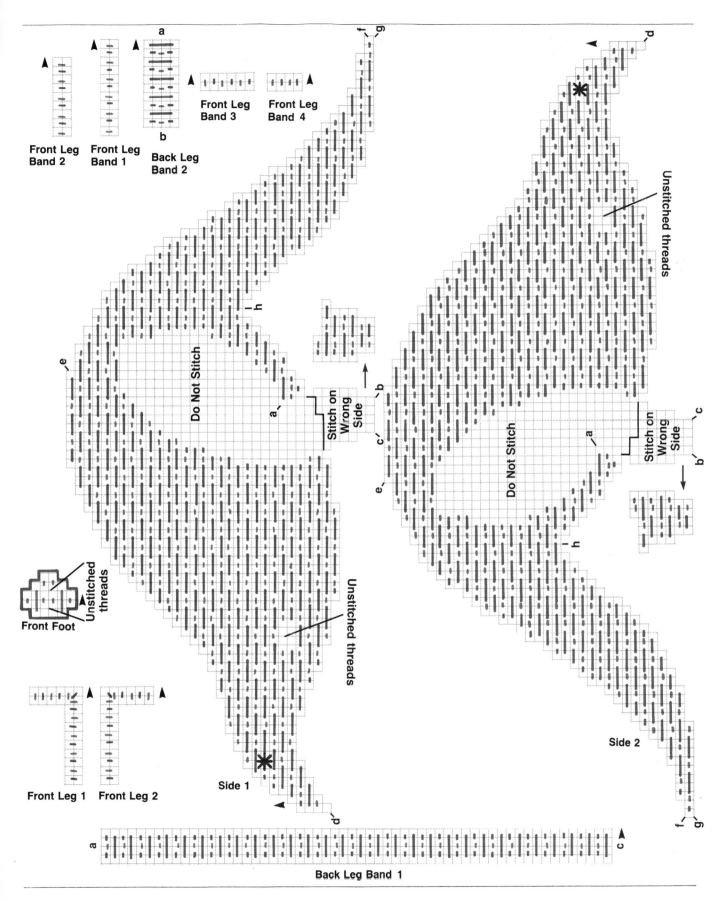

Front Leg
Band 2

Front Leg
Band 1

Back Leg
Band 2

a

b

Front Leg
Band 3

Front Leg
Band 4

a

f g

d

Unstitched
threads

Do Not Stitch

e

a

h

Stitch on
Wrong
Side

b

c

e

Do Not Stitch

a

Stitch on
Wrong
Side

c

b

h

Unstitched threads

Front Foot

Unstitched
threads

Front Leg 1

Front Leg 2

Side 1

Side 2

d

f g

a

c

Back Leg Band 1

9. Work the spine and upper tail bands in Parisian stitch. Put in the long stitches first, using Dark Lime yarn; then work the short stitches, using Lime yarn. (The unstitched plastic threads will be used in assembly.)

10. Work the underbelly and lower tail bands in Parisian stitch. Put in the long stitches first, using Dark Lime yarn; then work the short stitches, using Lime yarn.

Color

 Dk. Lime

 Lime

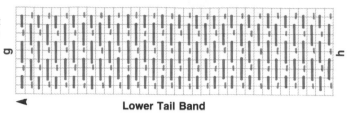

Lower Tail Band

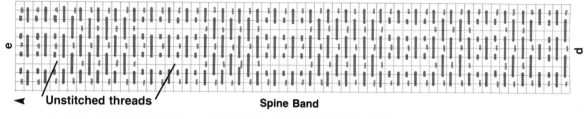

Unstitched threads   Upper Tail Band

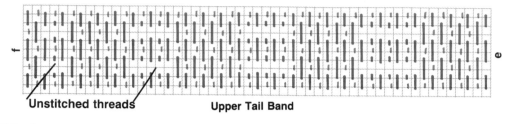

Unstitched threads   Spine Band

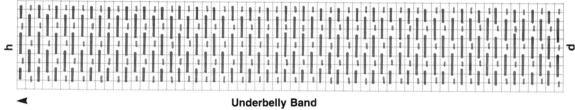

Underbelly Band

Assembly/Stegosaurus

Do all joining using two strands of Dark Lime yarn.

Back Leg Preassembly

The two back leg bands are joined on their long sides to the outline edge of the back leg on the right side of side 1 and to each other on one of their short sides, forming an open box the shape of the back leg. Refer to the stitch diagrams for the join placement points of the bands along the edges of the back leg.

Place the side 1 piece right side up. Wrong side up, place one long side of one back leg band 2 piece against the lower back edge of the back leg, matching the **b** end of the band to the **b** end of the leg and the **a** end of the band to the **a** point of the leg. Flush join these two matched edges.

With wrong sides up, flush join the **a** end of one back leg band 1 piece to the **a** end of the previously joined back leg band 2 piece.

Curving the joined bands upward so their wrong sides face each other and the center of the leg, match the **c** end of back leg band 1 to the **c** end of the leg. Starting at this point, flush join the long side of back leg band 1 adjacent to side 1 to the remaining outline edge of the leg on the right side of side 1.

Join the remaining two back leg bands to the right side of side 2 and each other the same way the two back leg bands were joined to side 1.

Front Legs

With wrong sides up, match the long sides of one front leg band 1 and one front leg band 3 to the outside edges of one front leg 1 piece. Flush join these matched edges.

With wrong sides up, match the long sides of one front leg band 2 and one front leg band 4 to the inside edges of the front leg 1 piece. Flush join these matched edges.

Turn the four bands upward so their wrong sides face each other and the center of the leg. Flush join the adjacent short edges of each set of two bands, forming two L-shape angles.

With right side up, place one front leg 2 piece over the top edges of the assembled front leg bands. Flush join the top edges of the bands to the two L-shape inside and outside edges of the leg as the front leg 1 piece was joined.

Join the second set of front leg and front leg band pieces the same way the first set was joined.

Match the square-shape edges of the short side of one leg to the square-shape outline edges of the unstitched plastic threads on the lower front of the right side of side 1. Flush join the leg to side 1 along these matched squares.

Join the second front leg to the right side of side 2 the same way the first front foot was joined to side 1.

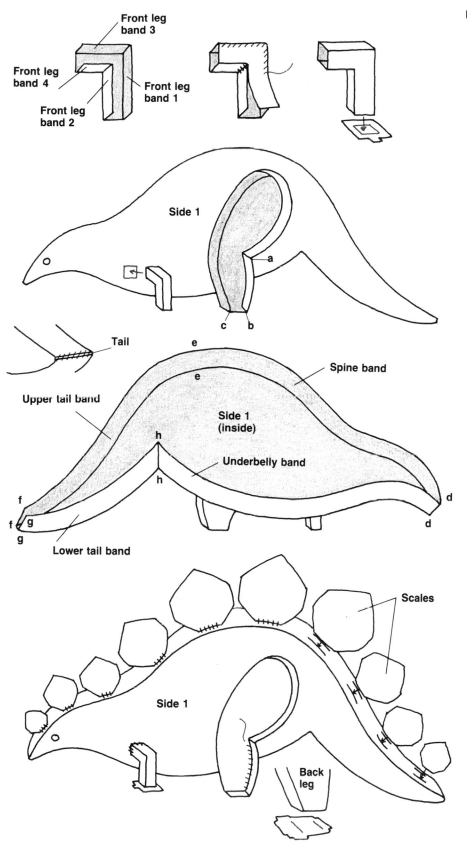

Front leg band 3

Front leg band 4

Front leg band 1

Front leg band 2

Side 1

a

c   b

Tail

e

Upper tail band

e

Spine band

Side 1 (inside)

h

Underbelly band

h

f

f   g

g

Lower tail band

d

d

Scales

Side 1

Back leg

Body

The four body bands, pieces 15 through 18, are joined on their long sides to the edges of side 1 and to each other on their short sides, forming an open box. Refer to the stitch diagrams for these pieces for the join placement points of the bands along the edges of side 1.

Place the side 1 piece right side up. With right side up, place the **d** end of the spine band against the **d** join placement point on side 1. Starting at **d,** flush join the long edge to side 1, easing the band around the outward curves of the dinosaur's head and back, ending at join point **e.**

With right side up, flush join the **e** end of the upper tail band to the **e** end of the spine band.

Starting at point **e,** flush join the long edge of the upper tail band to the adjacent edge of side 1, easing the band around the downward curve of the upper tail, ending at join point **f.**

With right side up, flush join the **d** end of the underbelly band to the **d** end of the spine band.

Starting at point **d,** flush join the long edge of the underbelly band to the adjacent edge of side 1, easing the band around the inward curve of the dinosaur's jaw and the outward curve of the belly, ending at join point **h.** When joining the band to the back leg, the outline edge of side 1 is the edge above the reversed Parisian stitches.

With right side up, flush join the **h** end of the lower tail band to the **h** end of the underbelly band.

Starting at join point **h,** flush join the long edge of the lower tail band to the adjacent edge of side 1, easing the band around the outward curve of the lower tail, ending at join point **g.**

The two broken parallel lines of unstitched plastic threads on the spine and upper tail bands are for joining the scales. With side 1 and the scales right sides up and starting at the dinosaur's nose, flush join the bottom edges of half of the scales to each of the segments of the broken line closest to side 1 in the following order: Scale 1, Scale 2, Scale 3, Scale 4, Scale 5, Scale 6, Scale 5, Scale 4, Scale 3, Scale 2.

Turn the dinosaur's body wrong side up. With right sides out, flush join the bottom edges of the remaining set of scales to each of the segments of the second broken line, following the placement order in which the first set of scales was joined.

With the dinosaur's body still wrong side up, join the right side up edges of the side 2 piece to the second side of long edges on the bands. Start and stop the band joins on side 2 at the same join placement points as side 1, following the same order of joining as side 1.

To complete the dinosaur body, flush join the **f** end of the upper tail band to the **g** end of the lower tail band.

Leg Finishing

Place the dinosaur right side up. Place back leg 1 right side up over the top edges of the assembled back leg bands. Flush join the top edges of the bands to the edges of back leg 1. Start and stop the band joins at the same join placement

points as the back leg preassembly, following the same order of joining.

With the right side up, place one back foot below the back leg. Match the unstitched plastic thread at the back of the foot to the bottom edge of back leg band 2. Match the unstitched plastic thread at the center of the foot to the bottom edge of back leg band 1. These two unstitched threads and the two perpendicular threads that join them form a square. Flush join this square to the square-shape bottom edge of the back leg.

With right side up, place one front foot below the front leg, with the two-hole end of the foot toward the dinosaur's nose and

the four-hole end of the foot facing the tail. Match the square shape of the two unstitched plastic threads at the center and back of the foot and the two perpendicular threads that join them to the square-shape bottom edge of the front leg. Flush join these pieces along these matched squares.

Join the back leg 2 piece to side 2 of the dinosaur the same way the back leg 1 piece was joined to side 1 of the dinosaur.

Join the second set of front and back leg feet to the front and back legs on side 2 of the dinosaur the same way the first set of feet was joined to the legs on side 1 of the dinosaur.

Materials/Dimetrodon

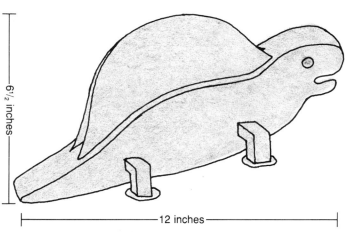

6½ inches

12 inches

- W. T. Rogers Quick-Count clear 7-mesh plastic canvas:
  one sheet 10½″ × 13½″ (70 holes × 90 holes)
  one sheet 10½″ × 13½″ cut to 3″ × 13½″ (22 holes × 90 holes)

- Brunswick Windrush Yarn:

#9044	Dark Green	12 yards
#9095	Dark Lime	135 yards
#9093	Lime	68 yards
#90921	Misty Lime	10 yards
#9008	Saffron	2 yards
#9025	Scarlet	2 yards

- no. 16 tapestry needle

Cutout Diagrams/Dimetrodon

Pattern Pieces

Follow the cutting diagrams carefully, making sure to count the holes accurately and to cut the right number of pieces.

1. Side 1. Cut one piece 80 holes wide × 23 holes high.
2. Side 2. Cut one piece 80 holes wide × 23 holes high.
3. Fin 1. Cut one piece 46 holes wide × 30 holes high.
4. Fin 2. Cut one piece 46 holes wide × 30 holes high.
5. Front Leg 1. Cut two pieces 5 holes wide × 7 holes high.
6. Front Leg 2. Cut two pieces 5 holes wide × 7 holes high.
7. Front Leg Band 1. Cut two pieces 2 holes wide × 7 holes high.
8. Front Leg Band 2. Cut two pieces 2 holes wide × 5 holes high.
9. Front Leg Band 3. Cut two pieces 5 holes wide × 2 holes high.
10. Front Leg Band 4. Cut two pieces 3 holes wide × 2 holes high.
11. Back Leg 1. Cut two pieces 5 holes wide × 6 holes high.

12. Back Leg 2. Cut two pieces 5 holes wide × 6 holes high.
13. Back Leg Band 1. Cut two pieces 2 holes wide × 6 holes high.
14. Back Leg Band 2. Cut two pieces 2 holes wide × 4 holes high.
15. Back Leg Band 3. Cut two pieces 5 holes wide × 2 holes high.
16. Back Leg Band 4. Cut two pieces 3 holes wide × 2 holes high.
17. Feet. Cut four pieces 4 holes wide × 5 holes high.
18. Spine Band. Cut one piece 10 holes wide × 71 holes high.
19. Head Band. Cut one piece 10 holes wide × 27 holes high.
20. Mouth Back Band. Cut one piece 10 holes wide × 2 holes high.
21. Mouth Band. Cut one piece 10 holes wide × 7 holes high.
22. Underbelly Band. Cut one piece 10 holes wide × 56 holes high.
23. Lower Tail Band. Cut one piece 10 holes wide × 27 holes high.

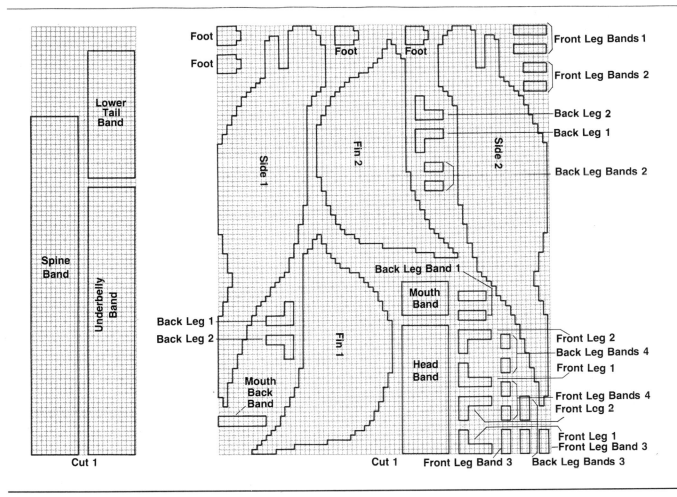

Foot

Foot

Front Leg Bands 1

Front Leg Bands 2

Back Leg 2

Back Leg 1

Back Leg Bands 2

Lower Tail Band

Foot

Foot

Fin 2

Side 1

Side 2

Spine Band

Underbelly Band

Back Leg Band 1

Mouth Band

Front Leg 2

Back Leg Bands 4

Front Leg 1

Back Leg 1

Back Leg 2

Fin 1

Head Band

Front Leg Bands 4

Front Leg 2

Mouth Back Band

Front Leg 1

Front Leg Band 3

Cut 1

Cut 1

Front Leg Band 3

Back Leg Bands 3

Stitching Diagrams/Dimetrodon

Stitches Used

Tent stitch (see page 12)
Gobelin stitch (see page 15)
Satin stitch (see page 16)
Parisian stitch (see page 17)
Cross stitch (see page 18)
Rhodes stitch (see page 18)
Whip stitch (see page 21)

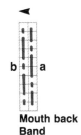

a   e

Mouth Band

b   a

Mouth back Band

c

b

Head Band

The Stitching

Work tent stitch, cross stitch, and Rhodes stitch using one strand of yarn. Work Parisian stitch, gobelin stitch, satin stitch, and whip stitch using two strands of yarn. Stitch the pieces as diagrammed in the following order:

1. Work the head band in Parisian stitch, beginning with the two-color stitches first. Following the diagram carefully, put in the long stitches, using Dark Lime yarn, then work the short stitches, using Lime yarn. Work the rest of the band using Dark Green yarn.

2. Work the mouth back band in Parisian stitch, using Dark Green yarn.

3. Work the tongue on the mouth band in satin stitch, using

g   f

Lower tail band

Color

Dk. Green   Lime

Dk. Lime   Scarlet

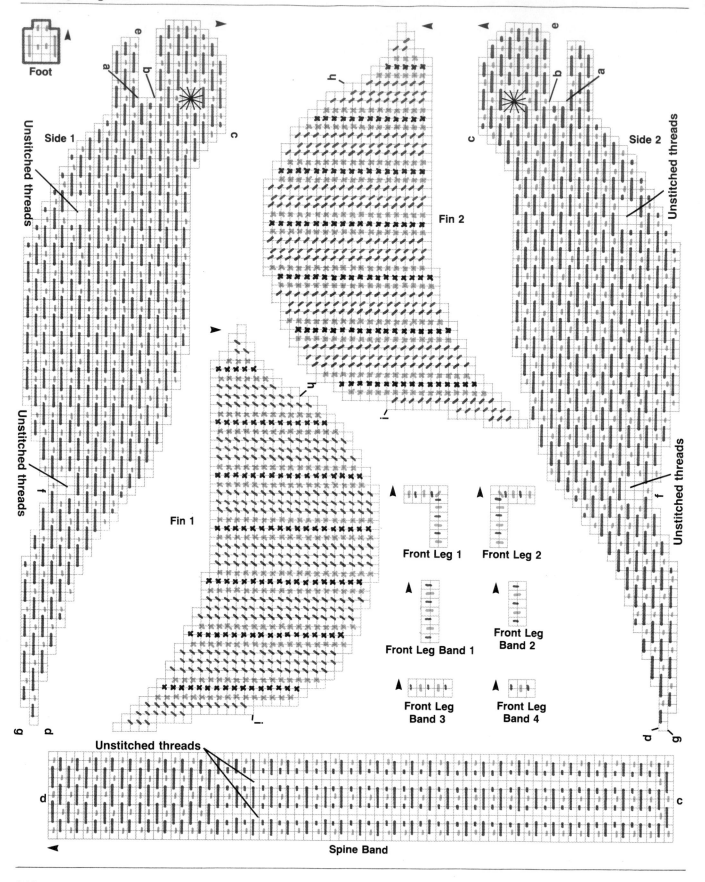

Foot

e

a

b

Side 1

c

Unstitched threads

Unstitched threads

f

g

p

h

Fin 2

c

e

b

a

Side 2

Unstitched threads

Unstitched threads

f

d

g

Fin 1

u

i

i.

Front Leg 1

Front Leg 2

Front Leg Band 1

Front Leg Band 2

Front Leg Band 3

Front Leg Band 4

Unstitched threads

d

c

Spine Band

Color

✏ (Dk. Green)	Dk. Green
✏ (Dk. Lime)	Dk. Lime
✏ (Lime)	Lime
✖ (Misty Lime)	Misty Lime
╱ (Saffron)	Saffron

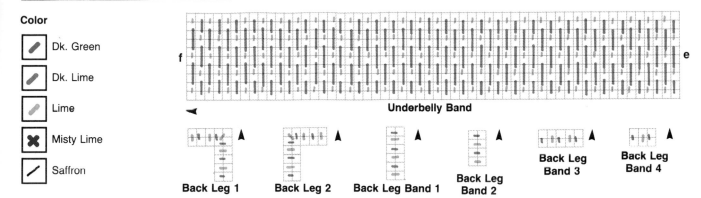

f ◄ Underbelly Band ► e

Back Leg 1 **Back Leg 2** **Back Leg Band 1** **Back Leg Band 2** **Back Leg Band 3** **Back Leg Band 4**

Scarlet yarn. Work the rest of the band in Parisian stitch, using Dark Green yarn.

4. Work the spine band in Parisian stitch. Work the long stitches first, using Dark Lime yarn; then the short lines, using Lime yarn. (The unstitched plastic threads will be used in the assembly.)

5. Work the lower tail and underbelly bands in Parisian stitch. Work the long stitches first with Dark Lime yarn, then the short stitches with Lime yarn.

6. Work the two sides of the dimetrodon in Parisian stitch, working one side at a time. Following the stitch diagram carefully, work the long stitches first, using Dark Lime yarn; then work the short lines with Lime yarn. Add the eyes in Rhodes stitch, using Saffron yarn. (The unstitched plastic threads will be used in the assembly.)

7. Work the two fin pieces next. Alternate three-stitch columns of tent stitch and cross stitch. Work the columns from right to left, using Dark Green yarn and Dark Lime yarn for the tent stitch

columns and Lime yarn and Misty Lime yarn for the cross stitch columns.

8. Work the two front leg pieces in gobelin stitch, alternating Dark Lime and Lime yarn. Work the Dark Lime stitches first, then the Lime.

9. Work the eight front leg band pieces in gobelin stitch, alternating Dark Lime and Lime yarn. Work the Dark Lime stitches first, then the Lime.

10. Work the two back leg pieces in gobelin stitch, alternating Dark Lime and Lime yarn. Work the Dark Lime stitches first, then the Lime.

11. Work the eight back leg band pieces in gobelin stitch, alternating Dark Lime and Lime yarn. Work the Dark Lime stitches first, then the Lime.

12. Work the four feet pieces in Parisian stitch, using Lime yarn. Work whip stitch to overcast the edges, using Dark Lime yarn. (The unstitched plastic threads will be used in the assembly.)

Assembly/Dimetrodon

Do all overcasting and joining using two strands of Dark Lime yarn unless otherwise indicated.

Front Legs and Back Legs

With wrong sides up, match the long sides of one front leg band 1 and one front leg

band 3 to the outside edges of one front leg 1 piece. Flush join these matched edges.

With wrong sides up, match the long sides of one front leg band 2 and one front leg band 4 to the inside edges of the front leg 1 piece. Flush join these matched edges.

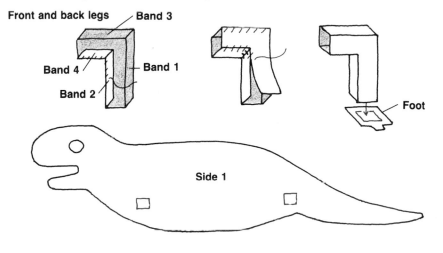

Front and back legs — Band 3

Band 4 — Band 1

Band 2

Side 1

Foot

Turn the four bands upward so their wrong sides face each other and the center of the leg. Flush join the adjacent short edges of each set of two bands, forming two L-shape angles.

With right side up, place one front leg 2 piece over the top edges of the assembled front leg bands. Flush join the top edges of the bands to the two L-shape inside and outside edges of the leg the same way the front leg 1 piece was joined.

Join the second set of front leg and front leg band pieces the same way the first set was joined.

Match the square edges of the short side of one leg to the square outline edges on the unstitched plastic threads on the lower front of the right side of side 1. Flush join the leg to side 1 along this matched square.

Place one foot right side up below the front leg, with the two-hole end of the foot toward the dinosaur's nose and the four-hole end toward the tail. Match the square shape of the two unstitched plastic threads at the center and back of the foot and the two perpendicular threads that join them to the square-shape bottom edge of the front leg. Flush join these pieces along these matched threads.

Join the second front leg to side 2 of the dinosaur in the same way the first front leg was joined to side 1.

Join a foot to the bottom edge of the second front leg the same way the foot was joined to the bottom of the first front leg.

The back legs are slightly smaller than the front legs, but they are assembled the same way. Assemble both back legs and join them to the square of the unstitched plastic threads on the lower back of the right sides of side 1 and side 2. Join the feet to the bottom edges of the back legs the same way the feet were joined to the front legs.

Body

Except for pieces 20 and 21, the six body bands, pieces 18 through 23, are joined on their long sides to the edges of side 1 and to each other on their short sides, forming an open box. Pieces 20 and 21 join the other bands on their long sides and the edges of side 1 on their short sides. Refer to the stitch diagrams of side 1 and of the bands for the join placement points of the bands along the edges of side 1.

Place the side 1 piece wrong side up. Place the **a** end of the mouth back band right side up against the **a** join placement point on side 1. Starting at **a**, flush join the short edge to side 1, ending at point **b.**

Flush join the **b** end of the head band right side up to the **b** end of the mouth back band, using Dark Green yarn.

Starting at point **b,** flush join the long edge of the head band to the adjacent edge of side 1, easing the band around the outward curve of the dinosaur's head, ending at join point **c.**

With right side up, flush join the **c** end of the spine band to the **c** end of the head band.

Starting at point **c,** flush join the long edge of the spine band to the adjacent edge of side 1, easing the band around the inward curves of the dinosaur's neck and the upper tail, ending at join point **d.**

With right side up, flush join the **a** end of the mouth band to the **a** end of the mouth back band, using Dark Green yarn.

Starting at point **a,** flush join the short edge of the mouth band to the adjacent edge of side 1, ending at join point **e.**

With right side up, flush join the **e** end of the underbelly band to the **e** end of the mouth band.

Starting at point **e,** flush join the long edge of the underbelly band to the adjacent edge of side 1, easing the band around the inward curve of the dinosaur's jaw and the outward curve of the belly, ending at join point **f.**

With right side up, flush join the **f** end of the lower tail band to the **f** end of the underbelly band.

Starting at point **f,** flush join the long edge of the lower tail band to the adjacent edge of side 1, easing the band around the outward curve of the dinosaur's lower tail, ending at join point **g.**

The two parallel lines of unstitched plastic threads on the spine band are for joining the two fin pieces. With side 1 and fin 1 both right side up, place the bottom edge of the fin along the line of unstitched plastic threads closest to side 1. Flush join the fin bottom to the spine band along this line.

Turn the dinosaur's body wrong side up. Flush join the bottom edge of the second fin right side out to the second line of unstitched threads on the spine band the same way the first was joined.

Join the edges of the side 2 piece right side up to the second set of side edges on the bands. Start and stop the band joins on side 2 at the same join placement points as side 1, following the same order of joining as side 1.

Flush join the **d** end of the spine band to the **g** end of the lower tail band.

To join the two fin pieces, temporarily tack the two pieces together at points **h** and **i** marked on the stitch diagram.

Beginning at the base of the fin along the upper tail, flush join the edges of the two fins. Join the edges between the spine band and tack points **h** and **i** loosely, creating elongated triangles from the band to the tack points. Join the edges between tack points **h** and **i** tightly, the edge of one fin meeting the edge of the other. Remove the temporary tacks as you come to them.

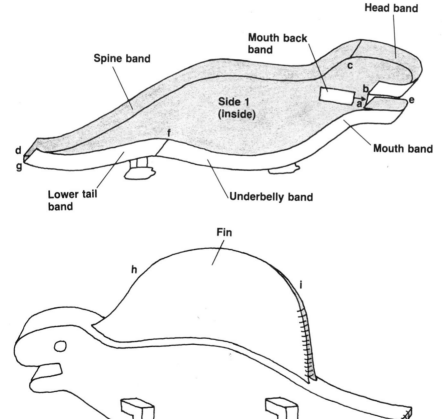

Victorian Lamppost Photo Cube

Intermediate

This delightful Victorian lamppost adds a decorative touch to a desk or table while displaying photographs of your favorite people. School photographs, incidentally, will fit perfectly in the four apertures. The lamppost is easy to stitch, but the construction is fairly complicated.

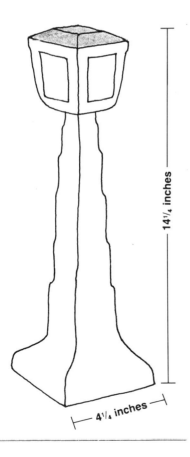

14¹/₄ inches

4¹/₄ inches

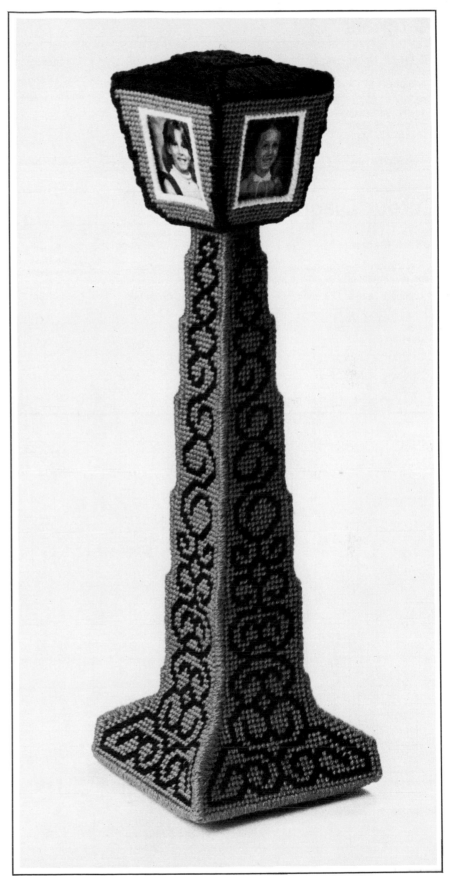

Materials

- Boye E-Z Count clear 10-mesh plastic canvas:
  one sheet 11″ × 14″ (110 holes × 140 holes)
  one sheet 11″ × 14″ cut to 4″ × 11″ (40 holes × 110 holes)
- Bernat 1–2–3 Ply Persian Type Yarn:
  #N04–942 Black   58 yards
  #N04–948 Gray   78 yards
  #N10–428 White   3 yards

- four photographs with a picture area 1½″ wide × 2″ high
- nos. 18 and 20 tapestry needles
- masking tape

Cutout Diagrams

Pattern Pieces

Follow the cutting diagrams carefully, making sure to count the holes accurately and to cut the right number of pieces.

1. Lamppost Base. Cut one piece 40 holes wide × 40 holes high.
2. Lamppost. Cut four pieces 40 holes wide × 110 holes high.
3. Lamp Base. Cut one piece 14 holes wide × 14 holes high.
4. Lamp Sides. Cut four pieces 28 holes wide × 26 holes high.
5. Lamp Cap Sides. Cut four pieces 28 holes wide × 9 holes high.
6. Lamp Cap. Cut one piece 12 holes wide × 12 holes high.

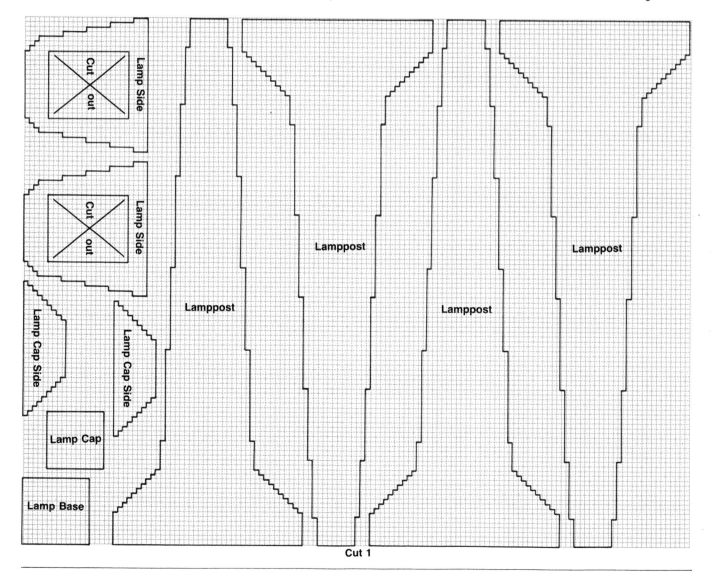

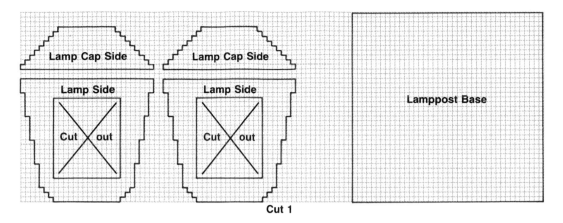

Cut 1

Stitching Diagrams

Stitches Used

Tent stitch (see page 12)
Satin stitch (see page 16)
Backstitch (see page 20)
Whip stitch (see page 21)

The Stitching

Work tent stitch and backstitch using two strands of yarn. Work satin stitch using three strands of yarn. Work whip stitch to overcast, using three strands of yarn. Use the no. 18 tapestry needle for all stitching. Stitch the pieces as diagramed in the following order:

1. Work the lamppost base In tent stltch, using Gray yarn.

2. Work the four lamp cap sides in satin stitch, using Black yarn.

3. Work the lamp base in tent stitch, using Gray yarn. (The unstitched plastic threads in the center are assembly points.)

Color

 Black

 Grey

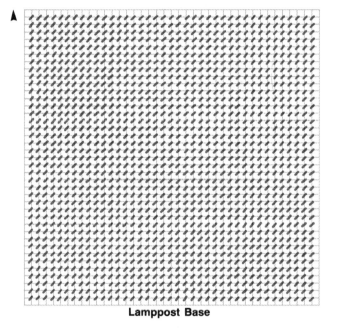

Lamppost Base

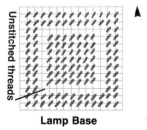

Lamp Base

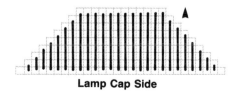

Lamp Cap Side

4. Work the four sides of the lamp in tent stitch, using Gray yarn. Work whip stitch with White yarn to overcast the center aperture in each piece.

5. Work the four lamppost pieces. Begin by working the grillwork in tent stitch, using Black yarn. Then work the background in tent stitch, using Gray yarn.

6. Work the lamp cap in satin stitch, using Black yarn. Work the backstitch as shown, using Black yarn.

Color

  Black

 Gray

 White

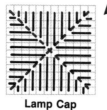

Lamp Cap

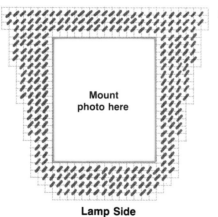

Lamp Side

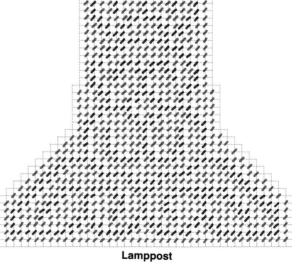

Lamppost

Assembly

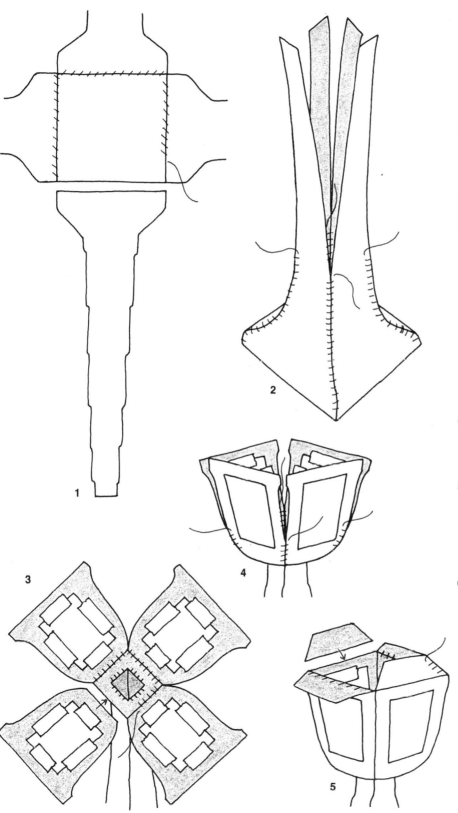

1

2

3

4

5

Do all overcasting and joining using three strands of yarn and the no. 20 tapestry needle.

Lamppost

1. With right sides up and in consecutive order, flush join the edges of the base of the lamppost to the bottom edges of the four lamppost pieces, using Gray yarn.

2. With right sides out, flush join the adjacent edges of the lamppost pieces, using Gray yarn. It is easiest to assemble it by joining the four sides concurrently, working upward at approximately 1-inch intervals.

Lamp

3. Place the lamp base, wrong side up, on the top edge of the assembled lamppost, matching the edge of the post to the square of unstitched threads in the center of the lamp base. Flush join, using Gray yarn.

   Using masking tape, mount one photograph on the wrong side of each of the sides of the lamp. To be secure, the photographs should be at least $1/2$ inch larger than the frame on each side.

   With wrong sides up and in consecutive order, flush join the bottom edges of the four sides of the lamp to the edges of the lamp base, using Black yarn.

4. With right sides out and in consecutive order, flush join the lamp sides concurrently, working upward at approximately $1/2$-inch intervals. Use Black yarn.

5. With wrong sides up and in consecutive order, flush join the bottom edges of the four lamp cap sides to the top edges of the four lamp sides, using Black yarn.

   With right sides out, flush join the adjacent edges of the lamp cap sides, using Black yarn.

6. With right side up and in consecutive order, flush join the edges of the lamp cap to the top edges of the four lamp cap sides, using Black yarn.

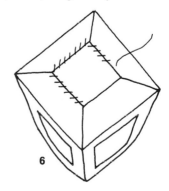

6

Dollhouse
Advanced

The design of this magnificent three-story dollhouse is based on a Georgian town house. This is an ambitious project. Not only the outer walls and roof but the inner walls, ceilings, and floors are all done in needlepoint. The construction is complex. Foam-core board, available in art supply shops, placed between the outer and inner walls makes the dollhouse sturdy. And once it is completed, it will surely become a prized family heirloom.

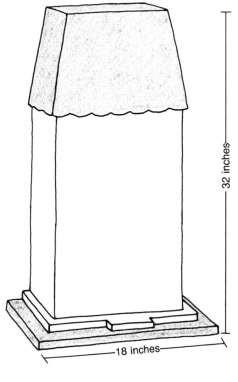

32 inches

18 inches

Materials

- W. T. Rogers Quick-Count Artist Size clear 7-mesh plastic canvas:
  one sheet 13½" × 21½" (90 holes × 145 holes)
  one sheet 13½" × 21½" cut to 13½" × 18½" (90 holes × 131 holes)
  one sheet 13½" × 21½" cut to 13½" × 17" (90 holes × 119 holes)
  one sheet 13½" × 21½" cut to 13½" × 15½" (90 holes × 109 holes)
  two sheets 13½" × 21½" cut to 13½" × 13½" (90 holes × 91 holes)

- W. T. Rogers Quick-Count clear 7-mesh plastic canvas:
  twelve sheets 10½" × 13½" (70 holes × 90 holes)
  two sheets 10½" × 13½" cut to 10½" × 10½" (70 holes × 71 holes)
  five sheets 10½" × 13½" cut to 10" × 10½" (67 holes × 70 holes)
  four sheets 10½" × 13½" cut to 9½" × 10½" (63 holes × 70 holes)

- Brunswick Windrush Yarn:

#9010	White	1010 yards
#90621	Grey Heather	178 yards
#90622	Medium Grey Heather	55 yards
#90623	Dark Grey Heather	185 yards
#9002	Light Blue	75 yards
#90111	Light Powder Blue	168 yards
#90112	Medium Powder Blue	49 yards
#90113	Dark Powder Blue	66 yards
#9020	Spring Leaf	25 yards
#9083	Meadow Green	70 yards
#9085	Earth Green	9 yards
#9003	Yellow	24 yards
#90383	Dark Goldenrod	44 yards
#90013	Larkspur Heather	30 yards
#90025	Sugar Plum	48 yards
#9026	Flame	68 yards
#9024	Maroon	5 yards
#90090	Peach	90 yards
#90452	Pale Desert Flower	190 yards
#9045	Light Desert Flower	18 yards
#90453	Dark Desert Flower	150 yards
#9066	Denim Blue Heather	345 yards
#90731	Caramel	7 yards

- Bernat 1–2–3 Ply Persian Type Yarn:
  #N10–428 White   4 yards

- no. 16 tapestry needle

- one piece gray felt 18" × 12¼", matching yarn color #90623 Dark Grey Heather

- fabric glue

- no. 14 white florist's wire, cut in the following lengths:
  four pieces 21½" long
  four pieces 18" long
  four pieces 13½" long
  four pieces 12¼" long
  one piece 10¼" long
  eight pieces 9¾" long
  two pieces 9¼" long

- wire cutters

- gray magic marker, matching yarn color #90623 Dark Grey Heather

- Foam core, cut in the following dimensions:
  one piece 17¾" × 12"
  four pieces 13¼" × 9¾"
  one piece 12" × 9½"
  one piece 9¾" × 9¾"
  four pieces 9¼" × 9¾"

- T square

- 24" ruler

- mat or craft knife

- plastic bubble paper (small bubbles), as necessary, cut to match the foam-core pieces

- transparent tape

- gold nail head or thumbtack with a ⅝"-diameter circular head

- 280 red miniature artificial flowers

Cutout Diagrams

Pattern Pieces

Follow the cutting diagrams carefully, making sure to count the holes accurately and to cut the right number of pieces.

Base

1. Upper Base and Floor 1. Cut one piece 119 holes wide × 81 holes high.
*2. Lower Base. Cut one piece 119 holes wide × 81 holes high.
3. Base Bands 1a and 1b. Cut two pieces 119 holes wide × 4 holes high.
4. Base Bands 2a and 2b. Cut two pieces 4 holes wide × 81 holes high.

Foundation

*5. Foundation 1a and 1b. Cut two pieces 89 holes wide × 4 holes high.
*6. Foundation 2a and 2b. Cut two pieces 4 holes wide × 67 holes high.
*7. Foundation 3a and 3b. Cut two pieces 4 holes wide × 63 holes high.

Stoop and Flower Box

8. Stoop. Cut one piece 99 holes wide × 78 holes high.
9. Stoop Band 1. Cut one piece 27 holes wide × 3 holes high.

10. Stoop Bands 2a and 2b. Cut two pieces 3 holes wide × 7 holes high.
11. Stoop Bands 3a and 3b. Cut two pieces 36 holes wide × 3 holes high.
12. Stoop Bands 4a and 4b. Cut two pieces 3 holes wide × 71 holes high.
13. Stoop Bands 5a and 5b. Cut two pieces 4 holes wide × 3 holes high.

Outside Walls—First Floor

14. Outside Wall 1a. Cut one piece 67 holes wide × 67 holes high.
15. Outside Wall 1b. Cut one piece 89 holes wide × 67 holes high.
16. Outside Wall 1c. Cut one piece 67 holes wide × 67 holes high.

Outside Walls—Second Floor

17. Outside Wall 2a. Cut one piece 67 holes wide × 69 holes high.
18. Outside Wall 2b. Cut one piece 89 holes wide × 69 holes high.
19. Outside Wall 2c. Cut one piece 67 holes wide × 69 holes high.

Wall Braces—Third Floor

*20. Outside Walls 3a and 3c. Cut two pieces 67 holes wide × 63 holes high.

*21. Outside Walls 3a and 3c Bands. Cut two pieces 67 holes wide × 6 holes high. (Bendable gable band.)
*22. Outside Wall 3b. Cut one piece 89 holes wide × 69 holes high.

Roof—Third Floor

23. Roof 1. Cut one piece 91 holes wide × 70 holes high.
24. Roof 2a and 2b. Cut two pieces 71 holes wide × 70 holes high.
25. Roof 3. Cut one piece 91 holes wide × 70 holes high.
26. Roof 4. Cut one piece 71 holes wide × 71 holes high.

Outside Bands

27. Outside Bands 1a, 1b, 1c and 1d. Cut four pieces 4 holes wide × 65 holes high. (Vertical bands between inside and outside walls.)
28. Outside Bands 2a and 2b. Cut two pieces 89 holes wide × 4 holes high. (Separates floors and ceilings.)
29. Outside Bands 3a and 3b. Cut two pieces 4 holes wide × 62 holes high. (Behind roof on front.)

*Indicates pieces not stitched

Pattern Pieces

30. Outside Band 4. Cut one piece 67 holes wide × 4 holes high. (Separates ceiling and roof 4.)

Inside Walls—First Floor

31. Inside Walls 1a and 1c. Cut two pieces 63 holes wide × 65 holes high.
32. Inside Wall 1b. Cut one piece 89 holes wide × 65 holes high.

Inside Walls—Second Floor

33. Inside Walls 2a and 2c. Cut two pieces 63 holes wide × 65 holes high.
34. Inside Wall 2b. Cut one piece 89 holes wide × 65 holes high.

Inside Walls—Third Floor

35. Inside Walls 3a and 3c. Cut two pieces 63 holes wide × 60 holes high.
36. Inside Walls 3a and 3c Bands. Cut two pieces 63 holes wide × 3 holes high. (Bendable baseboard.)
37. Inside Wall 3b. Cut one piece 81 holes wide × 63 holes high.

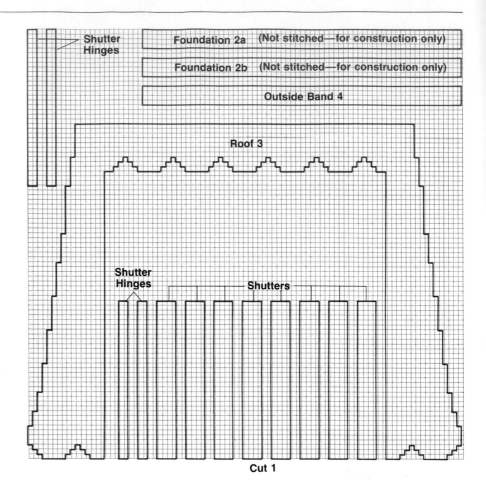

Shutter Hinges

Foundation 2a (Not stitched—for construction only)

Foundation 2b (Not stitched—for construction only)

Outside Band 4

Roof 3

Shutter Hinges

Shutters

Cut 1

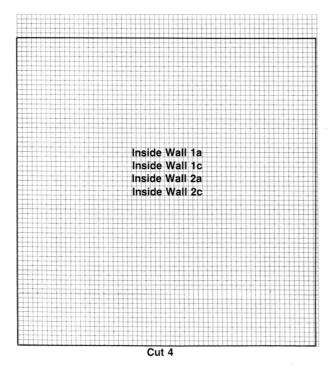

Inside Wall 1a
Inside Wall 1c
Inside Wall 2a
Inside Wall 2c

Cut 4

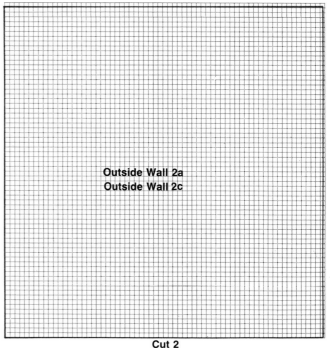

Outside Wall 2a
Outside Wall 2c

Cut 2

Pattern Pieces

Shutters—First Floor

38. Shutters. Cut eight pieces
    4 holes wide × 33 holes high.
39. Shutter Hinges. Cut four pieces
    2 holes wide × 33 holes high.

Floors

40. Floor 2. Cut one piece
    89 holes wide × 67 holes high.
41. Floor 3. Cut one piece
    89 holes wide × 67 holes high.

Ceilings

42. Ceiling 1. Cut one piece
    89 holes wide × 67 holes high.
43. Ceiling 2. Cut one piece
    89 holes wide × 67 holes high.
44. Ceiling 3. Cut one piece
    67 holes wide × 67 holes high.

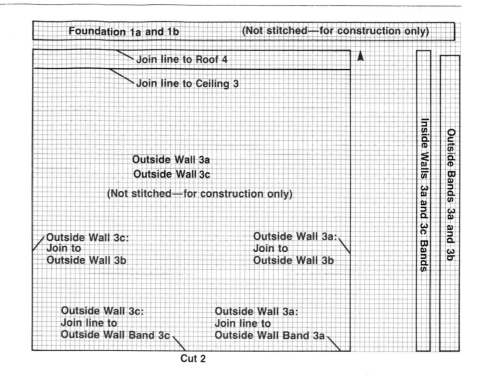

Foundation 1a and 1b   (Not stitched—for construction only)

Join line to Roof 4

Join line to Ceiling 3

Outside Wall 3a
Outside Wall 3c

(Not stitched—for construction only)

Outside Wall 3c:
Join to
Outside Wall 3b

Outside Wall 3a:
Join to
Outside Wall 3b

Outside Wall 3c:
Join line to
Outside Wall Band 3c

Outside Wall 3a:
Join line to
Outside Wall Band 3a

Inside Walls 3a and 3c Bands

Outside Bands 3a and 3b

Cut 2

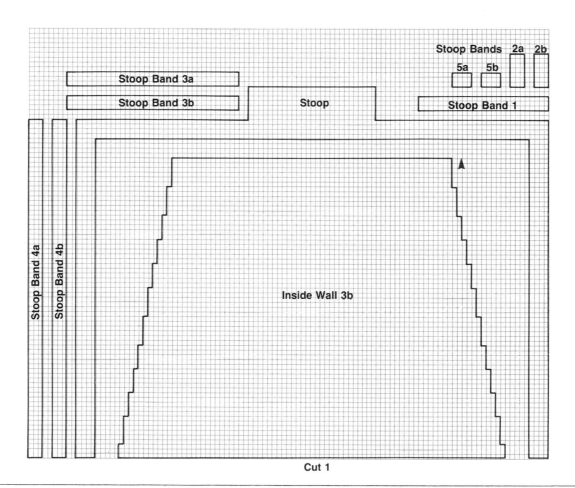

Stoop Bands   2a   2b

Stoop Band 3a   5a   5b

Stoop Band 3b   Stoop   Stoop Band 1

Stoop Band 4a

Stoop Band 4b

Inside Wall 3b

Cut 1

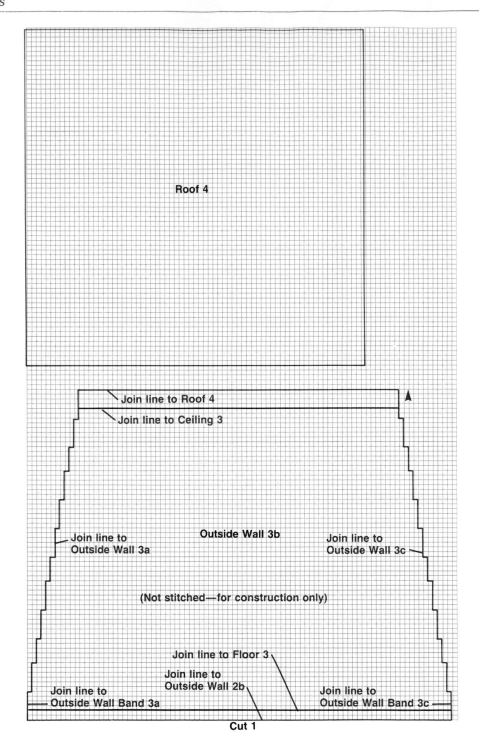

Roof 4

Join line to Roof 4

Join line to Ceiling 3

Join line to
Outside Wall 3a

Outside Wall 3b

Join line to
Outside Wall 3c

(Not stitched—for construction only)

Join line to Floor 3

Join line to
Outside Wall 2b

Join line to
Outside Wall Band 3a

Join line to
Outside Wall Band 3c

Cut 1

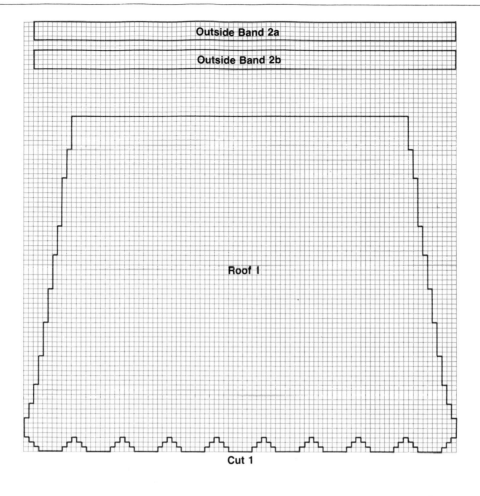

Outside Band 2a

Outside Band 2b

Roof 1

Cut 1

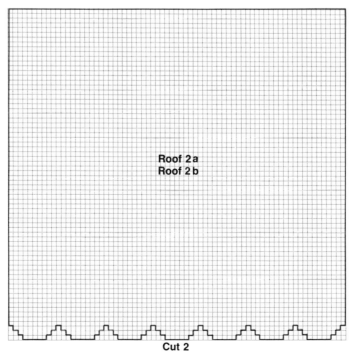

Roof 2 a
Roof 2 b

Cut 2

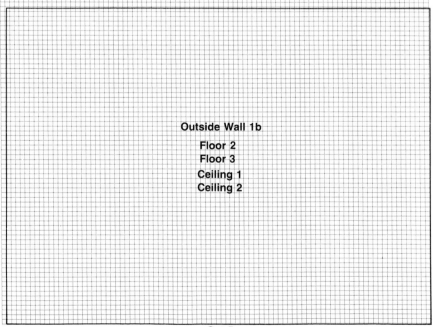

Base Band 1a

Base Band 2a

Base Band 2b

Upper Base and Floor 1

Cut 1

Outside Wall 1b

Floor 2
Floor 3
Ceiling 1
Ceiling 2

Cut 5

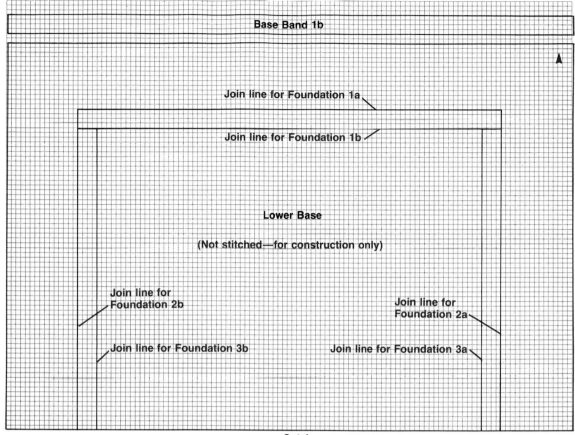

Base Band 1b

Join line for Foundation 1a

Join line for Foundation 1b

Lower Base

(Not stitched—for construction only)

Join line for
Foundation 2b

Join line for
Foundation 2a

Join line for Foundation 3b

Join line for Foundation 3a

Cut 1

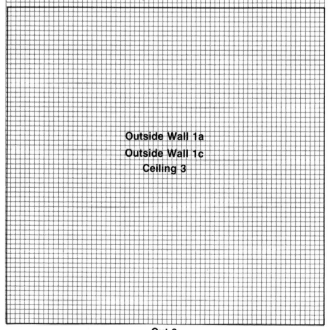

Outside Wall 1a
Outside Wall 1c
Ceiling 3

Cut 3

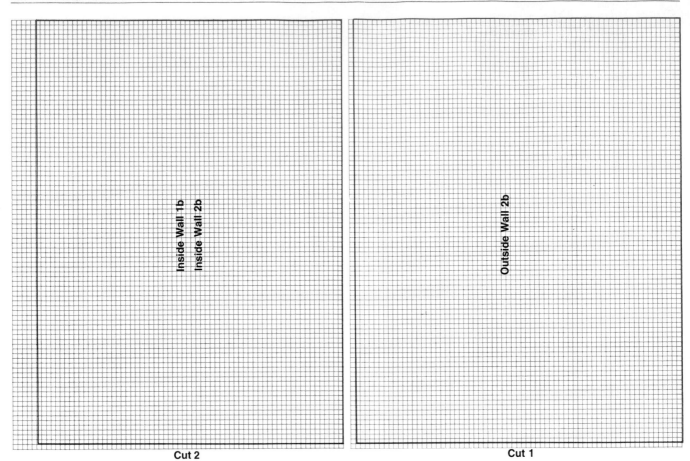

Inside Wall 1b
Inside Wall 2b

Outside Wall 2b

Cut 2

Cut 1

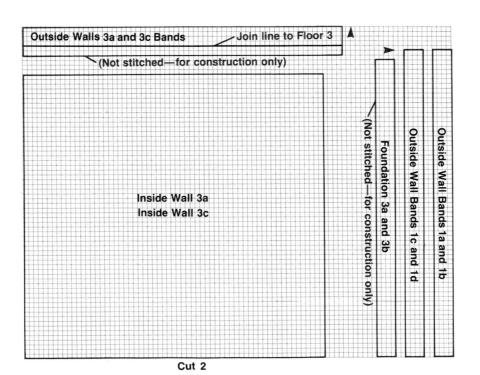

Outside Walls 3a and 3c Bands

Join line to Floor 3

(Not stitched—for construction only)

Inside Wall 3a
Inside Wall 3c

(Not stitched—for construction only)

Foundation 3a and 3b

Outside Wall Bands 1c and 1d

Outside Wall Bands 1a and 1b

Cut 2

Stitching Diagrams

Stitches Used

Tent stitch (see page 12)
Slanted gobelin stitch (see page 13)
Mosaic stitch (see page 14)
Cashmere stitch (see page 14)
Gobelin stitch (see page 15)
Satin stitch (see page 16)
Brick stitch (see page 16)
Hungarian diamond stitch (see page 17)
Cross stitch (see page 18)
Double cross stitch (see page 18)
Rhodes stitch (see page 18)
Double leviathan stitch (see page 19)
Algerian eye stitch (see page 20)
Backstitch (see page 20)
French knot (see page 21)
Whip stitch (see page 21)

Colors for the stitch diagrams are listed next to each diagram.

The Stitching

Work all stitches using Brunswick Windrush yarn. Work tent stitch, slanted gobelin stitch, mosaic stitch, cashmere stitch, cross stitch, double cross stitch, Rhodes stitch, double leviathan stitch, Algerian eye stitch, backstitch, and French knots using one strand of yarn. Work gobelin stitch, satin stitch, brick stitch, Hungarian diamond stitch, and whip stitch using two strands of yarn. Stitch the pieces as diagramed in the following order (the lower base, foundation, walls 3a and 3c, outside walls 3a and 3c bands, and outside wall 3b pieces are not stitched and are used only in the assembly):

To Change Colors

The yarn quantities used for stitching and assembly are listed by coordinated exterior and interior areas so the colors can be changed if desired.

Upper base and base bands 1 and 2:
Medium Grey Heather	55 yards
Dark Grey Heather	61 yards

Stoop and stoop bands 1–5:
White	33 yards
Earth Green	9 yards

Outside walls 1a, 1b, 1c, 2a, 2b, 2c and outside bands 1–4:
White	195 yards
Grey Heather	178 yards
Flame	46 yards
Maroon	5 yards
Light Powder Blue	22 yards
Light Blue	14 yards

Roofs 1–4:
Denim Blue Heather	300 yards
Dark Grey Heather	58 yards
White	28 yards
Flame	22 yards
Light Powder Blue	10 yards
Light Blue	12 yards

Inside walls 1a, 1b, 1c, shutters, shutter hinges:
White	195 yards
Light Powder Blue	56 yards
Medium Powder Blue	49 yards
Dark Powder Blue	11 yards
Light Blue	9 yards

Floor 1:
White	22 yards
Light Powder Blue	27 yards
Dark Powder Blue	55 yards
Dark Goldenrod	44 yards

Ceiling 1:
White	90 yards

Inside walls 2a, 2b, and 2c:
White	38 yards
Pale Desert Flower	97 yards
Dark Desert Flower	120 yards
Light Blue	10 yards
Light Powder Blue	10 yards
Meadow Green	9 yards

Floor 2:
Pale Desert Flower	11 yards
Light Desert Flower	18 yards
Dark Desert Flower	20 yards
Meadow Green	61 yards

Ceiling 2:
White	86 yards

Inside walls 3a, 3b, and 3c and inside walls 3a and 3c bands:
White	148 yards
Peach	63 yards
Pale Desert Flower	45 yards
Larkspur Heather	30 yards
Spring Leaf	25 yards

Floor 3:
Caramel	7 yards
Peach	13 yards
Pale Desert Flower	26 yards
Sugar Plum	26 yards
Light Powder Blue	33 yards
Yellow	24 yards
Light Blue	18 yards

Ceiling 3:
White	28 yards
Peach	4 yards
Pale Desert Flower	5 yards
Sugar Plum	22 yards
Light Blue	12 yards
Light Powder Blue	10 yards

Assembly Yarn Measurements

Upper base, lower base, base bands 1 and 2, and foundation 1–3:
Dark Grey Heather	55 yards
White	2 yards

Stoop and stoop bands 1–5:
White	28 yards

Outside walls 1a, 1b, 1c, 2a, 2b, 2c, 3a, 3b, 3c, outside walls 3a and 3c bands, and outside bands 1–4:
White	151 yards

Roofs 1–4:
Denim Blue Heather	44 yards
Dark Grey Heather	11 yards

Inside walls 1a, 1b, 1c, floor 1, ceiling 1, shutters, and shutter hinges:
White	37 yards

Interior walls 2a, 2b, 2c, floor 2, and ceiling 2:
White	9 yards
Pale Desert Flower	4 yards
Dark Desert Flower	11 yards

Inside walls 3a, 3b, 3c, inside walls 3a and 3c bands, floor 3, and ceiling 3:
White	13 yards
Peach	11 yards

Color

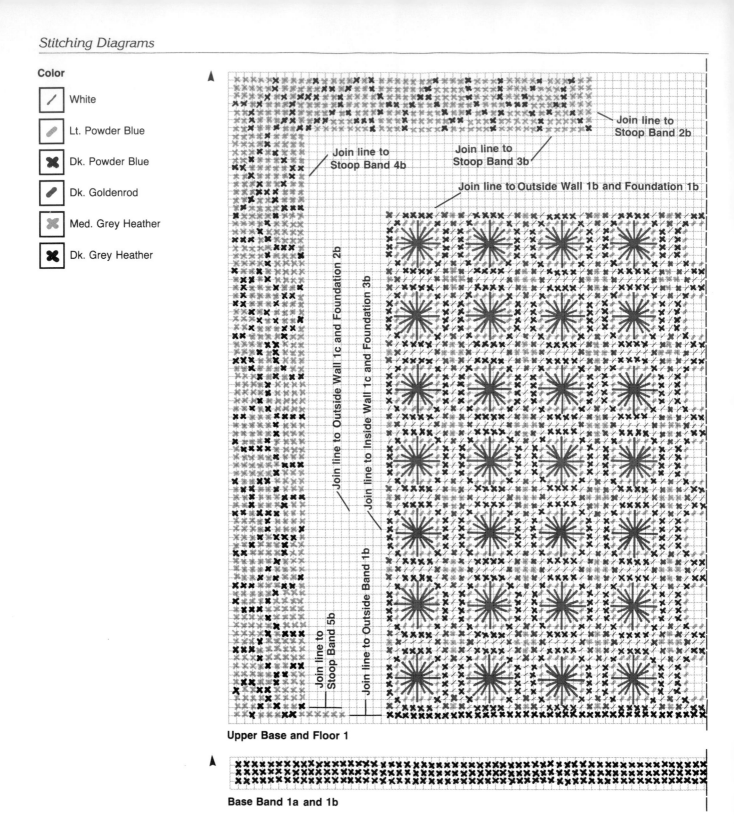

/ White

/ Lt. Powder Blue

✕ Dk. Powder Blue

/ Dk. Goldenrod

✕ Med. Grey Heather

✕ Dk. Grey Heather

Join line to Stoop Band 4b

Join line to Stoop Band 3b

Join line to Stoop Band 2b

Join line to Outside Wall 1b and Foundation 1b

Join line to Outside Wall 1c and Foundation 2b

Join line to Inside Wall 1c and Foundation 3b

Join line to Outside Band 1b

Join line to Stoop Band 5b

Upper Base and Floor 1

Base Band 1a and 1b

1. The upper base of the dollhouse is divided into two areas, a flagstone courtyard and floor 1. Work the L-shape halves of the courtyard in cross stitch. Following the diagram carefully, work the cement grouting first, using Dark Grey Heather yarn; then work the stones in Medium Grey Heather yarn. Begin the floor area by working one horizontal row of cross stitch along the outside edge, using Dark Grey Heather yarn. Following the diagram carefully, outline the octagonal tiles, working cross stitch, using Dark Powder Blue yarn. Outline the diamond shapes between the tiles by working cross stitch, using Dark

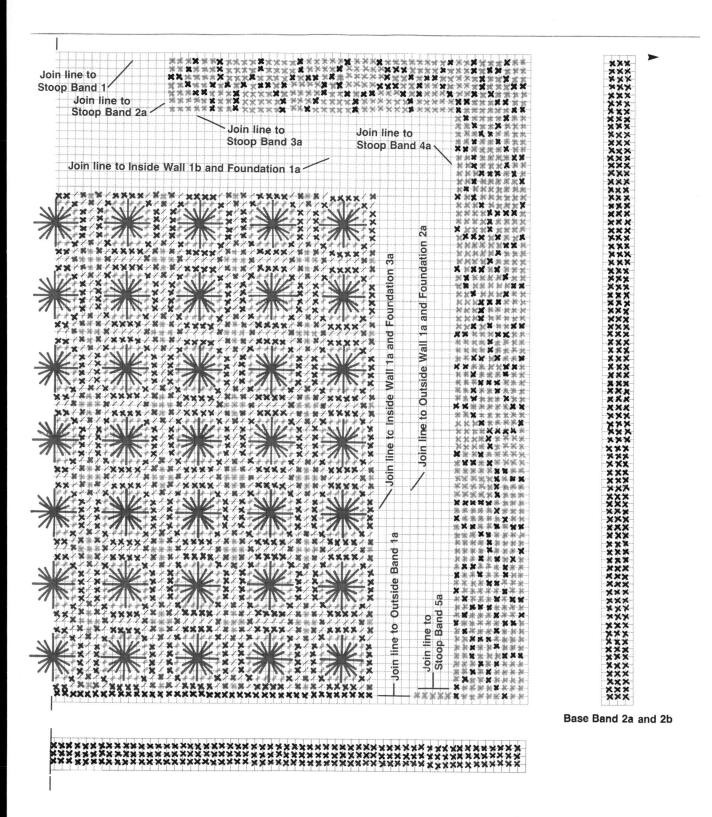

Join line to
Stoop Band 1

Join line to
Stoop Band 2a

Join line to
Stoop Band 3a

Join line to
Stoop Band 4a

Join line to Inside Wall 1b and Foundation 1a

Join line to Inside Wall 1a and Foundation 3a

Join line to Outside Wall 1a and Foundation 2a

Join line to Outside Band 1a

Join line to
Stoop Band 5a

Base Band 2a and 2b

Goldenrod yarn. Put In the centers of these diamonds in cross stitch, using Light Powder Blue yarn. Add the outlines between the tiles and the diamonds in tent stitch, using White yarn. Outline the inside edge of each tile in tent stitch, using Light Powder Blue yarn. Work the center of each tile in double

leviathan stitch, using Dark Goldenrod yarn. (The unstitched plastic threads will be used in the assembly.)

2. Work the four base band pieces in cross stitch, using Dark Grey Heather yarn.

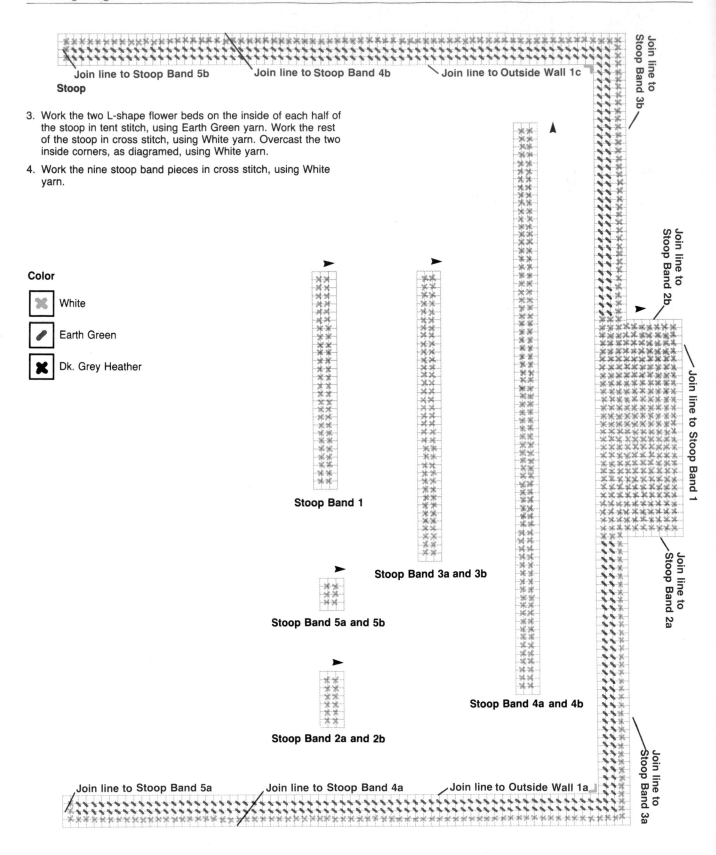

Stoop

3. Work the two L-shape flower beds on the inside of each half of the stoop in tent stitch, using Earth Green yarn. Work the rest of the stoop in cross stitch, using White yarn. Overcast the two inside corners, as diagramed, using White yarn.

4. Work the nine stoop band pieces in cross stitch, using White yarn.

Color

White

Earth Green

Dk. Grey Heather

Join line to Stoop Band 5b

Join line to Stoop Band 4b

Join line to Outside Wall 1c

Join line to Stoop Band 3b

Join line to Stoop Band 2b

Join line to Stoop Band 1

Join line to Stoop Band 2a

Join line to Stoop Band 3a

Stoop Band 1

Stoop Band 3a and 3b

Stoop Band 5a and 5b

Stoop Band 2a and 2b

Stoop Band 4a and 4b

Join line to Stoop Band 5a

Join line to Stoop Band 4a

Join line to Outside Wall 1a

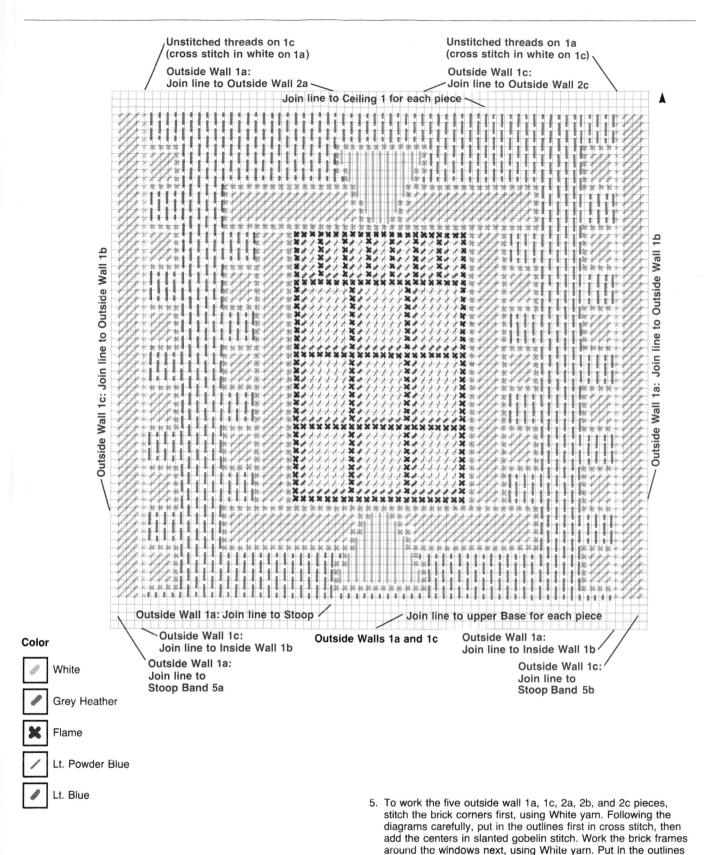

Unstitched threads on 1c
(cross stitch in white on 1a)

Unstitched threads on 1a
(cross stitch in white on 1c)

Outside Wall 1a:
Join line to Outside Wall 2a

Outside Wall 1c:
Join line to Outside Wall 2c

Join line to Ceiling 1 for each piece

Outside Wall 1c: Join line to Outside Wall 1b

Outside Wall 1a: Join line to Outside Wall 1b

Outside Wall 1a: Join line to Stoop

Join line to upper Base for each piece

Outside Wall 1c:
Join line to Inside Wall 1b

Outside Walls 1a and 1c

Outside Wall 1a:
Join line to Inside Wall 1b

Outside Wall 1a:
Join line to
Stoop Band 5a

Outside Wall 1c:
Join line to
Stoop Band 5b

Color

	White
	Grey Heather
✖	Flame
/	Lt. Powder Blue
	Lt. Blue

5. To work the five outside wall 1a, 1c, 2a, 2b, and 2c pieces, stitch the brick corners first, using White yarn. Following the diagrams carefully, put in the outlines first in cross stitch, then add the centers in slanted gobelin stitch. Work the brick frames around the windows next, using White yarn. Put in the outlines first in cross stitch, then add the centers in slanted gobelin

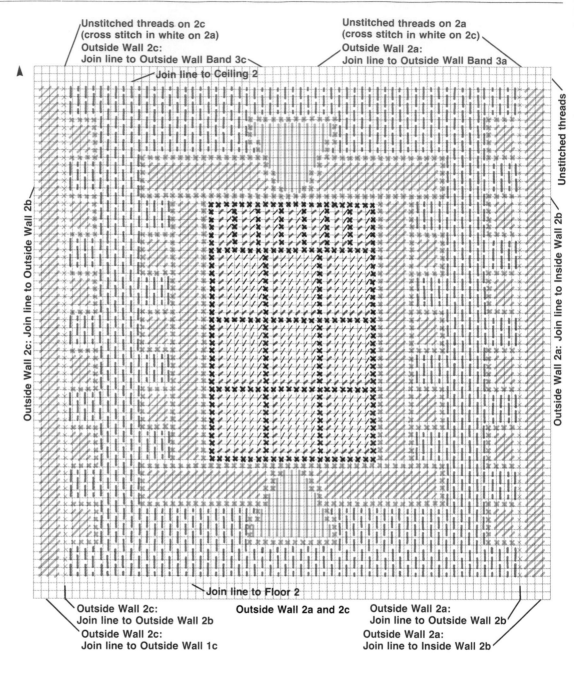

Unstitched threads on 2c
(cross stitch in white on 2a)
Outside Wall 2c:
Join line to Outside Wall Band 3c

Join line to Ceiling 2

Unstitched threads on 2a
(cross stitch in white on 2c)
Outside Wall 2a:
Join line to Outside Wall Band 3a

Unstitched threads

Outside Wall 2c: Join line to Outside Wall 2b

Outside Wall 2a: Join line to Inside Wall 2b

Join line to Floor 2

Outside Wall 2c:
Join line to Outside Wall 2b

Outside Wall 2c:
Join line to Outside Wall 1c

Outside Wall 2a and 2c

Outside Wall 2a:
Join line to Outside Wall 2b

Outside Wall 2a:
Join line to Inside Wall 2b

Color

/ White

❙ Grey Heather

✖ Flame

/ Lt. Powder Blue

/ Lt. Blue

stitch and satin stitch. Work the window frames in cross stitch, using Flame yarn. Work the windowpanes in tent stitch. Put in the shadows first, using Light Powder Blue yarn; then work the rest of each pane in Light Blue yarn. Work the background in brick stitch, using Grey Heather yarn. (The unstitched plastic threads will be used in the assembly.)

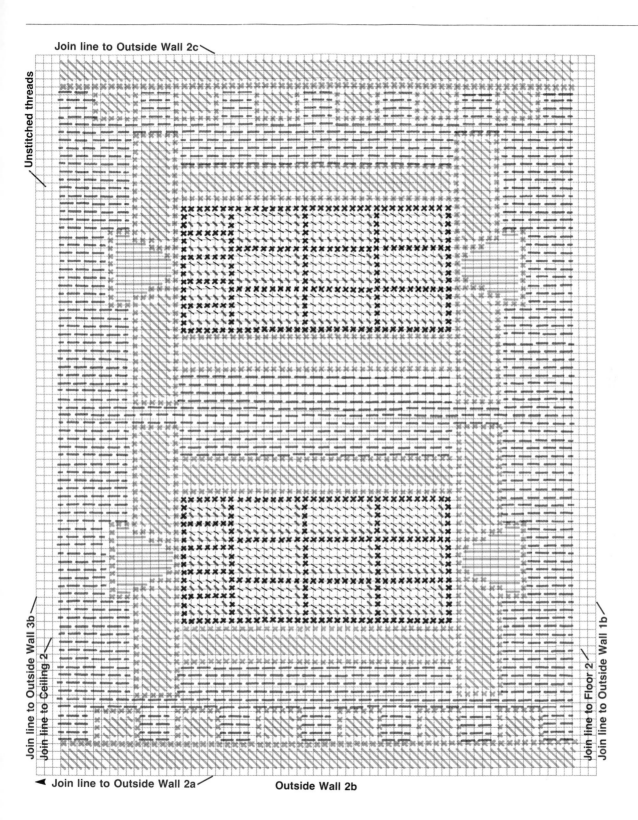

Join line to Outside Wall 2c

Unstitched threads

Join line to Outside Wall 3b

Join line to Ceiling 2

◄ Join line to Outside Wall 2a

Outside Wall 2b

Join line to Floor 2

Join line to Outside Wall 1b

163

Color

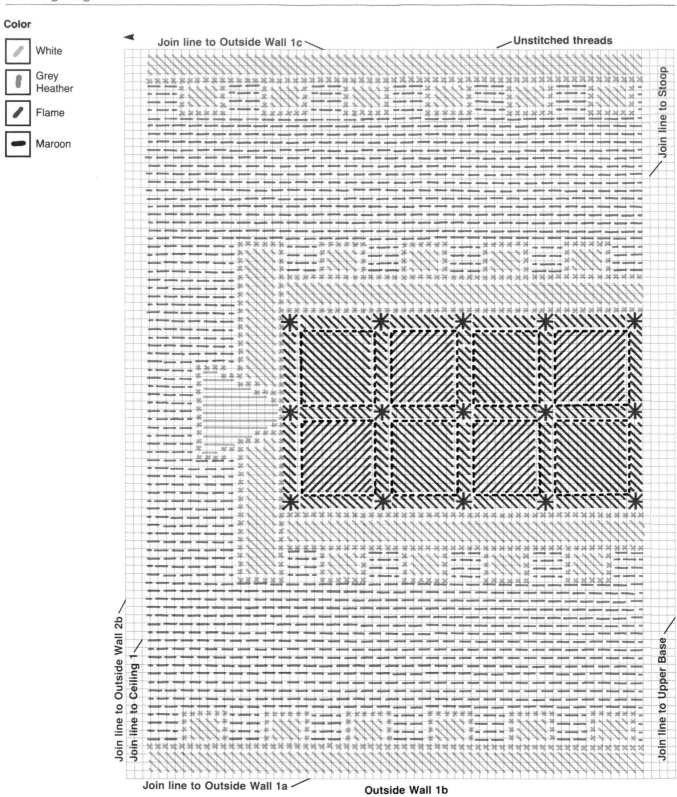

6. Stitch the brick corners on outside wall 1b, using White yarn. Following the diagram carefully, put in the outlines first in cross stitch; then add the centers in slanted gobelin stitch. Work the brick frame around the door next, using White yarn. Put in the

outlines first in cross stitch; then add the centers in slanted gobelin stitch and satin stitch. Work the narrow horizontal and vertical bands of the door frame in slanted gobelin stitch, using Flame yarn. Work the corners between these bands in double

Color

▯	Denim Blue Heather
▬	Dk. Grey Heather

Roof 1

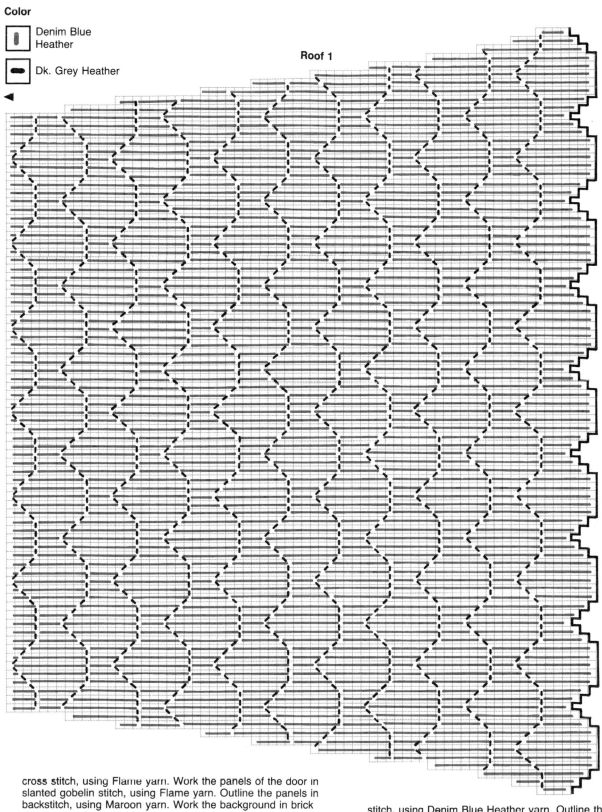

cross stitch, using Flame yarn. Work the panels of the door in slanted gobelin stitch, using Flame yarn. Outline the panels in backstitch, using Maroon yarn. Work the background in brick stitch, using Grey Heather yarn.

7. Work the shingles on the three roof 1 and 2 pieces in satin stitch, using Denim Blue Heather yarn. Outline the shingles in backstitch, using Dark Grey Heather yarn. Overcast the edges in whip stitch, as diagramed, using Dark Grey Heather yarn.

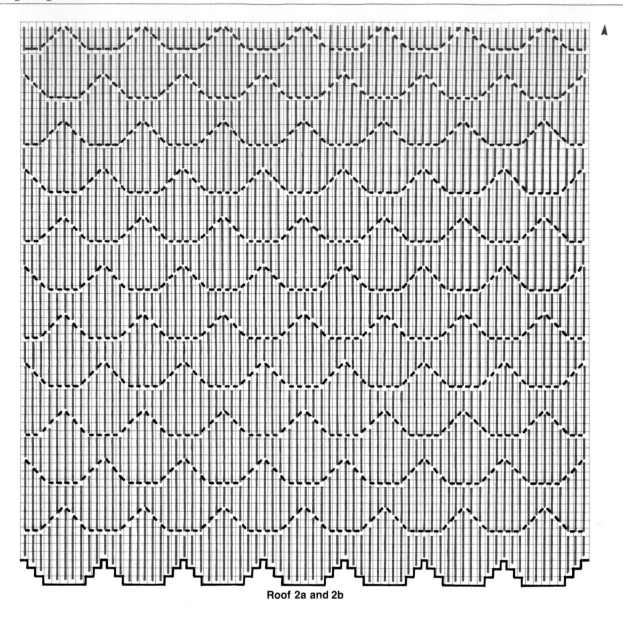

Roof 2a and 2b

Color

Denim Blue
Heather

Dk. Grey Heather

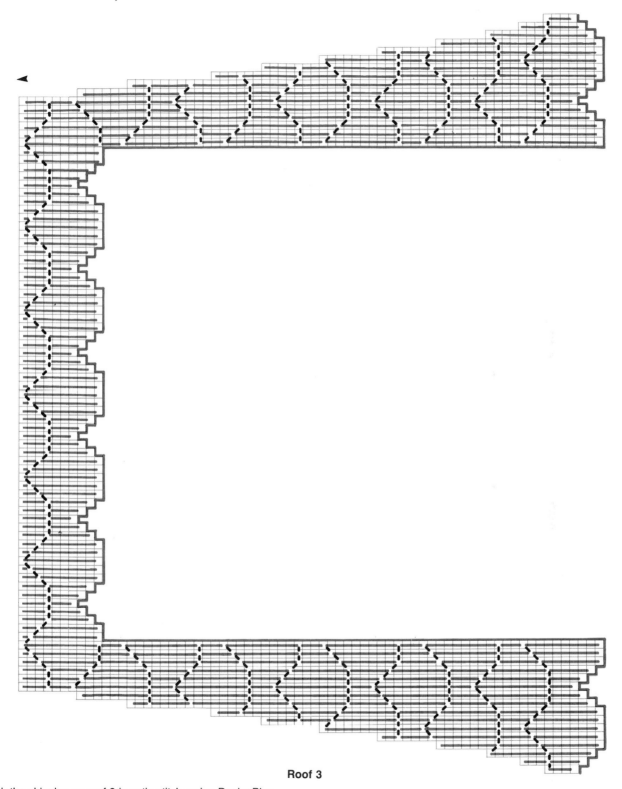

Roof 3

8. Work the shingles on roof 3 in satin stitch, using Denim Blue Heather yarn. Outline the shingles in backstitch, using Dark Grey Heather yarn. Overcast the edges in whip stitch, as diagramed, using Dark Grey Heather yarn along the scalloped edges and Denim Blue Heather yarn along the straight edges.

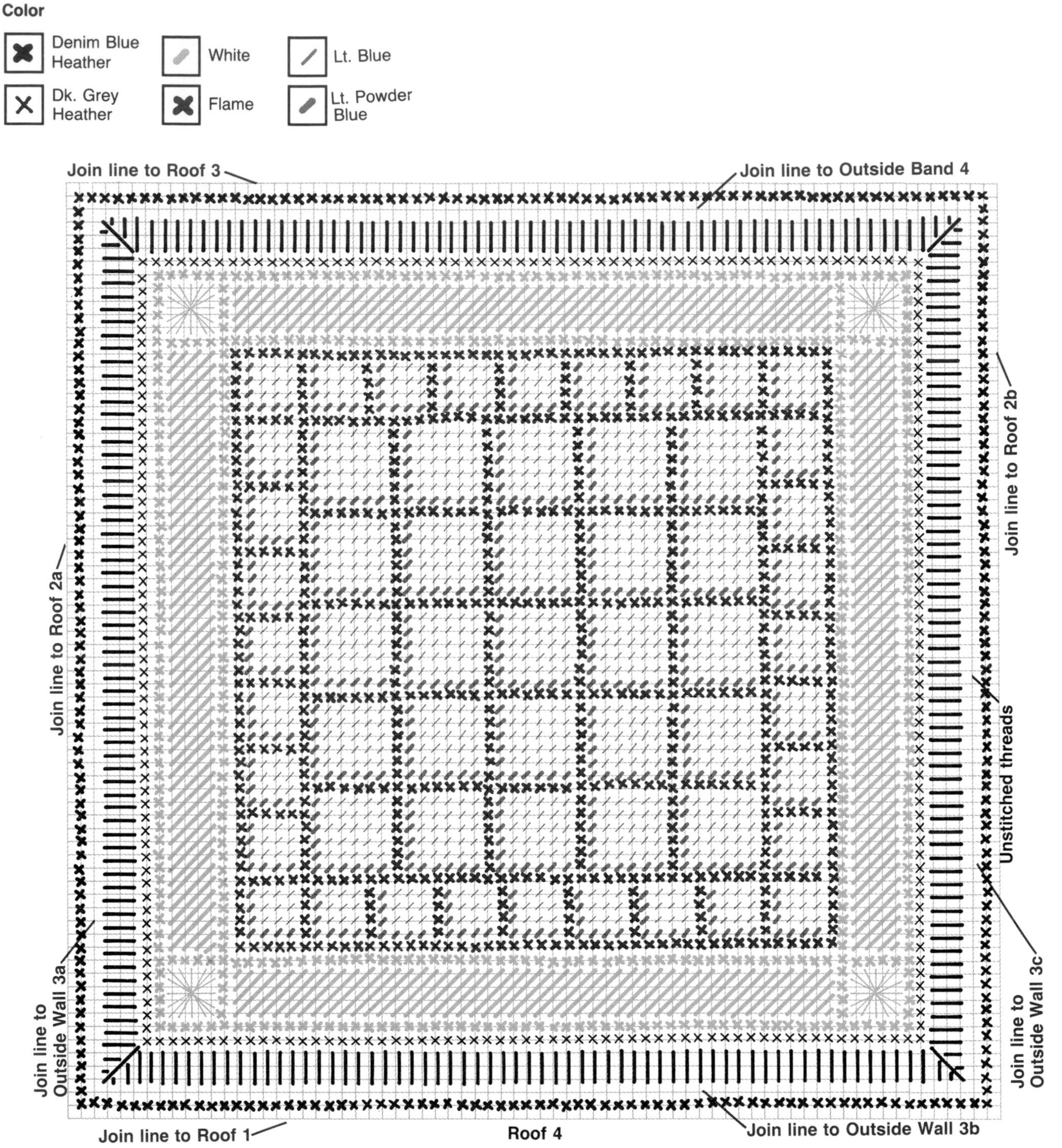

Color

✖ Denim Blue Heather	⬮ White	╱ Lt. Blue
✕ Dk. Grey Heather	✖ Flame	⬮ Lt. Powder Blue

Join line to Roof 3

Join line to Outside Band 4

Join line to Roof 2a

Join line to Roof 2b

Join line to Outside Wall 3a

Unstitched threads

Join line to Roof 1

Roof 4

Join line to Outside Wall 3b

Join line to Outside Wall 3c

9. Work the outline edge of roof 4 in cross stitch, using Denim Blue Heather yarn. Work the border of shingles in gobelin stitch, using Denim Blue Heather yarn. Put in the shadow in the center of this border in cross stitch, using Dark Grey Heather yarn. Work the wood frame around the skylight in White yarn. Put in the outlines first in cross stitch; then add the corners in double leviathan stitch and the horizontal and vertical bands in slanted gobelin stitch. Outline the windowpanes in cross stitch, using Flame yarn. Work the windowpanes in tent stitch. Put in the shadows first, using Light Powder Blue yarn; then work the rest of each pane in Light Blue yarn. (The unstitched plastic threads will be used in the assembly.)

10. Work the nine outside band pieces in slanted gobelin stitch, using White yarn.

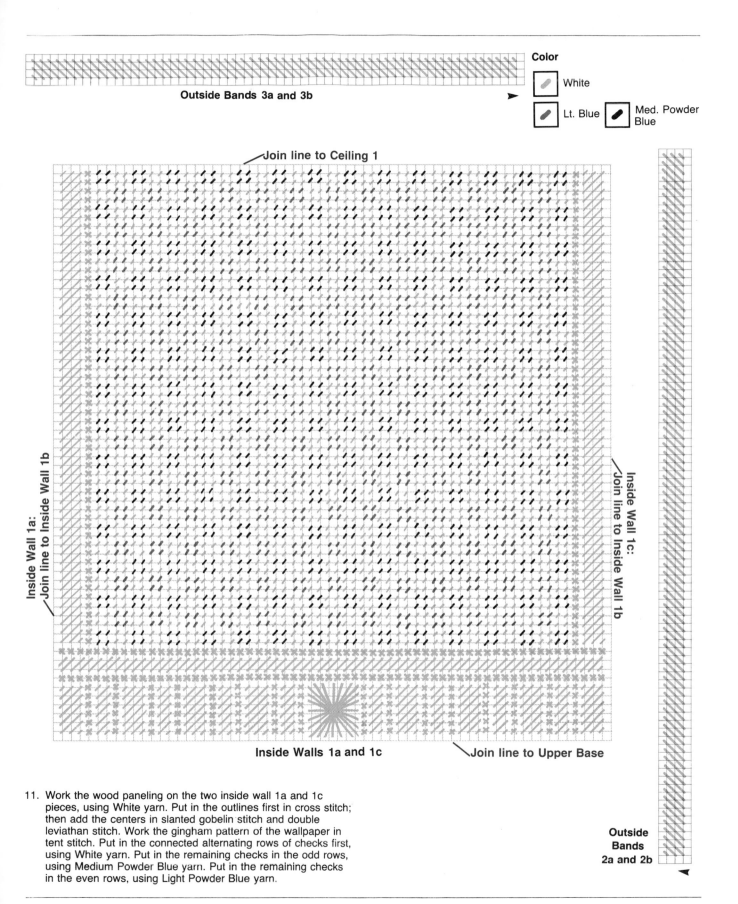

Outside Bands 3a and 3b ▶

Color

	White
	Lt. Blue
	Med. Powder Blue

Join line to Ceiling 1

Inside Wall 1a:
Join line to Inside Wall 1b

Inside Wall 1c:
Join line to Inside Wall 1b

Inside Walls 1a and 1c

Join line to Upper Base

Outside Bands 2a and 2b ◀

11. Work the wood paneling on the two inside wall 1a and 1c pieces, using White yarn. Put in the outlines first in cross stitch; then add the centers in slanted gobelin stitch and double leviathan stitch. Work the gingham pattern of the wallpaper in tent stitch. Put in the connected alternating rows of checks first, using White yarn. Put in the remaining checks in the odd rows, using Medium Powder Blue yarn. Put in the remaining checks in the even rows, using Light Powder Blue yarn.

Color

White	
Lt. Blue	
Lt. Powder Blue	
Med. Powder Blue	
Dk. Powder Blue	

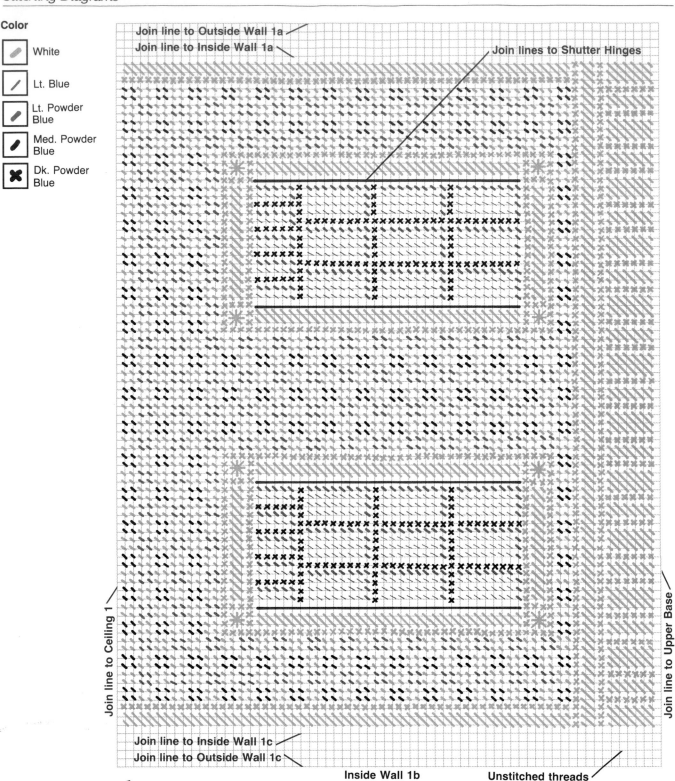

Join line to Outside Wall 1a

Join line to Inside Wall 1a

Join lines to Shutter Hinges

Join line to Ceiling 1

Join line to Upper Base

Join line to Inside Wall 1c

Join line to Outside Wall 1c

Inside Wall 1b

Unstitched threads

12. Work the wood paneling on inside wall 1b, using White yarn. Put in the outlines first in cross stitch. Then add the centers in slanted gobelin stitch. Work the wood frames outlining the windows in White yarn. Put in the outlines first in cross stitch.

Then add the corners in double cross stitch and the horizontal and vertical bands in slanted gobelin stitch. Outline the windowpanes in cross stitch, using Dark Powder Blue yarn. Work the windowpanes in tent stitch. Put in the shadows first,

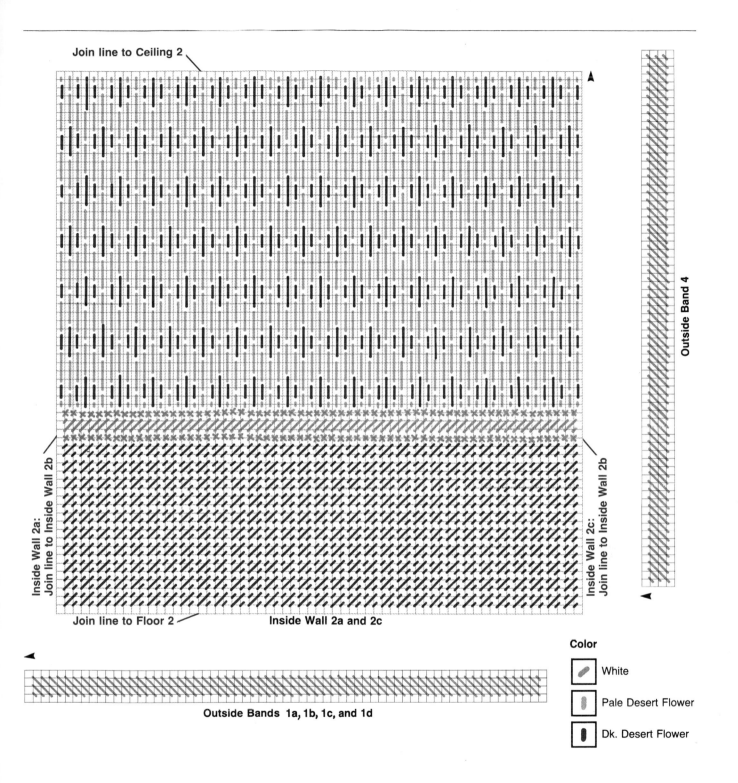

Join line to Ceiling 2

Inside Wall 2a:
Join line to Inside Wall 2b

Inside Wall 2c:
Join line to Inside Wall 2b

Outside Band 4

Join line to Floor 2

Inside Wall 2a and 2c

Outside Bands 1a, 1b, 1c, and 1d

Color

White

Pale Desert Flower

Dk. Desert Flower

using Light Powder Blue yarn. Work the rest of each pane, using Light Blue yarn. Work the gingham pattern of the wallpaper in tent stitch. Put in the connected alternating rows of checks first, using White yarn. Put in the remaining checks in the odd rows, using Medium Powder Blue yarn. Put in the remaining checks in the even rows, using Light Powder Blue yarn. (The unstitched plastic threads will be used in the assembly.)

13. Work the solid color wallpaper on the two inside wall 2a and 2c pieces in mosaic stitch, using Dark Desert Flower yarn. Work the horizontal strip of wood paneling in White yarn. Put in the outlines first In cross stitch; then add the centers in slanted gobelin stitch. To work the patterned wallpaper, put in the zigzag background first in satin stitch, using Pale Desert Flower yarn. Then work the diamond pattern in Hungarian diamond stitch, using Dark Desert Flower yarn.

Color

White	
Pale Desert Flower	
Dk. Desert Flower	
Lt. Blue	
Lt. Powder Blue	
Meadow Green	

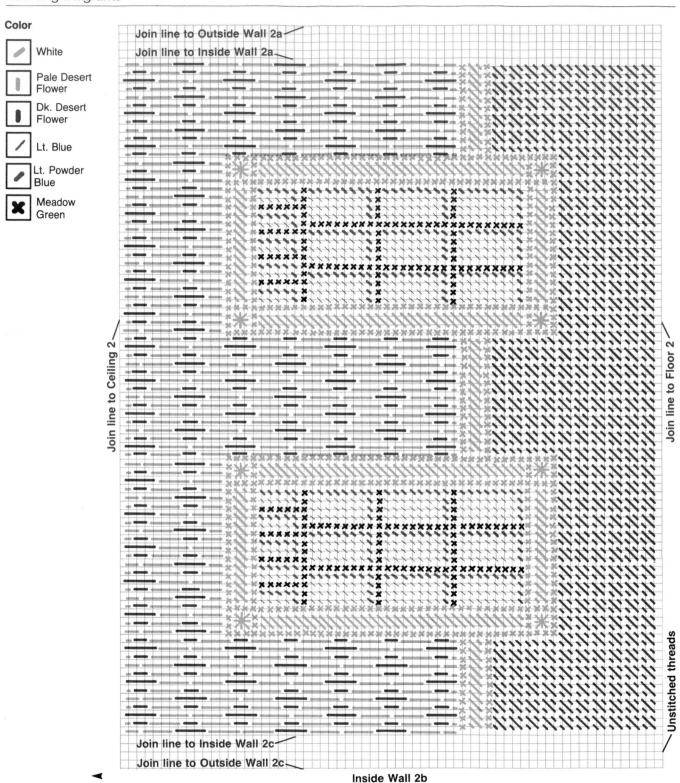

Join line to Outside Wall 2a

Join line to Inside Wall 2a

Join line to Ceiling 2

Join line to Floor 2

Unstitched threads

Join line to Inside Wall 2c

Join line to Outside Wall 2c

Inside Wall 2b

14. Work the solid color wallpaper on inside wall 2b in mosaic stitch, using Dark Desert Flower yarn. Work the frames outlining the windows in White yarn. Put in the outlines first in cross stitch. Then add the corners in double cross stitch and the horizontal and vertical bands in slanted gobelin stitch. Outline the windowpanes in cross stitch, using Meadow Green yarn. Work the windowpanes in tent stitch. Put in the shadows first, using Light Powder Blue yarn. Work the rest of each pane, using Light Blue yarn. Work the horizontal strip of wood paneling in White yarn. Put in the outlines first in cross stitch;

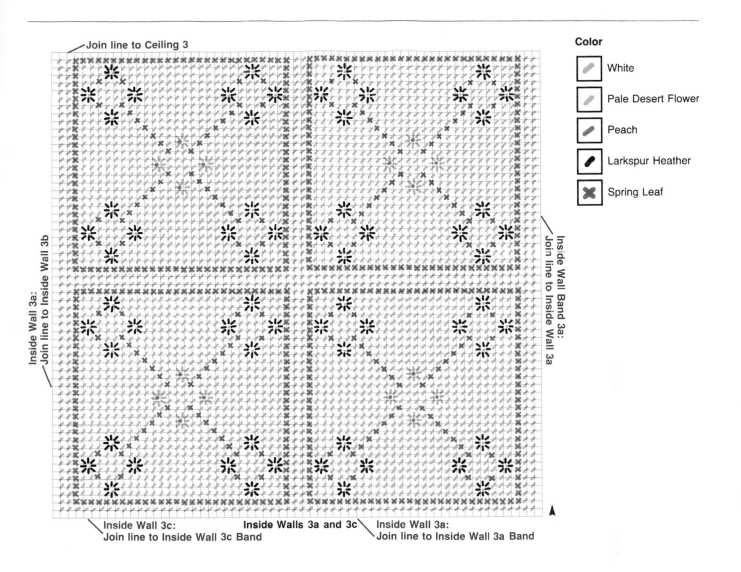

Join line to Ceiling 3

Color

White

Pale Desert Flower

Peach

Larkspur Heather

Spring Leaf

Inside Wall 3a:
Join line to Inside Wall 3b

Inside Wall Band 3a:
Join line to Inside Wall 3a

Inside Wall 3c:
Join line to Inside Wall 3c Band

Inside Walls 3a and 3c

Inside Wall 3a:
Join line to Inside Wall 3a Band

Inside Wall 3a and 3c Band

then add the centers in slanted gobelin stitch. To work the patterned wallpaper, put in the zigzag background first in satin stitch, using Pale Desert Flower yarn. Then work the diamond pattern in Hungarian diamond stitch, using Dark Desert Flower yarn. (The unstitched plastic threads will be used in the assembly.)

15. Work the two inside wall 3a and 3c pieces by outlining the four square wallpaper panels first in cross stitch, using Pale Desert Flower yarn. Then work the three vertical bands and two horizontal bands between the square panels in tent stitch, using Peach yarn. Working one square panel at a time, put in the four diamond-shaped groups of four flowers at the top and bottom of each panel in Algerian eye stitch, using Larkspur Heather yarn.

Work a French knot in the center of each of the sixteen flowers, using Peach yarn. Put in the center diamond-shaped group of four flowers, using Algerian eye stitch and Peach yarn. Work a French knot in the center of each of the four flowers, using Pale Desert Flower yarn. Connect the four flowers in each of the five diamonds by working a single cross stitch between each flower, using Spring Leaf yarn. Work the four diagonal lines connecting the outside groups of flowers to the center group of flowers in cross stitch, using Spring Leaf yarn. Now work the background of each panel in tent stitch, using White yarn.

16. Work the two inside wall 3a and 3c band pieces in slanted gobelin stitch, using White yarn.

173

Color ▭ White ▭ Pale Desert Flower ▭ Peach ▭ Larkspur Heather ✖ Spring Leaf

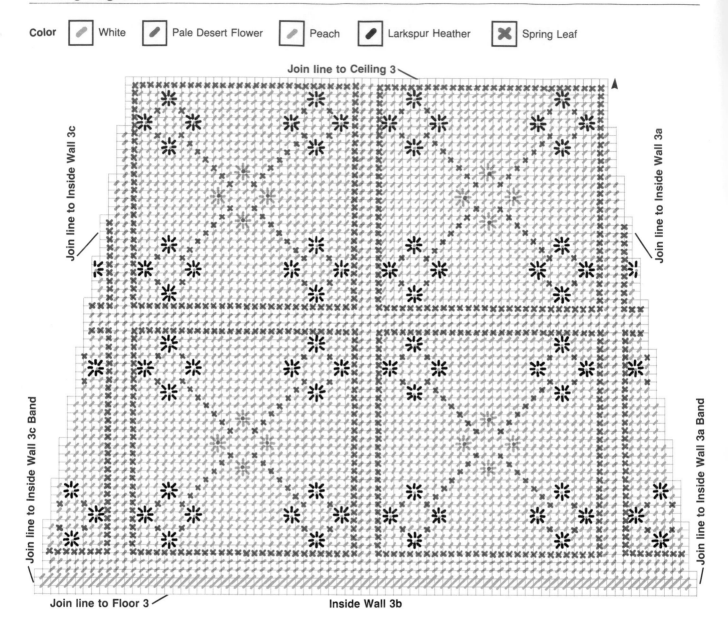

Join line to Ceiling 3

Join line to Inside Wall 3c

Join line to Inside Wall 3a

Join line to Inside Wall 3c Band

Join line to Inside Wall 3a Band

Join line to Floor 3

Inside Wall 3b

17. Work inside wall 3b by putting in the horizontal band of wood paneling at the bottom first in slanted gobelin stitch, using White yarn. Then outline the four square wallpaper panels in the center and the four partial wallpaper panels on the side edges in cross stitch, using Pale Desert Flower yarn. Next work the three vertical bands and two horizontal bands between the square panels and the partial panels in tent stitch, using Peach yarn. Working one square panel at a time, put in the four diamond-shaped groups of four flowers at the top and bottom of each panel in Algerian eye stitch, using Larkspur Heather yarn. Work a French knot in the center of each of the sixteen flowers, using Peach yarn. Put in the center diamond-shaped group of four flowers, using the Algerian eye stitch and Peach yarn. Work a French knot in the center of each of the four flowers, using Pale Desert Flower yarn. Connect the four flowers in each of the five diamonds by working a single cross stitch between each flower in Spring Leaf yarn. Work the four diagonal lines connecting the outside groups of flowers to the

center group of flowers in cross stitch, using Spring Leaf yarn. Now work the background of each panel in tent stitch, using White yarn. Work the two half flowers in the top two partial wallpaper panels in Algerian eye stitch, using Larkspur Heather yarn. Work a French knot in the center of each partial flower, using Peach yarn. Complete the background of these two partial panels by working tent stitch in White yarn. Work the four flowers in each of the bottom two partial wallpaper panels in Algerian eye stitch, using Larkspur Heather yarn. Work a French knot in the center of each flower, using Peach yarn. Work the two cross stitches adjacent to the top flower and the four cross stitches adjacent to the bottom flowers in Spring Leaf yarn. Complete the background of each of these partial panels by working tent stitch in White yarn.

18. Work the floor 2 piece in satin stitch. Put in the connected center zigzag first, using Meadow Green yarn. Working outward from this center, put in the remaining disconnected zigzags, using Meadow Green yarn. Working one yarn color at a time,

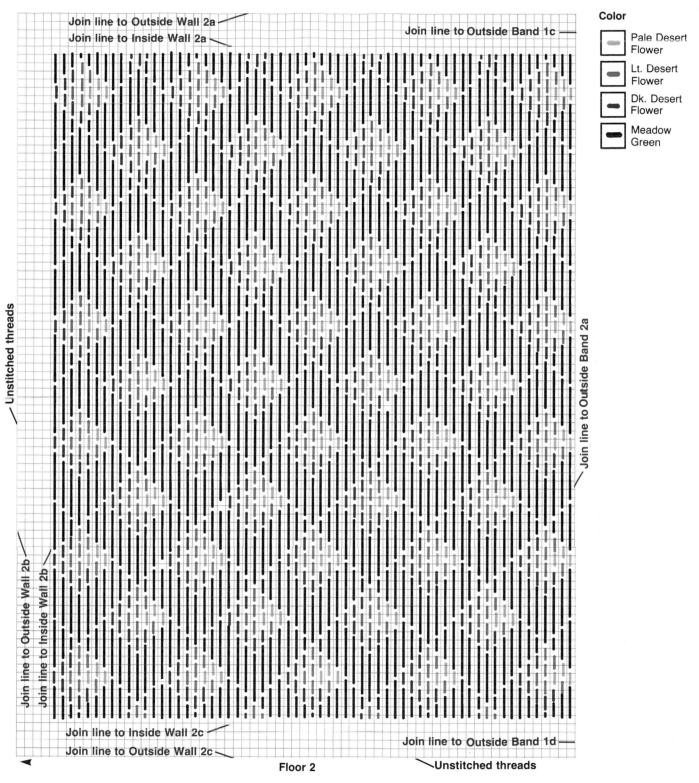

Join line to Outside Wall 2a
Join line to Inside Wall 2a
Join line to Outside Band 1c

Unstitched threads

Join line to Outside Band 2a

Join line to Outside Wall 2b
Join line to Inside Wall 2b

Join line to Inside Wall 2c
Join line to Outside Wall 2c

Join line to Outside Band 1d

Unstitched threads

Floor 2

Color

Pale Desert Flower

Lt. Desert Flower

Dk. Desert Flower

Meadow Green

complete the diamonds between the zigzags. Work seven stitches at the top and left side of each diamond in Dark Desert Flower. Work six stitches in the center and right edge of each diamond, using Light Desert Flower. Work the remaining three stitches in the center and bottom of each diamond, using Pale

Desert Flower. Work the three stitches in the partial diamonds on the right edge in Dark Desert Flower. Work the top stitch in the partial diamonds on the left edge in Dark Desert Flower. Work the bottom two stitches in Light Desert Flower. (The unstitched plastic threads will be used in the assembly.)

Color

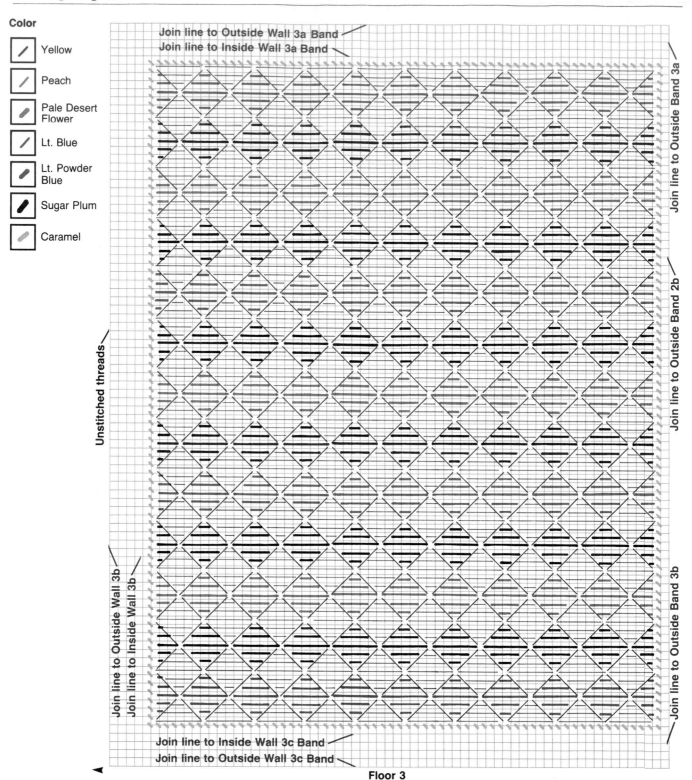	Yellow
	Peach
	Pale Desert Flower
	Lt. Blue
	Lt. Powder Blue
	Sugar Plum
	Caramel

Join line to Outside Wall 3a Band

Join line to Inside Wall 3a Band

Join line to Outside Band 3a

Join line to Outside Band 2b

Join line to Outside Band 3b

Unstitched threads

Join line to Outside Wall 3b

Join line to Inside Wall 3b

Join line to Inside Wall 3c Band

Join line to Outside Wall 3c Band

Floor 3

19. Work the outline edge of the floor 3 piece in tent stitch, using Caramel yarn. Work the columns of diamonds in the center, using Hungarian diamond stitch and five yarn colors. Work the first column of half diamonds on the right edge, using Light Blue yarn. Work the second column of full diamonds, using Light Powder Blue yarn; the third column, using Light Blue yarn; the fourth column, using Sugar Plum yarn; the fifth column, using Peach yarn; the sixth column, using Pale Desert Flower yarn; the seventh column, using Peach yarn; and the eighth column, using Sugar Plum yarn. Starting with Light Blue yarn again,

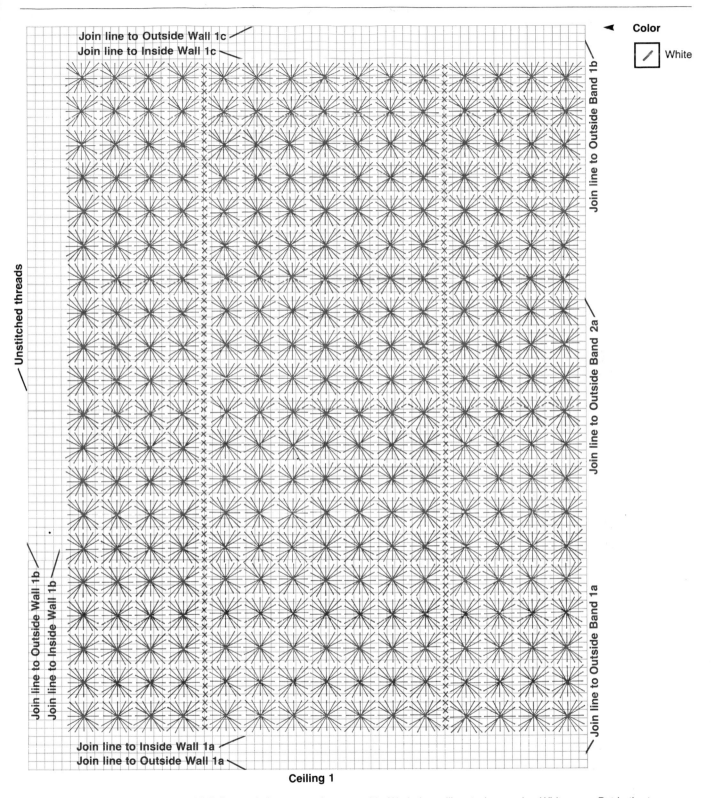

Join line to Outside Wall 1c
Join line to Inside Wall 1c

Unstitched threads

Join line to Outside Band 1b

Join line to Outside Band 2a

Join line to Outside Wall 1b
Join line to Inside Wall 1b

Join line to Outside Band 1a

Join line to Inside Wall 1a
Join line to Outside Wall 1a

Ceiling 1

continue working the columns of full diamonds in consecutive order, repeating this eight-color sequence, ending on the left edge with a column of half diamonds worked in Light Blue yarn. Complete the piece by outlining the diamonds in backstitch, using Yellow yarn.

20. Work the ceiling 1 piece, using White yarn. Put in the two rows of cross stitch first, then the fifteen rows of double leviathan stitch. (The unstitched plastic threads will be used in the assembly.)

Color

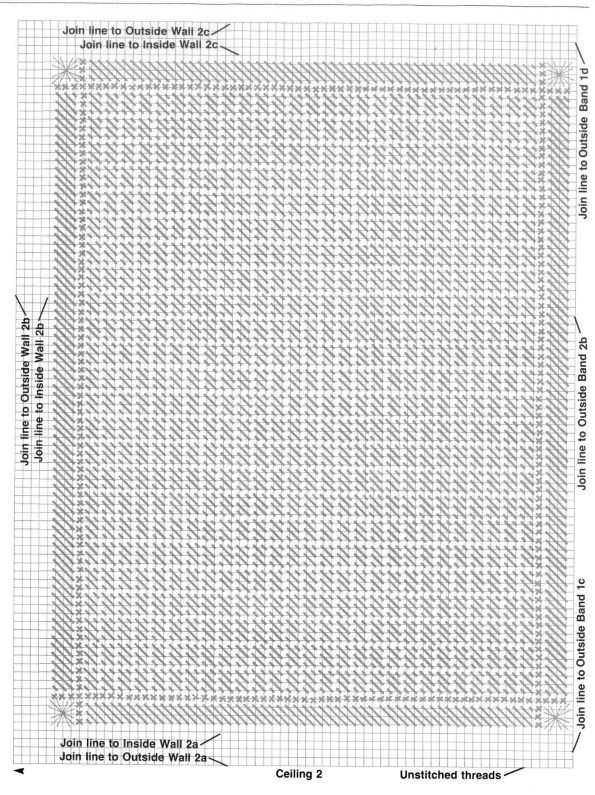

White

Join line to Outside Wall 2c

Join line to Inside Wall 2c

Join line to Outside Band 1d

Join line to Outside Wall 2b

Join line to Inside Wall 2b

Join line to Outside Band 2b

Join line to Outside Band 1c

Join line to Inside Wall 2a

Join line to Outside Wall 2a

Ceiling 2

Unstitched threads

21. Work the ceiling 2 piece, using White yarn. Work the border first, outlining the edges in cross stitch. Then work the corners in Rhodes stitch and the horizontal and vertical bands in slanted gobelin stitch. Complete by working the center in cashmere stitch. (The unstitched plastic threads will be used in the assembly.)

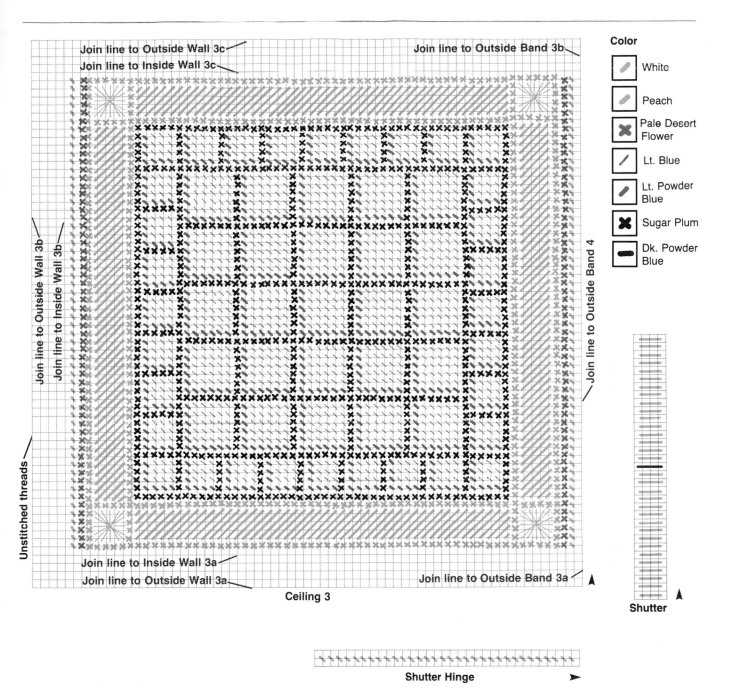

Color

⬱	White
⬱	Peach
✖	Pale Desert Flower
╱	Lt. Blue
⬱	Lt. Powder Blue
✖	Sugar Plum
▬	Dk. Powder Blue

Join line to Outside Wall 3c

Join line to Inside Wall 3c

Join line to Outside Band 3b

Join line to Outside Wall 3b

Join line to Inside Wall 3b

Unstitched threads

Join line to Outside Band 4

Join line to Inside Wall 3a

Join line to Outside Wall 3a

Join line to Outside Band 3a

Ceiling 3

Shutter

Shutter Hinge ➤

22. Start the ceiling 3 piece by working the wood frame around the skylight in White yarn. Put in the outlines first in cross stitch; then add the corners in double leviathan stitch and the horizontal and vertical bands in slanted gobelin stitch. Outline the windowpanes in cross stitch, using Sugar Plum yarn. Work the windowpanes in tent stitch. Put in the shadows first, using Light Powder Blue yarn. Then work the rest of each pane in Light Blue yarn. Work one row of cross stitch above and below the wood frame, using Pale Desert Flower yarn. Work one row of tent stitch above and below these two rows of cross stitch, using Peach yarn. (The unstitched plastic threads will be used in the assembly.)

23. Work the eight shutter pieces in gobelin stitch. Working one piece at a time, put in all the stitches but the center stitch, using White yarn; then add the center stitch, using Dark Powder Blue yarn.

24. Work the four shutter hinge pieces in tent stitch, using White yarn.

Assembly

The dollhouse is constructed of three stacked rooms resting on a base. A raised stoop surrounding the first floor rests on top of the base. Each room has both inside and outside walls, a floor, and a ceiling. The roof hides the outside walls of the top room.

The outside wall and band pieces form the outside of the dollhouse. The inside wall and band pieces and the floor and ceiling pieces form the inside. The pieces that make each room, both inside and outside, are divided by floors. Pieces labeled **1** make the first floor; those labeled **2** make the second floor; and pieces labeled **3** make the third floor. The walls labeled **b** are center walls. The walls and bands labeled **a** and **c**, except for the base bands and outside bands, are side walls and bands.

Seams separate the base pieces, the inside and outside walls of each room, and the ceilings and floors between each room. These seams are padded with pieces of foam core for extra support and are sealed with a band. The two base pieces are separated by foundation braces, which support the walls assembled vertically above them. Wire is encased at the outside joins of the base pieces, the outside walls to each other, and the outside bands to the outside walls and the inside walls for additional support.

The dollhouse is assembled floor by floor, starting at the base. Both the inside and outside walls for each floor are joined concurrently. When assembling each floor, refer to the stitch diagram charts for each canvas piece. The interior horizontal and vertical plastic threads and the edge plastic threads used for joining are marked on these diagrams. For pieces that are not stitched, refer to their cutout diagrams for the join lines.

The dollhouse will take many hours to assemble. Work slowly and follow the directions carefully. Work cross stitch joins using one strand of Brunswick Windrush yarn. Work blind cross stitch joins using one strand of Bernat 1–2–3 Ply yarn. Work all other joins in tent stitch or gobelin stitch, as desired, using two strands of Windrush yarn. Work cross stitch and blind cross stitch joins in rows.

The foam-core supports between the walls and floors should fit snugly. If extra padding is required, cut a piece of plastic bubble paper the same size as the foam-core piece. Tape the bubble paper to the foam core along the edges.

Note: Outside walls of third floor are not stitched and are hidden under roof.

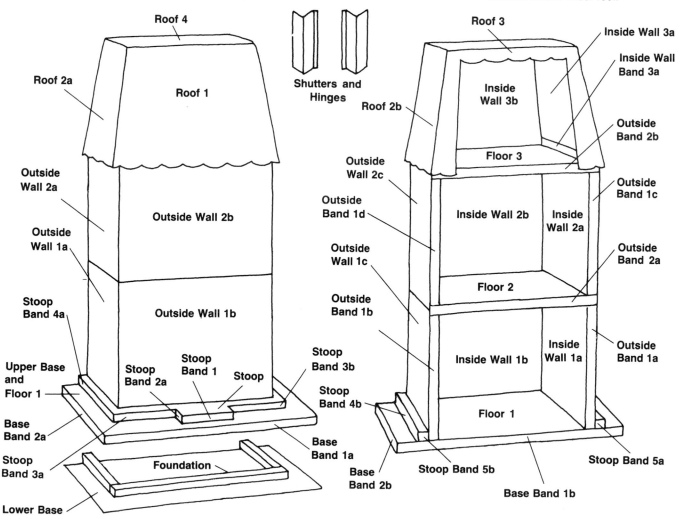

Shutters

1. Working two pieces at a time, place two shutters right side up side by side, matching two of their long edges. Flush join these edges, using White yarn.

2. Place two of the joined shutter panels right side up. Place a shutter hinge right side up along the right edge of each panel, matching their long edges. Flush join these edges, using White yarn.

   Place the remaining two joined shutter panels right side up. Place a shutter hinge right side up along the left edge of each panel, matching their long edges. Flush join these edges, using White yarn.

3. Place inside wall 1b right side up. Working one window at a time, place two shutter panels right side up on the right and the left of each window. Match the long edges of the shutter hinges to the unstitched vertical plastic threads along the inside frame of each window. Flush join the shutter hinges and these unstitched threads, using White yarn.

Overcast the outside plastic threads along the edges of each shutter panel, using White yarn. Adjust each of the shutter panels so the center joins are outward.

Base, Stoop, Foundation, and First Floor

1. Place the upper base piece right side up. Place the bottom edges of the nine stoop band pieces wrong sides up along the interior horizontal and vertical threads marked on the stitch diagram of the upper base. Flush join these matched edges and threads, using White yarn.

2. With wrong sides up, place the bottom edges of outside walls 1a and 1c against the right side of the upper base, along the vertical plastic threads marked on the stitch diagram of the upper base. Directly below these threads, on the wrong side of the upper base, match a long edge of each of the foundation 2 pieces. Working one wall

and foundation piece at a time, flush join these two matched edges and interior threads, using White yarn.

Place the bottom edge of outside wall 1b wrong side up against the right side of the upper base, along the horizontal plastic thread marked on the stitch diagram of the upper base. Directly below this thread, on the wrong side of the upper base, match a long edge of one foundation 1 piece. Flush join these two matched edges and interior thread, using White yarn.

3. Place the center inside edge of the stoop band right side up against the right side of outside wall 1b. The stoop center edge is two holes wider than outside wall 1b. Center the stoop so one hole extends beyond the wall on the right and the left. Match the stoop inside edge to the horizontal plastic thread marked on the stitch diagram of outside wall 1b. Flush join this matched edge and thread, using White yarn.

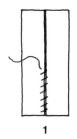 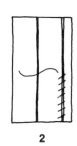 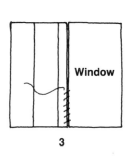

Window

1   2   3

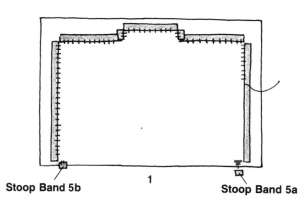

Stoop Band 5b   1   Stoop Band 5a

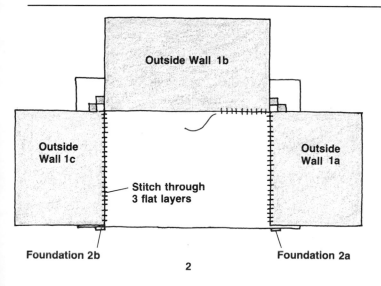

Outside Wall 1b

Outside Wall 1c   **Outside Wall 1a**

— Stitch through 3 flat layers

Foundation 2b   Foundation 2a

2

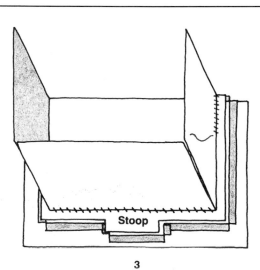

Stoop

3

Match the inside edge of the stoop adjacent to outside wall 1a to the horizontal plastic thread indicated on the stitch diagram of outside wall 1a. The stoop edge is one hole shorter than the wall. Starting at the left edge of the wall and working to the right edge, flush join the matched stoop edge and horizontal interior thread, using White yarn.

Match the inside edge of the stoop adjacent to outside wall 1c to the horizontal plastic thread indicated on the stitch diagram of outside wall 1c. The stoop edge is one hole shorter than the wall. Starting at the right edge of the wall and working to the left edge, flush join the matched stooped edge and horizontal interior thread, using White yarn.

4. With right sides facing each other, place the bottom edges of inside walls 1a and 1c against the right side of the upper base, along the vertical plastic threads marked on the stitch diagram of the upper base. Directly below these threads, on the wrong side of the upper base, match a long edge of each of the foundation 3 pieces. Working one wall and foundation piece at a time, flush join these two matched edges and interior threads, using White yarn.

With right side up, place the bottom edge of inside wall 1b against the right side of the upper base, along the horizontal plastic thread marked on the stitch diagram of the upper base. Directly below this thread, on the wrong side of the upper base, match a long edge of one foundation 1 piece. Flush join these two matched edges and interior thread, using White yarn.

5. Place the bottom edge of the outside band 1a piece wrong side up on the right side of the upper base, between outside wall 1a and inside wall 1a, along the horizontal plastic thread marked on the stitch diagram of the upper base. Flush join the edge and thread, using White yarn.

Place the bottom edge of the outside band 1b piece wrong side up on the right side of the upper base, between outside wall 1c and inside wall 1c, along the horizontal plastic thread marked on the stitch diagram of the upper base. Flush join the edge and thread, using White yarn.

6. Turn the upper base wrong side up. Flush join the edges of the two foundation 2 pieces and the outer foundation 1 piece. Flush join the edges of the two foundation 3 pieces to the adjacent threads of the inner foundation 1 piece. Flush join the edges of the inner foundation 1 piece to the adjacent threads of the foundation 2 pieces. Work all of these joins using White yarn.

7. Place the lower base piece on top of the joined foundation pieces on the

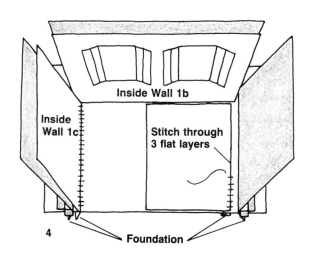

Inside Wall 1b

Inside Wall 1c

Stitch through 3 flat layers

4 — Foundation

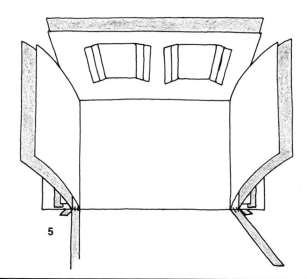

5

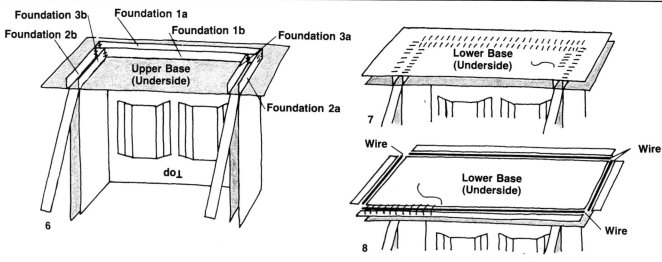

Foundation 3b
Foundation 1a
Foundation 2b
Foundation 1b
Foundation 3a

Upper Base (Underside)

Foundation 2a

Top

6

Lower Base (Underside)

7

Wire

Wire

Lower Base (Underside)

Wire

8

wrong side of the upper base. Match the long edges of the six foundation pieces to the horizontal and vertical threads marked on the stitch diagram of the lower base. Flush join these matched edges and threads, using Dark Grey Heather yarn.

8. Using the gray magic marker, stain the white thread on the outside of the 18-inch and the 12¼-inch pieces of florist's wire.

   With right sides out, place a long edge of each of the two base band 1 pieces against a long edge of the lower base. Lay a piece of 18-inch florist's wire along each of these matched edges. Flush join the two sets of matched edges, encasing the wire, using Dark Grey Heather yarn.

   With right sides out, place the long edges of each of the two base band 2 pieces against a short edge of the lower base. Lay a 12¼-inch piece of florist's

wire along each of these matched edges. Flush join the two sets of matched edges, encasing the wire, using Dark Grey Heather yarn.

   Glue the gray felt to the lower base piece. When dry, turn the piece so the upper base is right side up.

9. Match the edges of inside walls 1a and 1c adjacent to inside wall 1b to the vertical inside plastic threads marked on the stitch diagram of inside wall 1b. Flush join these matched edges and threads, using White yarn.

10. Match the edges of inside wall 1b adjacent to outside walls 1a and 1c to the inside vertical plastic threads marked on the stitch diagrams of outside walls 1a and 1c. Flush join these matched edges and threads in cross stitch, using White yarn. Start these joins at the upper base, below the stoop joins.

11. With wrong side up, place the ceiling 1

piece over the top edges of inside walls 1a, 1b, and 1c. Match these edges to the interior horizontal and vertical plastic threads marked on the stitch diagram of ceiling 1. Flush join these matched edges and threads, using White yarn.

12. Place a 13½-inch-wide × 9¾-inch-high piece of foam core in the seam between inside wall 1b and outside wall 1b.

   Match the edges of ceiling 1 adjacent to outside walls 1a, 1b, and 1c to the interior horizontal plastic threads marked on the stitch diagrams of outside walls 1a, 1b, and 1c. Flush join these matched edges and threads in cross stitch, using White yarn.

13. Beginning at the upper base, below the stoop join, flush join the adjacent edges of outside walls 1a and 1b and outside walls 1c and 1b, using White yarn. Before working each join, place a 21½-

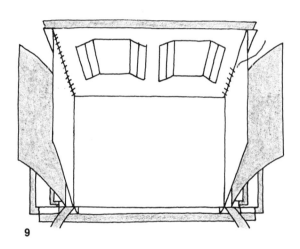

9

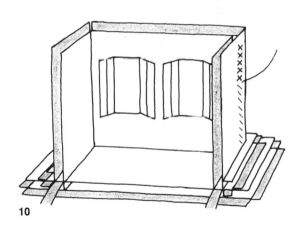

10

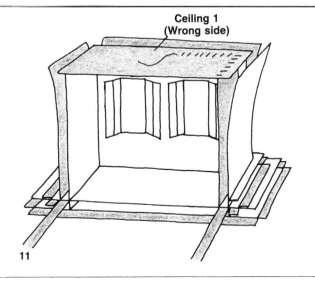

Ceiling 1
(Wrong side)

11

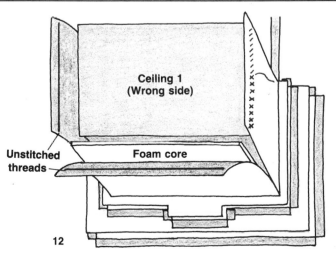

Ceiling 1
(Wrong side)

Foam core

Unstitched
threads

12

inch piece of wire vertically along the outside of the edges to be joined, with one end resting on the upper base. Encase these pieces of wire within the joins along each edge.

14. With right sides out, flush join the edges of the two stoop band 5 pieces adjacent to outside walls 1a and 1c to the vertical interior plastic threads marked on the stitch diagrams of outside walls 1a and 1c. Work these joins using White yarn.

    With right sides out, flush join the adjacent edges of each of the stoop band 1 through 5 pieces, using White yarn.

    Flush join the outside edges of the stoop to the top edges of the stoop band 1 through 5 pieces, using White yarn.

15. Using the mat or craft knife, cut the 17¾-inch-wide × 12-inch-high piece of foam core into a U shape, by cutting a centered 13½-inch-wide × 10½-inch-high rectangle from one long edge.

    Insert this U-shape piece of foam core

between the upper and lower base pieces, on the outside of the foundation pieces. Insert the 12-inch-wide × 9½-inch-high piece of foam core between the upper and lower base pieces, on the inside of the foundation pieces.

Flush join the adjacent edges of each two base band pieces, using Dark Grey Heather yarn.

Flush join the adjacent edges of the upper base and base band pieces, using Dark Grey Heather yarn. Encase an 18-inch piece of florist's wire within the joins along the long edges of the upper base. Encase a 12¼-inch piece of florist's wire within the joins along the short edges of the upper base.

16. Insert a 9½-inch-wide × 9¾-inch-high piece of foam core into the seams between inside wall 1a and outside wall 1a and between inside wall 1c and outside wall 1c.

    With right sides out, join a long edge of the outside band 2a piece to the remaining long edge of ceiling 1, using

White yarn. Before working this join, place a 13½-inch piece of florist's wire horizontally along the outside of the edges to be joined. Encase this piece of wire within the join. While working this join, join the top edge of the two partially attached outside band 1 pieces as well by matching the top edge of each of the outside band 1 pieces to the outside edges of the outside band 2a and ceiling pieces.

17. Flush join the adjacent edges of the outside band 1 and inside wall 1a and 1c pieces, using White yarn. Before working these joins, place a 9¾-inch piece of florist's wire vertically along the outside of the edges to be joined, starting at the upper base. Encase these pieces of wire within the joins.

    Flush join the adjacent edges of the outside band 1 and outside wall 1a and 1c pieces, using White yarn. Before working these joins, place a 21½-inch piece of florist's wire vertically along the outside of the edges to be joined, starting at the upper base. Encase these pieces of wire within the joins.

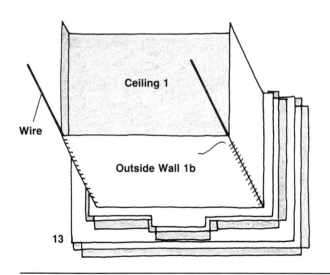

Ceiling 1

Wire

Outside Wall 1b

13

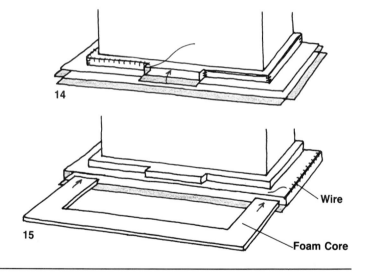

14

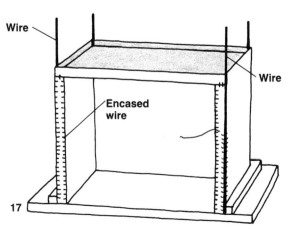

15

Wire

Foam Core

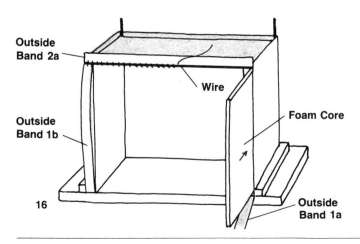

Outside Band 2a

Wire

Outside Band 1b

Foam Core

16

Outside Band 1a

Wire

Wire

Encased wire

17

Second Floor

1. With right side out, place the bottom edge of outside wall 2a against the top edge of outside wall 1a. Flush join, using blind cross stitch. With right side out, place the bottom edge of outside wall 2b against the top edge of outside wall 1b. Flush join, using blind cross stitch. With right side out, place the bottom edge of outside wall 2c against the top edge of outside wall 1c. Flush join, using blind cross stitch.

2. Flush join the adjacent edges of outside walls 2a and 2b and outside walls 2c and 2b, using White yarn. Work each join for four holes only, and continue to encase the 21¼-inch pieces of wire.

3. The top edge of outside wall 1a has one unstitched horizontal plastic thread. The bottom edge of outside wall 2a has two unstitched horizontal plastic threads. Using one strand of White yarn, work slanted gobelin stitch over the joined edges of outside walls 1a and 2a, covering the unstitched plastic thread on outside wall 1a and the bottom unstitched interior plastic thread on outside wall 2a. Work the diagonal of the stitch in the same direction as the diagonal of the slanted gobelin stitches on the right sides of the outside walls. When complete, one plastic horizontal thread should separate the slanted gobelin stitches and the pattern stitches on outside wall 2a.

Overstitch the joined edges of outside walls 1b and 2b and outside walls 1c and 2c in slanted gobelin stitch, as the joined edges of outside walls 1a and 2a were overstitched.

4. With right sides facing each other, place the bottom edges of inside walls 2a and 2c against the right side of the floor 2 piece, along the vertical plastic threads marked on the stitch diagram of floor 2. Flush join these sets of matched threads and edges, using Dark Desert Flower yarn.

With right side up, place the bottom edge of inside wall 2b against the right side of the floor 2 piece, along the horizontal plastic thread marked on the stitch diagram of floor 2. Flush join this matched edge and thread, using Dark Desert Flower yarn.

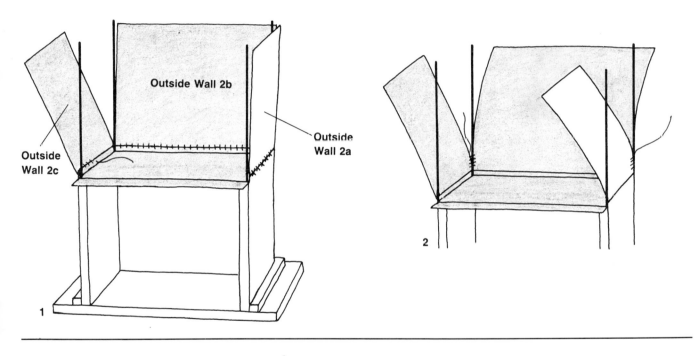

Outside Wall 2b

Outside Wall 2a

Outside Wall 2c

2

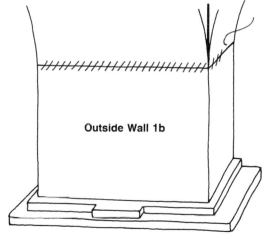

Outside Wall 1b

3

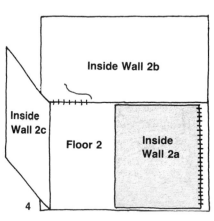

Inside Wall 2b

Inside Wall 2c

Floor 2

Inside Wall 2a

4

5. Place floor 2 right side up above the wrong side of ceiling 1. Match the edges of floor 2 adjacent to outside walls 2a, 2b, and 2c to the interior horizontal plastic threads marked on the stitch diagrams of outside walls 2a, 2b, and 2c. Flush join these matched edges and threads in cross stitch, using White yarn.

6. Match the edges of inside walls 2a and 2c adjacent to inside wall 2b to the interior vertical plastic threads marked on the stitch diagram of inside wall 2b. Flush join these matched edges and threads, matching the color order and placement of the adjacent pattern stitches.

7. Match the edges of inside wall 2b adjacent to outside walls 2a and 2c to the interior vertical plastic threads marked on the stitch diagrams of outside walls 2a and 2c. Flush join these matched edges and threads in cross stitch, using White yarn.

8. With wrong side up, place ceiling 2 over

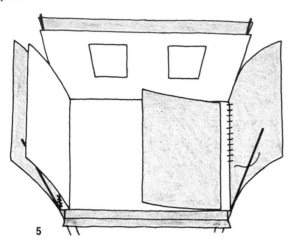

5

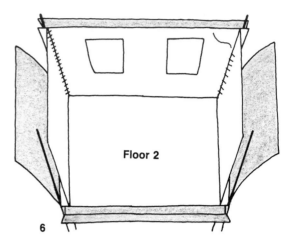

Floor 2

6

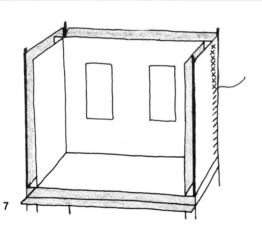

7

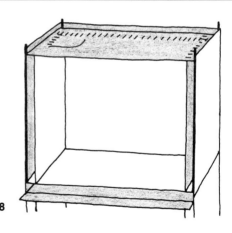

8

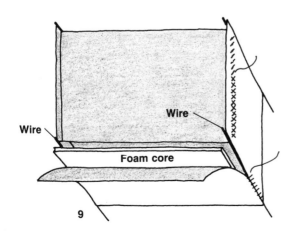

Wire

Wire

Foam core

9

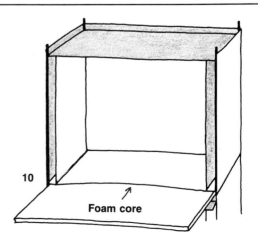

10

Foam core

the top edges of inside walls 2a, 2b, and 2c. Match these edges to the interior horizontal and vertical plastic threads indicated on the stitch diagram of ceiling 2. Flush join these matched edges and threads, using Pale Desert Flower yarn.

9. Place a 13¼-inch-wide × 9¾-inch-high piece of foam core inside the seam between inside wall 2b and outside wall 2b.

Match the edges of ceiling 2 adjacent to outside walls 2a, 2b, and 2c to the interior horizontal plastic threads marked on the stitch diagrams of outside walls 2a, 2b, and 2c. Flush join these matched edges and threads in cross stitch, using White yarn.

Flush join the adjacent edges of outside walls 2a and 2b and outside walls 2c and 2b, using White yarn, continuing to encase the two 21¼-inch pieces of wire.

10. Insert a 13¼-inch-wide × 9¾-inch-high piece of foam core in the seam between ceiling 1 and floor 2.

11. Join the remaining long edge of the partially joined outside band 2a piece to the adjacent edge of floor 2, using White yarn. Before working this join, place a 13½-inch piece of florist's wire horizontally along the outside of the edges to be joined. Encase this piece of wire within the join. While working this join, join the bottom edges of the two outside band 1c and 1d pieces as well by matching the bottom edge of each of the right sides of the outside band 1 pieces to the outside edges of floor 2 and outside band 2a pieces.

12. Insert a 9¼-inch-wide × 9¾-inch-high piece of foam core in the seams between inside wall 2a and outside wall 2a and inside wall 2c and outside wall 2c.

With the right side out, join the long edge of the outside band 2b piece to the remaining long edge of ceiling 2,

using White yarn. Before working this join, place a 13½-inch piece of florist's wire horizontally along the outside of the edges to be joined. Encase this piece of wire within the join. While working the join, join the top edge of the two partially attached outside band 1 pieces as well by matching the top edge of each outside band 1 piece to the outside edges of ceiling 2 and outside band 2b pieces.

13. Flush join the adjacent edges of the outside band 1 and inside wall 2a and 2c pieces, using White yarn. Before working these joins, place a 9¾-inch piece of florist's wire vertically along the outside of the edges to be joined. Encase these pieces of wire within the joins.

Flush join the edges of the two outside band 1 pieces to the adjacent edges of outside walls 2a and 2c, using White yarn and continuing to encase the two pieces of 21¼-inch wire.

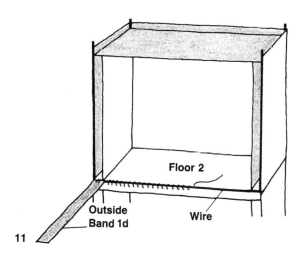

Floor 2

Wire

Outside Band 1d

11

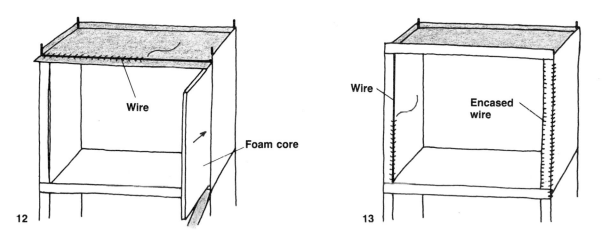

Wire

Foam core

12

Wire

Encased wire

13

Third Floor

1. Place a long edge of each of the outside wall 3a and 3c bands against the top edges of outside walls 2a and 2c. Flush join these edges, using blind cross stitch. Place the longest straight edge of outside wall 3b against the top edge of outside wall 2b. Flush join these edges, using blind cross stitch.

2. Using one strand of White yarn, work a row of slanted gobelin stitch, covering the unstitched horizontal plastic thread on outside wall 2a, the blind cross stitch join between outside wall 2a and outside wall 3a band, and the first horizontal interior plastic thread on exterior wall 3a band. Work the diagonal of the stitch in the same direction as the slanted gobelin stitches on the right sides of the outside walls.

Overstitch the joined edges of outside

walls 2b and 3b and outside wall 2c and outside wall 3c band in slanted gobelin stitch, as the joined edges of outside wall 2a and outside wall 3a band were overstitched.

3. Place the longest edges of the two outside wall 3a and 3c pieces against the top edges of the outside wall 3a and 3c bands. Flush join these matched edges, using White yarn.

4. With right sides facing each other, place

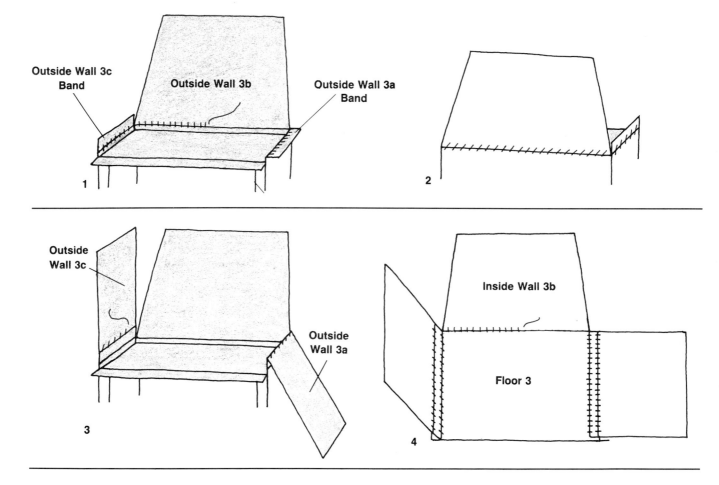

Outside Wall 3c Band

Outside Wall 3b

Outside Wall 3a Band

1

2

Outside Wall 3c

Outside Wall 3a

Inside Wall 3b

Floor 3

3

4

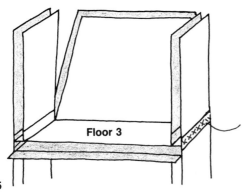

Floor 3

5

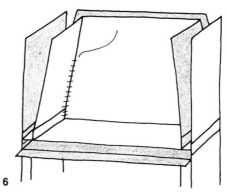

6

the bottom edges of the inside wall 3a and 3c bands against the right side of the floor 3 piece, along the vertical plastic threads marked on the stitch diagram of floor 3. Flush join these sets of matched edges and threads, using White yarn.

With right sides facing each other, place the bottom edges of the inside wall 3a and 3c pieces against the top edges of the inside wall 3a and 3c bands. Flush join these matched edges, using Peach yarn.

With right side up, place the bottom edge of the inside wall 3b piece against the right side of the floor 3 piece, along the horizontal plastic thread marked on the stitch diagram of floor 3. Flush join these matched edges and threads, using White yarn.

5. With right side up, place floor 3 above the wrong side of ceiling 2. Match the edges of floor 3 adjacent to outside wall bands 3a and 3c and outside wall 3b to the interior horizontal plastic threads marked on the stitch diagram of outside wall 3b and the cutout diagram of outside wall bands 3a and 3c. Flush join these matched edges and threads in cross stitch, using White yarn.

6. Flush join the edges of inside walls 3a and 3c and inside wall bands 3a and 3c to the adjacent edges of inside wall 3b, using White yarn.

7. With wrong side up, place ceiling 3 over the top edges of inside walls 3a, 3b, and 3c. Match these edges to the interior horizontal and vertical plastic threads marked on the stitch diagram of ceiling 3. Flush join these matched edges and threads, using Peach yarn.

8. Match the edges of ceiling 3 adjacent to outside walls 3a, 3b, and 3c to the interior horizontal plastic threads marked on the cutout diagrams of outside walls 3a, 3b, and 3c. Flush join these matched edges and threads, using White yarn.

9. Flush join the adjacent edges of outside wall bands 3a and 3c and outside wall 3b, using White yarn and completing

the encasement of the two 21¼-inch pieces of wire.

Flush join the adjacent edges of outside walls 3a and 3b and 3c and 3b, using White yarn. Before working these joins, place a 9¾-inch piece of florist's wire vertically along the outside of the edges to be joined. Encase these pieces of wire within the joins.

10. Insert a 13½-inch-wide × 9¾-inch-high piece of foam core in the seam between ceiling 2 and floor 3.

11. Join the remaining long edge of the partially joined outside band 2b piece to the adjacent edge of floor 3, using White yarn. Before working this join, place a 13½-inch piece of florist's wire horizontally along the outside of the edges to be joined. Encase this piece of wire within the join. While working this join, join the bottom edges of the two outside band 3 pieces as well by matching the bottom edges of each of the outside band 3 pieces to the outside edges of floor 3 and outside band 2b pieces.

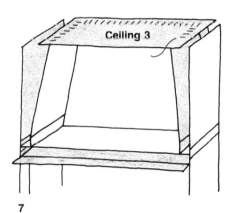

7

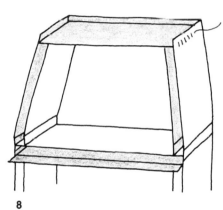

8

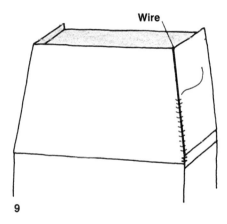

9

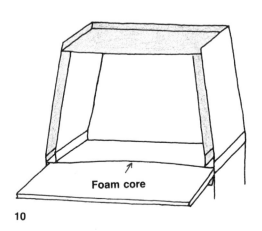

10

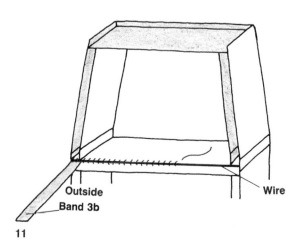

11

12. With right side out, join a long edge of outside band 4 to the remaining long edge of ceiling 3, using White yarn. Before working this join, place a 10¼-inch piece of florist's wire horizontally along the outside of the edges to be joined. Encase this piece of wire within the join. While working this join, join the top edge of the two partially attached outside band 3 pieces as well by matching the top edge of each of the outside band 3 pieces to the outside edges of ceiling 3 and outside band 4 pieces.

13. Flush join the edges of the outside band 3 pieces to the adjacent edges of the outside wall 3a and 3c bands, using White yarn, completing the encasement of the two 21¼-inch pieces of wire.

   Flush join the edges of the outside band 4 piece and the outside band 3 pieces to the adjacent edges of outside walls 3a and 3c, using White yarn. Before working these joins, place a 9¾-inch piece of florist's wire vertically along the outside of the edges to be joined. Encase these pieces of wire within the joins.

14. Flush join the edges of the outside band 3 pieces to the adjacent edges of the inside wall 3a and 3c bands and inside walls 3a and 3c, using White yarn. Before working these joins, place a 9¼-inch piece of florist's wire vertically along the outside of the edges to be joined. Encase these pieces of wire within the joins. Start these joins at the top of the walls and work downward. The inside wall bands will bow inward.

Roof

1. Place the 9¾-inch × 9¾-inch piece of foam core on top of the wrong side of ceiling 3.

2. Place the roof 4 piece right side up over the top edges of the outside wall 3a, 3b, and 3c pieces and the outside band 4 piece. Match the top edges of these four pieces to the wrong side of the roof 4 piece, along the unstitched horizontal and vertical threads marked on the stitch diagram of roof 4. Flush join these matched edges and threads by working cross stitch, using Dark Grey Heather yarn.

3. Flush join the top edges of the four roof 1, 2, and 3 pieces to the outside edges of the roof 4 piece, placing the roof 1, 2, and 3 pieces against the edges marked on the stitch diagram of roof 4. Work these joins using Denim Blue Heather yarn.

4. Flush join the adjacent edges of the roof 1, 2, and 3 pieces, using Denim Blue Heather yarn.

Finishing

1. Add a doorknob to the door by placing a nail head or thumbtack over the center double cross stitch on the right side of the door.

2. Plant a flower garden by placing the wire stems of the artificial flowers between the green tent stitches of the flower box on the stoop.

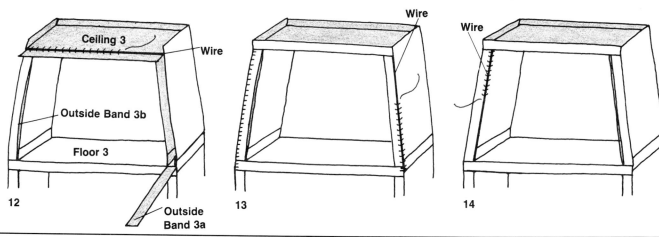

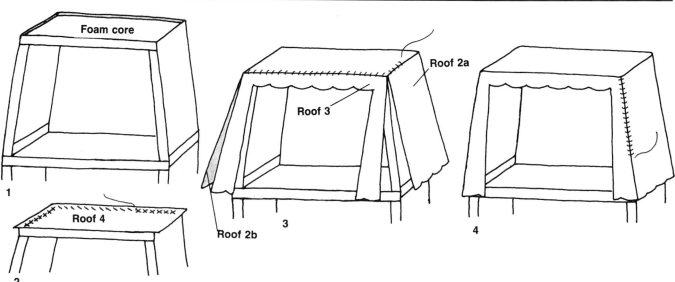

Sources of Supplies

The materials listed in this book may be purchased by mail from the following sources. When ordering materials, mention the title of this book as a reference for the supplier.

Plastic Canvas

Plastic canvas may be purchased at needlepoint shops, craft and hobby stores, and in the yarn departments of discount stores and department stores. If you are unable to purchase plastic canvas locally, you can order it from the following mail order sources. When ordering by mail, send an initial query with a self-addressed stamped envelope for a reply, describing the canvas you require (manufacturer, brand name, sheet size, canvas mesh, canvas color, and number of sheets desired) and requesting the price per sheet; shipping, handling, and sales tax charges; preferred payment method; and specific order placement instructions.

Boye E-Z Count canvas:
  Boye Needle Company
  Customer Service Department
  4343 North Ravenswood
  Chicago, Illinois 60613

Columbia-Minerva FashionEase canvas:
  Columbia-Minerva Division
  Caron International, Inc.
  Consumer Service Department
  P.O. Box 500
  Robesonia, Pennsylvania 19551

W. T. Rogers Quick-Count canvas:
  J. P. Roberts Company
  Fritz Road
  Route 2
  Verona, Wisconsin 53593

Westex Industries canvas:
  Revere Yarn and Crafts
  10 Depot Street
  Uxbridge, Massachusetts 01569

Yarn

Yarn may be purchased at yarn shops, needlepoint shops, craft and hobby stores, and in the yarn departments of discount stores and department stores. If you are unable to purchase yarn locally, you can order it from the following mail order sources. When ordering by mail, send an initial query with a self-addressed stamped envelope for a reply, describing the yarn you require (manufacturer, brand name, color numbers and/or names, and yardage required per color) and requesting the yardage and price per skein; shipping, handling, and sales tax charges; preferred payment method; and specific order placement instructions.

Bernat Berella "4" Yarn, 1–2–3 Ply Persian Type Yarn, and Tabriz Needle Art Yarn:
  Art Needlecraft
  P.O. Box 394
  Uxbridge, Massachusetts 01569

Brunswick Windrush Yarn:
  Brunswick Yarns
  Customer Service
  P.O. Box 276
  Pickens, South Carolina 29671

Coats and Clark Red Heart 4-Ply Handknitting Yarn:
  Coats and Clark Sales
  Consumer Service Educational Mail Department
  P.O. Box 1010
  Toccoa, Georgia 30577

Columbia-Minerva Nantuk Yarn and Caron Sayelle Yarn:
  Caron International, Inc.
  Customer Service Department
  P.O. Box 300
  Rochelle, Illinois 61068

Columbia-Minerva FashionEase Yarn for Needlepoint:
  Columbia-Minerva Division
  Caron International, Inc.
  Consumer Service Department
  P.O. Box 500
  Robesonia, Pennsylvania 19551

DMC Size 3 Pearl Cotton:
  American Needlewoman
  P.O. Box 6472
  Fort Worth, Texas 76115

Gemini 1/4" Ribbons Yarn:
  Studio Needlecraft
  720 East Jericho Turnpike
  Huntington Station, New York 11746

Phildar Sunset 330 Yarn:
  Creative Needles
  436 Avenue of the Americas
  New York, New York 10011

Opaque Paint Markers

Marvy Deco Color Opaque Paint Markers may be purchased at art supply stores and stationery stores. If you are unable to purchase these markers locally, write to the manufacturer for the closest mail order source.

  Uchida of America Corporation
  69-31 51st Avenue
  Woodside, New York 11377

Clock Movement

A clock movement may be purchased at craft and hobby stores. The Ultra Thin-Ultra Small Quartz Clock Movement specified may be purchased from the following mail order source. When ordering by mail, send an initial query with a self-addressed stamped envelope for a reply. Describe the clock movement by its product number and complete name and request its price; a description of its hour/minute hand options; shipping, handling, and sales tax charges; preferred method of payment; and specific order placement instructions.

  National Artcraft Co.
  23456 Mercantile Road
  Beachwood, Ohio 44122

Acknowledgments

My grateful thanks to Sue Zeckendorf and Adrienne Ingrum, for believing in me and this project; to Mary Anne Symmons Brown, Jack Godler, Joel Hecker, Marge Raphaelson, Mary Roby, Ed Smith, and Gail Tauber, for their valued and valuable advice and support; to Glorya Hale, whose hovering and honing made the concept of a manuscript the reality of a book; to Zuelia Ann Hurt, for lending her special talent and eye to the photography styling and for being there as a friend, personally and professionally; to Olympia Pena and Toshiko Tanaka, for stitching the project models with such expert hands and caring attention; to Melissa Carlson, for tackling with precision and care the tedious task of typing the seemingly endless pages of corrections and revisions; to Bernat Yarn and Craft Corporation, Boye Needle Company, Brunswick Worsted Mills, Inc., Caron International, Inc., Coats and Clark, Inc., Columbia-Minerva, The DMC Corporation, Gemini Innovations in Needlepoint, Inc., National Artcraft Co., W. T. Rogers Company, Uchida of America Corporation, and Westex Industries, for their generous contributions of materials from which the project models were developed; to The Gazebo and B. Schackman and Co., for their generous loan of the rag rug and dollhouse furniture that gloriously complemented the projects in photography; and to Susan Goldsmith, whose enthusiasm and confidence fatefully inspired me to think dimensionally.